CATCH ME BEFORE I FALL

Rosie Childs
with
Diane Taylor

TED SMART

Some of the names in this book have been changed for legal reasons.

First published in Great Britain in 2006 by
Virgin Books Ltd
Thames Wharf Studios
Rainville Road
London
W6 9HA

A catalogue record for this book is available from the British Library.

ISBN 185227 3410

This edition produced for The Book People,
Hall Wood Avenue, Haydock, St Helens, WA11 9UL

Typeset by TW Typesetting, Plymouth, Devon
Printed and bound in Great Britain by
Mackays of Chatham PLC

PROLOGUE

I am fifty-two years old and have changed my name seven times so far. I have never been able to understand why most people keep the same name from birth until death. My names change when my life changes. Perhaps those whose names don't change have lives that don't change either.

For a while I tried to keep my names separate – independent life spans with beginnings, middles and ends – but that doesn't work any more. They used to chase each other around in a blur, a perpetual process of fast forward, rewind and a few pauses in the present, but now they're still. All my names have caught up with each other.

I was born Clare Malone, the name my mother gave me. I was ten years old and living at Park Hall, a children's home in Liverpool run by an order of nuns, when I found out my mother had given me a dishonest name.

I was at Mass with my five brothers and sisters and was standing at the back of the chapel where the fumes of religion seemed more diluted. Sister Maria tapped me sharply on the shoulder. She bent down, her habit bristling, and whispered disapprovingly in my ear that my mother had arrived unexpectedly (as she always did). Sister Maria gave me a grudging nod to leave the service and I ran into the high, dark hallway. My heart always lifted when my mother turned up, although I knew hers remained steady in her chest.

She was slender and pale with elegant bones; her genes seemed to have avoided me entirely.

'Mum,' I whispered, hoping that the other nuns wouldn't catch me dodging God. 'Should we go and sit in the visitors' room?'

It was always impossible to gauge what my mother's reaction to anything would be but she didn't seem interested in sending me back to Mass. She was never a hugger and I knew that if I tried to fling my short, brown body against her in pursuit of a cuddle she would recoil. She took a step back and moved her eyes up and down me.

'Hello, Clare. How are you keeping? You seem well enough here. A bit less skinny by the looks of things.' My mother was born in Chorley and had been brought up in Preston. She moved to Liverpool before I was born and she spoke in flat Lancashire vowels rather than the accentuated 'ews' and 'euws' of Liverpool.

We went to the room with the maroon sofas and faded stripy curtains, which the children were never allowed into without the protective shield of a visiting adult. She turned her head away from me to stare out of the window. 'Yer sisters and brothers keepin' all right, Clare?'

'We're all fine, Mum,' I replied.

She draped herself over the radiator and drummed her roughened fingers against the windowsill. Her perfect limbs made her look expensive, although she rarely had any money at all. She wore a violently red blouse and black skirt, and her white-blonde hair was coiled elaborately into the nape of her neck. My mother never noticed housework. I doubted she had ever scrubbed a floor or scoured a sink the way we had to at Park Hall. Yet her hands belonged to someone who had led a harsh life and her bitten nails were as downtrodden as a scullery maid's.

The sky was a hopeless shade of grey. It looked as if it would retch sheets of metallic water forever. My mother had been on her way to the Queen's Head pub a few roads away when the downpour started. She didn't own an umbrella and impulsively decided to shelter at Park Hall.

'I'll turn up with rain tipping out of me hair and me lipstick smudged to bits,' she said, grumpily. 'And then what will Mick think? He likes to see me turned out like a proper lady.'

Her life was populated by men called Peter or Mick or Sam, who soaked up her time and her soul. I was never able to claim her the way I saw my friends at school lay claim to their mothers.

She lit a cigarette and inhaled with relief.

I knew that I had my mother to myself for as long as the rain fell and Mass lasted. It was probably the first time it had ever happened. As the two of us sat quietly I sensed I might never get another opportunity to ask the question I had always wanted to ask. My oldest brother, Damian, often sneered to me, 'You don't belong in our family, you're not like the rest of us. Look at that dark skin of yours. It doesn't look normal like ours.'

My five brothers and sisters all had creamy pink skin like my mother's and our father Sam's, while mine was a tough, dark brown. The difference was indisputable. Damian was usually right about things and I wondered often why I looked so different from the rest of the family. My mother had never said anything directly to me but I sensed she felt ashamed of me – the dark blot on the white landscape of her children. The imprint of that shame remains carved into me.

I trembled, then blurted, 'Mum, Damian told me I'm not from our family. I know I don't look like the rest of you. Am I from somewhere else? Are you really my mum and is Sam really my dad?'

Sam had been her husband before and after I was born, but had disappeared without trace one day when I was four years old. Malone was his surname.

At first I thought my mother was going to slap me. An angry vertical furrow appeared between her eyebrows and her mouth twitched downwards. Then the anger cleared. She turned towards me and her pale blue eyes filled with tears. At that moment she acknowledged what the alcohol usually pushed away – that everything worthwhile in her life had been lost to her. It made her generous with me.

'Of course I'm your mother, Clare. How else would you have got into our family?' She tried to sound cross but was becoming dreamy. 'Sam isn't your father, though. Your father was a proper gentleman, second in command to the captain of a Chilean ship. I met him when his ship docked in Liverpool. Jorges Sherriema his name was. He was such a handsome man.'

I was reeling. Although I knew there was a difference between me and the others, I had no idea it involved an unknown, unimagined father. Was he still alive? Was he a kind man? Did he have a family, a proper, cosy family, not a fragmented, tumbledown one like ours? Did he know about me? Would he want me to go and live with him? But I couldn't ask any of the questions that swarmed through my mind. Mass was over. The door opened and my sisters and brothers filed in. My mother smiled weakly to all of them but cuddled none and her revelation ended abruptly.

Ours was by far the biggest family at Park Hall. The other children placed here arrived alone or with one other sibling, and if they didn't behave too badly managed to shrink into the wallpaper. But, because of the sheer volume of Malones, none of us was able to do that. All six of us had a different father; Damian, twelve, followed by Mary, eleven, then me, ten, Lucy, eight, Tom, six and John, four, were not only more in number, but scraggier and scruffier than the others too, at least when we first arrived. When it came to anonymity we didn't stand a chance.

We had only been at Park Hall for a few months that day my mother arrived to shelter from the rain. Soon afterwards John, Tom, Damian and Lucy were dispatched to various parts of the country to live with foster parents. Nobody ever chose Mary or me so we remained at Park Hall until we left school.

My mother's eyes kept swivelling away from us towards the sky, beseeching whoever made the rain fall to make it stop. She seemed desperate for a drink to stopper her memory. Talking to us only made her feel worse. Like Jorges we were another loss, another failure, looking her innocently in the eye. She wanted to skip away to the Queen's Head, sink into the corner booth, have three double whiskies quickly, smoke hard and let Mick rub her neck and drape his hand across her shoulder, grazing her breast, and whisper obscenities in her ear, to obliterate all thought.

She stood up, her face brightening as the sky cleared.

'Clare, make sure you braid your hair up nice and tidy. Lucy, you need to sponge that stain off your uniform or you'll have the sisters after you. Mary, make sure you're a good girl and watch over the others.'

She had once told me that she only wanted sons, and when she had another baby girl after the six of us, she looked away and handed her over for adoption as soon as the umbilical cord had been snipped. She told me, without a trace of emotion, about this seventh child much later, when I was fifteen. Perhaps because of my mother's deadpan delivery of the news, the discovery of another sister meant nothing to me. I promptly forgot about her.

My mother also muttered something about four more babies that she had miscarried or who had been stillborn after the seventh. These siblings who had never taken a breath outside the womb meant even less to me, and I didn't bother asking her for more details.

'Well, rain's stopped. I'd best be on me way. Behave all of you.' She gathered up a couple of carrier bags and, with a brief wave, eased herself out of the door. She was such a slight, unearthly presence in our lives that I began to doubt whether she had actually been in the room with us at all.

However, her words felt chunky and real. I didn't dare tell the others, as Damian would certainly gloat. I kept looking down at my brown arms and wondered about the face, the skin, the limbs of my Chilean father. All my life I had yearned for my skin to fade to the desirable pinkness of my siblings but, now I understood that my colour came from a proper gentleman, handsome too and from an exotic country I had never heard of, it was becoming, momentarily at least, a little less revolting to me. I was too young to erase the name Malone from my life but I vowed that, when I was free of the children's home, I would become Clare Sherriema. That was my first name change.

CLARE MALONE 1954–1970

Clare: a variant of my mother's name
Malone: the surname of my mother's husband, Sam

CHAPTER ONE

I was born on a dark-red couch in my mother's dirty, bare front room on 20 February 1954. She lived in a council house in Morgans Road, Page Moss, a poor area of Liverpool. Betty, the elderly lady who lived on our street and who acted as unofficial midwife to everyone in the neighbourhood, arrived just in time to witness my entry into the world.

I shot out of my mother powerfully and Betty caught me as I was about to tumble off the sofa on to the dusty floorboards. She screamed in horror: 'She's black! She's black!'

My mother's relief at expelling me from her womb was quickly replaced by panic. She tried to shush Betty in case other neighbours heard and came running to view the spectacle. My older sister, Mary, was eighteen months old at the time and says that Betty's screams that day are her earliest memory.

My mother gazed, revolted, at my coffee-coloured skin and placenta-splattered clumps of jet-black hair. I think she thought that, if she stared long and hard enough at me, I'd change into the colour of baby that she wanted me to be. She didn't seem to notice whether she'd given birth to a girl or a boy. My skin colour pushed everything else into the background.

'What on earth . . .?' Betty was stunned. I don't think she would have been any less surprised if my mother had given birth to a Martian. She placed a work-wrinkled hand over her thin mouth while thick strands of grey hair escaped from the usually immaculate bun she wore in the nape of her neck. It looked as if the shock of my arrival had sent an electric current through her head, splaying her hair in all directions. After a minute or two, she regained her equilibrium, wrapped her hair back into its place, and started to think through the consequences of this shocking birth.

'How did you produce a baby that colour, Clara? It's a first for this neighbourhood. You certainly know how to get the tongues wagging. I can't see your Sam being too pleased at being humiliated like that!'

Both my mother and her husband, Sam, had the palest pink skin and blond hair. Although my mother was a peroxide blonde, following the fashion at the time to look like Marilyn Monroe, she was naturally fair-haired. Betty wasn't one for gossip and hadn't heard the neighbours whispering about the affair my mother had been conducting with 'that tall, dark, handsome Chilean seaman'. Of course, Sam hadn't heard the whispers either, mainly because he spent most of his time away at sea. These days the neighbourhood is home to people from a variety of races, but then non-white faces were virtually unknown in Page Moss.

My mother lay back weakly on the sofa but her brain whirred and she fixed Betty with a feverish, glassy stare. The smell of dirt, dust and my mother's fresh sweat hung unpleasantly together in the air.

'Please hang on to her for me. Just till the fuss dies down, Betty. You know what it's like round here. Once the neighbours get wind of it, Sam'll also get wind of it as soon as his ship docks next week.' She squeezed her hands together as though she were praying, and beseeched Betty for all she was worth.

'Don't be silly, Clara. Everyone round here knows you've been pregnant. They'll all want to have a peek at the baby. You can't hide the poor little mite away. It's your baby and you should be close to her, cuddling her and nursing her. What are you going to call her?'

Although my mother kept her children in a filthy, almost entirely unfurnished house, which stank of urine because we all perpetually wet the bed, she didn't like to parade this squalor to the neighbours. The entire inventory of household furniture was: two beds, one belonging to my mother and one for the three girls and

Tom; one kitchen table covered with a sticky, plastic cloth; one twin-tub washing machine, which my mother sometimes hid stolen cigarettes inside; and a set of bunk beds in the box room for the other two boys. A single bar of carbolic soap adorned our bathroom, and the biggest attraction in our kitchen was the lighter for the gas stove. We used to hold the lighter to spoonfuls of sugar and pretend we were making toffee with it when my mother wasn't around. It always tasted wonderful and we took turns to dip our tongues into the brown syrup we had created. Although my mother owned a mop bucket, I never saw her use it, and all the surfaces in the house were either dusty or sticky or both.

Just as my mother wanted to keep our living conditions private, she didn't want her sex life to become a conversation point among the neighbours. She had been anxious about giving birth to me from the moment she discovered she was pregnant because she was unsure whether my father was Sam or Jorges, whom she had met and begun an affair with when his boat docked in Liverpool in the middle of 1953. Giving birth to a black baby meant that she could not conceal her affair from them and, for her, this was the most public humiliation imaginable. Although Page Moss at the time was a working-class area with many newly built, terraced council homes just like ours, it was considered to be a respectable part of Liverpool. I don't remember seeing any black families in the neighbourhood, although it's possible there were a few.

My mother had a friend called Pat who she went off with whenever she disappeared for days on end. One of the neighbours told me, years later, that the two of them went on to the ships when they docked in Liverpool to 'do all sorts' with the sailors. But most of the people in Page Moss weren't like my mother and Pat. The women worked hard to keep their front steps scrubbed to a shine, the cushions on their sofas plumped up invitingly and their rugs and carpets dust-free.

Our house had no carpets, only floorboards, which always felt gritty and dusty under my bare feet; a sofa without cushions, which was the sole item of furniture in the living room; and a bed without sheets. Sometimes a few of us would wake in the middle of the night and creep into my mother's bedroom. If she hadn't returned, we would climb into her bed to sleep because she had the luxury of sheets on her bed. But, if she was there, either alone or with one of the many men who she brought back for the night and who we would never see a second time, we scurried back to our prickly blankets and long, striped, tubular pillows without pillow cases. We had a scuffed, white bath in our bathroom. I don't remember ever having a bath in it. At night my mother told us to urinate into the mop bucket, which she left outside our bedroom door, instead of having to go to the outside toilet. As I lay whimpering on my mother's chest that February day, however, I was blissfully innocent of what lay ahead for me in Morgans Road.

'This goes against my better judgement, Clara,' Betty scolded. 'It's just not right for a mother to reject her little'un like this just because she's got the wrong skin colour. Sam's going to find out sooner or later.'

But my mother seemed to be getting more and more agitated about me and tried to hand me over to Betty, even though I was still connected to her by the umbilical cord. She shivered and sobbed and begged, and Betty finally relented.

'Once you start pleading with me, you know I always give in to you, Clara. But, mark my words, Sam will find out soon enough. Hush now and hold on to your little black baby while you can.' Betty snipped the cord and my mother shook her head when Betty tried to get her to continue to hold me.

'No, you take her for now, Betty love, I'm so bloody worn out.'

Distractedly she was finalising the details of her fib. What I represented was occupying all her brain space and she hadn't once glanced into my face to see who I was. 'I'll tell Sam I had a stillbirth,' she said, brightening at the prospect of getting herself out of trouble. She was so pleased with herself that she barely noticed the contractions as she expelled the placenta.

When, years later, I learned at school what purpose an umbilical cord served, I found it strange that my mother had ever grown one; she was an unlikely custodian of such a life-giving device. My mother adored alcohol and men. Poverty and marriage were no bars to her indulging in lots of both. When I was three or four years old, I watched her wistfully as she got ready to go out. As she rolled red lipstick around her mouth, she had a jittery, glittering excitement about her that she never had with us. She felt no personal shame about her excessive drinking, or about the men she had sex with when Sam's back was turned, at least some of them in exchange for money. But she felt deep shame about producing a black, bastard child and I felt she blamed me for opting for Jorges's skin in the womb rather than hers. When she shouted at me for what she considered to be an endless stream of misdeeds, I told myself that, if I'd looked like her, she would have loved me more.

Of course, Sam did eventually find out about me. The residents of Morgans Road couldn't keep a scandal like that to themselves for long. Scenting something amiss, a trickle of neighbours knocked on our door 'to peek at' the new arrival. At first my mother tried to fob them off, but, in the end, she wearily lifted me out of the pram that doubled as my cot and let everyone gasp.

'Ooh, I say,' said Mrs Jones from Number Five. 'You don't half make life difficult for yourself, Clara Malone. What's your Sam going to say when he gets back from sea?'

My mother shrugged. 'Well, what's he going to do? Put a gun to my head? He'll come round.' She tried to sound flippant, but shuddered under her smile. Sam's wrath filled my mother with infinitely more fear than the gossiping neighbours.

When Sam arrived home from sea the house was quiet. He was a tall man and his blond, shiny hair gave him an angelic appearance that was belied by his violent streak.

'Where's the baby, Clara? I can see you've had it. Have you given me a son and heir?'

'Oh, Sam,' she said, weeping real tears and nuzzling her cheek and lips so deep into his neck that they disappeared in the folds of his skin. 'The baby died. It was a girl but she never took a breath. We buried her quick.'

Sam looked her hard in the eye, not sure whether to believe her or not. Then he decided to give her the benefit of the doubt. 'Ah, poor little thing, you should take it easy, Clara. I'm off out but I'll be back later on and I'll bring you a nice pie and chips and a nip of whisky.'

She smiled and kissed him softly on the lips. 'Thanks, darlin'. You go and enjoy yerself now with yer mates. You're bound to be tired what with all that travellin'.'

She knew he would go straight to the pub and that someone there would take great pleasure in telling him the truth about me, but at least she'd bought herself some time. She sat on the couch knotting and unknotting a dirt-streaked handkerchief and rehearsing the pain of the punches. Everything was perfectly still.

Sam beat my mother regularly, and he had beaten her even harder while I was in her womb. I wonder if he suspected all along that she was carrying another man's child. As far as I could tell, nobody else in the neighbourhood got beaten the way my mother did. Sam beat her whenever he was drunk and, when he was home from sea, he was drunk most days. My mother's screams and pleas for him to stop raining blows anywhere he could punctured many of my nights huddled under the scratchy blankets.

'For pity's sake, Sam, let me be, let me be', my mother would cry. The broken fear in her voice chilled me more than the sound of the blows.

Sam arrived home after midnight, throwing open the front door back against the wall. It was the equivalent of a drum roll before the finale of a play. Years of slamming had hewn a handle-shaped depression in the wall; it softened the bang.

He dragged my mother up from the couch where she was still shredding the handkerchief. Her blonde hair was woven into two plaits, which she'd wrapped around her head; he ripped them free. She crumpled into a limp, paper woman in his presence, submitting to her fate. There was no trace of the stern, distant mother we knew. Cowering from Sam's rage she looked like a little girl.

'You fucking bitch, making a fool out of me like that. You'll pay for that you little whore.'

He screwed up his fists and started beating her systematically in her face and chest. She clamped her eyes and lips shut, glued her fingers across her face and lay on her back on the floor, legs pulled up in the foetal position, enduring the blows until Sam's anger was spent. Her plaits had unravelled and her long blonde hair flowed like glinting water across the floorboards, which were darkened with streaks of blood that had dripped from her punched nose.

'Get rid of that black bastard or I go,' he hissed.

I had been sleeping tranquilly in an old Moses basket in Betty's bedroom, unaware of the explosion my existence had caused.

I came home the next morning. Sam stayed and glowered.

CHAPTER TWO

I have no memories of the first three years of my life and no knowledge of whether my mother looked after me adequately or abandoned me for hours on end in the old, scratched Silver Cross pram that served as my bed and transport system. All my retrospective knowledge of those early years comes from Mary and from my friend Marie, Betty's grandchild. I also salvaged a few grudging titbits from my mother, which she divulged when she was in a mellow mood.

I do remember Betty saying to me often, 'You're a hardy one, Clare', so perhaps it was she who ensured I survived during my mother's absences. Betty always seemed to be watching over me, as if that initial shock when she had caught me in the first minute of my life had welded her to me. If I looked particularly hungry she used to cup a piece of white bread smeared with raspberry jam into the palm of her hand for me. Occasionally she mended the few clothes I had when they developed holes. Her wrinkled smile and pragmatism protected me a little during those early years.

Sam and my mother stayed unhappily together until I was four years old. Before getting the house in Morgans Road their relationship had been similarly turbulent. My mother had lived with Sam and his mother in her home nearby. She argued even more with Sam's mother than with Sam and, when her mother-in-law became sick and confined to her bed, she ignored her pointedly. Sam's mother died while he was away at sea and she lay undiscovered for three days because, although she lived under the same roof and no doubt noticed a bad smell, my mother refused to step over the threshold of her bedroom.

We were all sent to foster parents for periods, often when things were particularly hateful between my mother and Sam, returning home when things were calmer. We were moved in and out of Morgans Road a total of twelve times before we left for ever when I was nine. My mother and Sam seemed to sustain each other in a peculiar way: the fights were always followed by passionate reconciliations and the alcohol bound them yet more closely together. As husband and wife they took their obligation seriously to share whatever alcohol one or the other could afford equitably.

From the beginning of my memory I was conscious of the violence: it was the colour of yellow-grey fog with a bright orange fire burning through it. There was nowhere white and soothing to shelter. One night, when I was three years old, my mother's high-pitched screams and Sam's deeper shouts woke me. I peered through a hole in the bedroom floorboards and watched, screwing up one eye to get a better view. Sam had a knife in his hand and, despite the fact that I knew that knives were dangerous, it didn't occur to me that he might be trying to kill my mother with it.

Sam screamed, 'You fucking bitch, I'll get you for this.' I never found out what he was so angry about.

My mother ignored the knife he wafted under her nose and yelled back, 'Keep your hands away from me, you fucking bastard. Get out, get out, get out!'

The sounds eventually dulled and this was such a usual occurrence that I climbed back into bed and went to sleep.

A few months later Sam attacked my mother on the stairs. I was playing with a rusty toy car in the hallway. I instinctively ran to her side and handed her a child's umbrella to defend herself with.

'Hit him with this, Mum, hit him with this.' I thought that, if I tried to protect her, she would repay me with love.

She took the umbrella and made a feeble attempt to hit him with it. The umbrella snapped in half but Sam appeared unharmed. He spat on to the bare floorboards and strode out of the house.

I knew nothing of Sam's threats about me to my mother, which always took the same form: 'Get rid of that black bastard or I'm going.'

My mother told me that eventually she agreed to Sam's demand and contacted social services about having me adopted at the age of two. Though I remember nothing of this, my mother told me when I was sixteen, probably the time in my life that I saw her most.

'A childless couple from Whiston, near Liverpool, wanted to adopt you,' she said. 'They were a lovely couple in their thirties. The wife crocheted you a pretty little pink bonnet with lots of loops on it, which you used to poke your fingers through. You stayed with them for a few weekends so that you could all get to know each other.'

However, at the last moment my mother lost her nerve and refused to sign the adoption papers. Rather than feeling grateful to her for this demonstration of her affection towards me, when I found out I was very angry with her and pictured the stable life I might have had away from the harshness and deprivation of life in Morgans Road. Wisely, though, I said nothing about my near miss with what I was certain would have been a blissfully happy childhood.

I was aware that I was different from the other children in my family and in the neighbourhood, but I never knew exactly what it was about me that made so many children withdraw from me. I knew that we were usually hungry and that my mother often wasn't at home but I assumed that that was a general feature of childhood rather than something that was specific to our family. I wasn't really self-conscious about my colour when I was younger. It was only when I got to primary school and children started shouting 'Paki' at me that I started to look at my arms and legs and wonder why I had come out of my mother's belly a different colour from all her other children. We rarely received a bath or a wash and, before I started school, I presumed that the fact that my skin was several shades darker than the other children in my street was all down to accumulated grime rather than because of my different ethnic origin.

The pupils at school generally excluded me from their games and the only way I knew how to respond to being pushed away was to try and fight my way in, a tactic that didn't go down very well. I was a tiny little thing, weighing barely five pounds at birth, but, although I never grew very tall, I could punch and fight like a tough boy. As Betty said, I really was hardy. Perhaps I had unwittingly learned how to fight after witnessing so many violent exchanges between my mother and Sam.

By the time I was seven years old I understood in basic terms that my sisters and brothers and I were neglected by my mother, who was absent from the house for almost as many days and nights as she was present. I saw other children's mothers wait at the school gate with bars of chocolate and friendly waves at 3.30 p.m. We were always expected to take ourselves home and our mother never handed out chocolate bars to us. I became aware of the clothes the other children wore too. They looked neat and clean, while our clothes had holes in them and hems that hung down. Sometimes other children called us names like 'stinky' or 'smelly', which no non-Malone child ever seemed to get called.

I had always been small for my age and even when I started primary school looked little older than a toddler. I had thick, black, straight hair, cut just below my ears. Everyone in the neighbourhood remarked on how shiny my hair was – the kind you don't see on white, English people. I had huge brown eyes, a small button nose and one front tooth that overlapped the tooth next to it. Usually I wore a dress which had been given to me by one or other of my foster mothers. Invariably it was grubby, and my skinny arms and legs dangled out of it looking as snappable as matchsticks. Like my brothers and sisters I didn't have proper shoes; we all ran around in cheap black pumps whatever the weather.

But I still had no real understanding of having a different skin colour from everyone else, and certainly no grasp at all of the fact that my skin colour was down to my father.

One day when I was seven I got a shock. Marie, Betty's granddaughter, was the same age as me, a doll-like child with beautiful blue eyes and blonde hair. She decided to put me in her bath to try and excavate my white skin from beneath the layers of grime. She used Ajax and a scrubbing brush.

Marie's bathroom was a palace compared with ours. It had linoleum and a neat row of shampoos and bath cubes, and I lay back enjoying the luxuriously hot water and all the attention from Marie. I didn't even mind that she was rubbing my skin raw. I wanted to lie in her bath with the forest fern bath cube fizzing away for ever.

Betty came in while Marie was unwittingly attempting ethnic cleansing. Laughing, she asked, 'What on earth are you doing to Clare, Marie?'

'I'm trying to get all the brown dirt off, Gran,' she replied, slightly breathless with exertion. As with me, there was no reason for her to be aware that people had skin of all different colours.

I was the only child in my neighbourhood and in my school who was non-white.

'Leave her be, Marie. She was born like that,' Betty said in a pitying tone, as if one of my limbs were missing.

I adored Marie and I envied everything about her, from her skin colour to her home. 'Sorry, Marie,' I said, feeling responsible for her failed mission to reveal the true whiteness of my skin.

'Don't worry, Clare. Fancy you having skin that colour. Does it feel funny?'

'No, it just feels normal,' I said, amazed that I could be covered in such a skin. 'I always thought my skin was just like yours underneath, Marie.'

'Come on, Clare, let's go and play dolls,' said Marie, grabbing my Ajax-roughened hand. The revelation appeared not to have perturbed her at all.

'No, I'm going to go home now,' I said to Marie.

The fact that I couldn't peel off the layer of dirt to reveal soft, pink skin like Marie's was devastating. Perhaps that was why my mother and Sam didn't seem to love me. Sam had always raised his hand as if he was about to strike me when I walked past, so that ducking became a reflex action even when he didn't threaten me. I was very subdued for the rest of the day, trying to adjust to my brown-forever identity. I kept examining my arms and hands to see if I could detect even the vaguest hint of pink. But there was no sign. I was stuck with misfit brown. I sat on the floor in our bedroom comparing my life with Marie's. Tears plopped into the dust.

Marie's house had carpets throughout, pictures on the wall, a TV and a kitchen table covered with a pretty tablecloth. Although our house was only a few doors away, it might just as well have been on another continent. While everything in Marie's house was designed to maximise comfort and warmth and cosiness, everything in our house was cold and bare and shabby. Our house was described by the NSPCC, when they eventually intervened to remove us, as 'barely furnished'.

I frequently went around either without knickers or dirty ones dug out of the pile of clothes waiting to be washed. None of us owned pyjamas and we all slept in our clothes. Most of us wet the bed, probably because we were so anxious all the time. Would we get fed that day? Would Sam be around to swipe us over the head? And, if my mother was home, would she be shouting?

Occasionally my mother had enough money to buy coal and then she made a lovely, roaring fire. When we were warm her mood was more conciliatory. She took a long fork and made toast for us, bringing a bit of margarine from the kitchen. It was never butter, which my mother said was only for rich people. I had never seen butter in the house so had no idea why it was apparently a superior thing to spread on bread, but we were more than happy with the margarine. We all felt like we were at the Ritz.

But one time the fire became my downfall. I was nine years old and my mother had carefully counted out exactly the right number of shillings to pay the coal man for a bag of coal. She left the shillings on the mantelpiece. I kept looking and looking at the shiny pile of shillings lying tantalisingly unguarded and, in the end, managed to convince myself that neither my mother nor the coal man would notice if I just took a single shilling. As soon as I felt the hard, shiny coin in my hand I bolted down the road to the mobile shop – a little corner of paradise for me – and bought some sweets to share with my friends. Although sweets were very precious commodities, it never occurred to me not to share them, particularly with my younger siblings. Lucy, John and Tom were born in quick succession after me; as the oldest children, Damian and Mary were in charge of the rest of us. They usually organised their own sweets but I couldn't bear to think of the little ones going without Mars bars or sherbet lemons if I had them.

Later that day the coal man called and Mary handed over the pile of shillings. I held my breath as he counted them up. My heart started to race at the prospect of being found out and a guilty flush spread across my face. When I had seen the shiny silver pile of coins winking at me I couldn't envisage the consequences of my action, only instant gratification. The man, who had a decent, straightforward face, shook his head.

'There's a shilling missing from here, lass,' he said, after counting the money up twice.

Mary looked devastated, and he handed over the coal anyway. 'Just make sure it's right next time,' he said gently, and hopped back in his van, whistling.

Mary knew it was me who had taken the money. 'How dare you take that money? Is it more important to you to have sweets than for our family to be warm?'

She told my mother, who was even more furious. I was more distraught about Mary's betrayal than about the beating I knew would come from my mother. She raised her hand and delivered a few forceful punches to my head. The corners of her mouth were turned down sourly and she didn't flinch when she saw me trying to curve my head and body away from her blows. The pain was extreme and numbing. She was doing to me exactly what Sam had done to her. How could she inflict such pain when she knew how it felt to be paralysed with fear as blows rained down? Now I remembered what the sight of the coins had obliterated: that the consequence of doing wrong was pain. I didn't cry and waited for her to finish.

Shouting rather than physical violence was my mother's preferred way of communicating with us; she confined her blows to punishments for specific misdemeanours, unlike Sam who preferred using his hands to using his mouth. One day, when I was three years old, I wandered into the larder cupboard looking for something to eat. I noticed some small, red, shiny things on a plate which I had never seen before and tasted one. Although I didn't know what I was eating, they were sweet, juicy tomatoes. I ate them all and let the juice and seeds drizzle down my chin and dress. As I swallowed the last mouthful, Sam walked into the larder. His breath smelled stale and sour, a smell I hadn't yet learned came from whisky.

'And what do you think you're doing?' he growled. He looked at the empty plate of tomatoes, and then at the red stains around my mouth, and started to roar, 'You're a wicked, greedy girl.' He repeatedly smashed his hand into my head. I tried to shield my head with my tiny hands but they stood no chance against his big calloused ones. I screamed but no one came running to help. Then Sam deftly took his belt out of his trouser loops, flung me belly button down on to his knees and started beating me on the bottom with his belt. The pain was too strong for tears. When he had finished, he threw me on to the larder floor and strode off. I stayed very still for a long time until the pain had subsided enough to move and until I was sure Sam was no longer in the house.

Compared with that, my mother's slaps and tellings-off seemed mild. Although she often yelled 'get out of my sight' to all of us, now and again a softer, more loving side manifested itself. It was a glimpse from a 1950s American movie of perfect family life, which contrasted with the grainy war footage of daily existence. Life for my mother was hard. The babies just kept on coming and the fog of alcohol loosened her grip on an already chaotic situation at home. I don't think she was a bad woman, but she was one who coped badly with the circumstances she found herself in. She would probably have been happier not to have had any children but, in the pre-contraception world, it wasn't something she had any say in.

One time I had a high fever and my mother allowed me to lie on the sofa while she lit a roaring fire. Instead of going out she sat by me at the end of the sofa all night. She seemed anxious too – all in all a perfect scenario for me. I felt unconcerned about whatever was wrong with me and hardly noticed my shivery burning and pounding head. I basked in her love. Another time, when I had some kind of sore on my body, she was similarly gentle. She wound a grey poultice round and round me while I stood patiently in front of the fire enjoying the double warmth.

My mother's attitude to my illnesses and injuries was, however, as inconsistent as her attitude to everything else concerning her children. One day I was bitten on my leg by an Alsatian dog while I was playing out in the street. The pain was fierce but the sight of the dog's sharp, wet teeth piercing my flesh made it feel even worse. I screamed and screamed. My mother was out and a neighbour took me down to the local hospital's casualty department. A nurse with too much pillowy flesh and sharp, black-framed glasses beckoned me into a cubicle. She was unimpressed by my tears and the chewed gash. Coldly, she drew a circle in biro around the top of my thigh where I had been bitten.

'This is where I'm going to give you an injection,' she said bluntly.

I started to cry louder at the prospect of a needle piercing my skin so soon after the dog's teeth had done so. The nurse offered no words of comfort and summoned another nurse to hold my hands behind my back while she jabbed me. I screamed again and, at that moment, my mother appeared, looking irritated.

The nurse explained what had happened. 'You can take her home now, Mrs Malone, we're all done with her,' she said, in that fake polite voice adults use with each other.

My mother was furious and marched me out of the hospital without a word. As soon as we arrived home, she said, 'What the hell do you think you're doing getting yourself bitten by a dog like that?'

Although she was dangerously careless with us, she never liked other people to witness her poor parenting and seemed to think that, as long as nobody saw too much of what went on in our house, there was no harm done.

Deep down I believe she did care about me and my brothers and sisters but she didn't understand the mundanities of nurture and was incapable of showing or sustaining affection for us. Because she preferred boys, and because my skin colour told everyone about her infidelity to Sam, I must have been a double disappointment to her. Responding to her erratic behaviour was hard for me. When she became softer and more loving it took me by surprise. I was always on my guard and eventually learned how to mould my responses to her moods and always to expect nothing in the hope of avoiding disappointment.

I often wondered if my father knew I had been born. I have no recollection of him but my younger sister, Lucy, says she remembers a slender, dark-haired man, whom we called Uncle Jorges, coming to visit once when we all still lived in Morgans Road and handing out pennies to all the children.

In my mind I pictured my father clearly. He was smartly dressed in a sailor suit and sailor hat and was standing on the other side of a mist. He kept peering through the mist, trying to find me, to rescue me from Morgans Road and to carry me away to a life of love and comfort like Marie's.

When I returned to see the family home in Page Moss many years after we'd all left it, a neighbour told me that my father had come back looking for my mother and, I was convinced, for me too. By then all of us children were long gone. He had arrived too late to rescue me.

CHAPTER THREE

Auntie Doreen, Auntie Maureen, Mrs Savage and Mrs Cooper are the only foster mothers out of the twelve I had whose names I can still remember. Constant movement and uncertainty filled the first eight years of my life. When I was at home I was not sure how long I would be there, and when I was sent away to foster parents I was always poised for removal. Often a move from Morgans Road to a new foster carer meant a new school, so we were endlessly dislocated from any friends we had managed to make at school and from any teachers who had cared enough about us to offer extra support and encouragement. For the most part, our moves to foster parents seemed to coincide with those times when things between my mother and Sam were especially violent, with my mother's multiple pregnancies or with her unexplained bouts of perhaps alcohol-related ill health. I do remember her once being carried out of the bedroom on a stretcher. Sometimes she lay for days on end in her bedroom moaning quietly, but she never explained to us what was hurting her and we never dared ask.

The details of which foster mother did what have leaked together like cheap, watery paint in my memory. One kept a bell under the carpet so she could hear if I left my bedroom after I'd been put to bed. Another gave me oranges, which, for some reason, I was convinced were poisoned. One foster mother cut a circle of cardboard out of a cornflake box and wrote her name and phone number on it. I was made to go to school with this pinned to my sweater, like Hester Prynne's scarlet letter. I hated it and was teased by the other children. In the end I took it off and hid it in my pocket, pinning it back on to my chest once more before I reached the front door of my foster mother's house.

One of my foster families allowed us to go carol singing the Christmas just before I was nine. I decided that I'd knock on the door of a nice-looking house at the end of a very long driveway. I began to sing 'We Wish You a Merry Christmas', but nobody opened the front door. I was sure that someone was in the house because the light was on and I could hear rustling through the letterbox. I got so angry that no one came to the door that I pushed my mouth as far through the letterbox as it would go and swore loudly. As I got back to the end of the driveway a little old lady opened the door. I turned round and ran back up the path. She pressed a huge bag of pennies into my hand.

'Have a wonderful Christmas, dear,' she said in a faded, tinkling voice, and blew me a kiss. 'Sorry it takes me so long to get to the door.' She was oblivious to my ugly curses.

I was overjoyed, and overwhelmed with guilt for having judged her frailty to be Scrooge-like indifference. 'Thank you, thank you, thank you' were the only words I could say through my huge grin.

For the most part my stays with foster parents were brief but going to foster families was a chance to be treated like a proper child. We got regular food and could get clean. I was often given nice dresses. I thought the foster families were really rich because of the things they gave us. Mostly they weren't; they were only rich in comparison with our severely straitened circumstances.

Auntie Maureen was the foster mother I went to when I was about seven or eight, and who I wanted to stay with for always. She gave me affection, which I had never had before. And the more I got, the more I wanted. I hoped it would never end. She could always be counted on to say, 'Come over here, darling, and we'll have a nice cuddle.' She rocked me and sang nursery rhymes to me. She smelled of lemon soap and put her hair in curlers every night so that it bounced a bit on top of her head. Her expression was always pleasant. And when I did something wrong she sat down with me and treated me even more kindly than usual while she explained why I shouldn't hit the boys who teased me or snatch things from girls who sneered at me. Before Auntie Maureen I didn't know that calm, non-violent tellings-off like this existed.

I cried when the social worker came to pick me up to take me back home to my mother. I had been with Auntie Maureen for almost two months, a period of time that felt so long to me that I thought it was going to last for ever.

Once I was back home life quickly returned to normal and the kind mist of Auntie Maureen faded in my mind. My mother never seemed particularly pleased to see me, she continued to stay out at night and we all continued to be neglected.

My mother and Sam's mutual loathing had intensified after my birth. The lovey-dovey periods between the rows and the violence became increasingly infrequent. They no longer shared their alcohol, which I took as a bad sign. My mother went out drinking in various pubs around Liverpool while Sam sat glowering on the sofa cradling half bottles of whisky or drinking in separate pubs from my mother.

I and my siblings always seemed to be whispering words of warning to each other, like 'Keep out of the way, Dad's been down the boozer', or 'Watch out, he's steaming drunk', an expression my mother also sometimes used. My mother was away from the house even more than usual when Sam was around, in an attempt to avoid him, but spent a bit more time with us whenever he went back to sea.

Sam rarely spoke to me unless his words preceded a beating, and he pretended I didn't live in the house. Perhaps the colour of my skin perpetually taunted him. He wasn't that much better with my siblings, also aiming sidelong swipes at their heads when they walked past him, and swearing when they enquired timidly whether he had any pennies for sweets. 'Get out of my way, the whole fucking, snivelling lot of you' was one of his favourites; 'You're all just parasites' was another. None of us knew what the word meant, but Mary asked Betty.

'It's when you scrounge off people,' said Betty, not knowing why Mary had asked.

Mary hung her head and told us to be extra careful to keep out of Sam's way and not to ask him for anything.

Then, inexplicably, when I was four years old, Sam went missing. My mother seemed mildly anxious. She didn't know whether he was dead or alive, and I'm not sure if her anxiety was because she thought he was dead or because she thought he was still alive. I, however, experienced no such ambivalence. His vanishing meant freedom from shouts and blows. I owned one battered doll and fetched two glasses from the kitchen, which I filled with water. I raised a glass as I had seen my mother do when she was drinking whisky, tried to wrap my doll's plastic hand around the other glass, and said, in my best drunken voice, 'Cheers!'

A police officer came round to get a description of Sam. My mother had no photos of him so she went up to Mary, pushed the fringe back from her forehead and said, 'He looks just like her.'

The police never managed to trace him and none of us ever saw him again.

My mother shed no tears. Although she continued to stay away from home and to react to the slightest transgression from any of us with a punch, life without a man on the premises felt blissful.

It didn't last for long. A couple of months later my mother found herself a new boyfriend. His name was Peter and he was a short man with an enormous belly. He had piercing blue eyes that were too small for his flabby face, like tiny, glittering buttons lost in enormous buttonholes. Both his cheeks and jawbones were completely hidden by drapes of flaccid skin. He was always making jokes, and usually laughed more heartily at them than whoever happened to be listening to him.

'This is Peter. Uncle Peter to you,' said my mother, proudly, when she introduced him to us all.

Although I instinctively shied away from Peter he was always very friendly towards me. He wasn't violent towards me or my mother and seemed to be in a perpetually jolly mood, something very unusual in our house. I don't know whether Peter gave my mother money but we were looked after a little bit better after he arrived.

For some reason Peter seemed to prefer me to the other children. Until then I had only been singled out for negative treatment – even though I had never heard the expression 'Black sheep of the family', that was the role I inhabited – and to be the favoured one was an emotional luxury. The attention was flattering and it drew me towards him. Often he singled me out for gifts of sweets and penny toys. I basked in the attention and briefly felt almost powerful.

'Come over here, princess,' he said softly, smacking his fat knees to indicate that I should perch on them. Pretending to be a magician, he first showed me an empty hand and then, with some not-very-good concealment, he filled it with sweets.

'Der derr,' he said triumphantly. 'I can do magic, princess.'

I laughed, not at his cleverness, but with the anticipation of filling my rumbling stomach with something sugary. I could smell my release from hunger and, moments later, I was tipping a sherbet fountain or barely chewed liquorice Allsorts down my throat. My favourite sweets were Uncle Joe's mint balls, which lasted a good ten minutes if I sucked them slowly, and they set my mouth on fire.

Sometimes, when Peter beckoned to me to sit on his lap, he told me stories. We didn't have any books in the house so he always made them up. School was the only place I had ever seen books and the class teacher sometimes read the first- and second-year primary school children tales of Snow White and Cinderella. I was entranced by the stories, identified strongly with Cinderella's life, at least the first part of it, and dreamed of Snow White's happy ending for my own life. Peter's stories were rather less gripping and always sounded the same to me. They were all about beautiful young girls who found themselves in terrible predicaments – dragons, cruel stepmothers, starvation, battles – and always a mature, wise and powerful man came to their rescue and whisked them away to live happily ever after in his golden mansion. It never occurred to me that the man was always him.

One day Peter said he was going to take me to the café down the road for tea as a special treat. I was six years old and the invitation made me feel as if I'd grown a foot taller. I felt extremely loved and important. It wasn't every day that such outings were on offer to either me or to any of my sisters and brothers. I dived into the pile of dirty washing in the corner of the kitchen and tried to find something less dirty than the coarse blue skirt and threadbare yellow blouse I had on. I fished out a few things and eventually chose a pale blue dress of Mary's, even though I knew it would be too big for me, on the basis that it had a more diluted smell of unwashed bodies than everything else in the pile. My mother often moaned about the mountain of washing but rarely seemed to bother loading up our twin-tub.

'Come on, princess,' said Peter, laughing. 'Off we go. You can choose anything you like from the menu.' He put my tiny, bony hand into his fat, spongy ball of a hand and we set off down the street. I skipped with happiness.

The café was crowded when we arrived. It was a small place run by Bessie, an enormous, cheerful woman, with arms as thick as sides of beef coming out of her too-tight nylon overall. It was full of men smoking, men in oily clothes from the local garage, sailors home from sea and assorted painters, decorators and plumbers. I hated the thick smoke and kept waving at the air in front of me to clear it away.

The food at Bessie's was what she described as 'honest, no-nonsense fare'. In the kitchen, which was visible at the back of the shop, I could see diamond droplets of oil falling from chips she had just lifted out of the fryer, more eggs frying in one pan than I'd ever seen before in my life, and strips of bacon, with crispy, curling fatty edges. We never had any of those things at home and I decided that Bessie's café fitted my rather modest vision of heaven.

Peter chose a table in the corner and handed me a menu spotted with grease. I could barely read or write so I was completely unaware of all the misspelled words like 'bacen' and 'freid bred'.

Peter ordered for both of us. 'We'll have two bacon, eggs and fried bread please, Bessie.'

He looked hard at Bessie's tightly curled, fake-yellow hair, her huge breasts that looked as if they were panting to free themselves from her too-tight overall and those enormous arms.

'Yer a fine looking woman, Bessie,' said Peter, his eyes flitting expertly between her face and her breasts, like a spider moving back and forth across its web.

'And you're an old flatterer. You should hush your mouth. I'm old enough to be your mother. Will you be wanting garnishers with yer meal?'

'What's garnishers?' I asked.

'A little bit of lettuce and cucumber and tomato,' she explained.

'Yes, definitely,' I replied. We never got to eat food like that at home and when we had salad with school dinners I always loved the raw, crunchy novelty of it. Food at home was usually overcooked and ended up as grey, pulverised slop on our plates.

Peter talked to me like a real grown-up while we waited for our food. He told me about his job as a warehouse manager near the docks and asked me who my favourite teacher was at school.

'I haven't really got a favourite teacher. They all shout at me and don't like me, and say I'm thick and that I'm a bad girl. I'm always getting into trouble and getting told off for it.'

'Oh no, no, no, Clare, we can't have you talking like that. You mark my words: you'll go far in life. You're a very special little girl. You're my special little girl.'

I giggled and imagined being a famous ballerina, something I had dreamed of since I saw a storybook at one of my foster mother's homes. The story was mainly pictures with just one line of writing, which I couldn't read, on each page. It was about a little girl who wore a frilly ballerina dress and delicate pink ballet shoes with soft ribbons wrapped around her ankles.

Our food arrived so hot that when I bent my head towards the plate to breathe in the bacon fumes the steam burned my nose. It was a long time since I'd felt so contented with my lot. Things really were looking up since Peter had arrived. With his patronage life at home and life with (and often without) my mother seemed much rosier. I wolfed down the bacon and then pierced the yolks of the fried eggs with my fork, watching them stream towards the bread, dying it yellow. Everything tasted perfect.

I saved the salad until last and was about to scoop up a forkful of lettuce when I noticed that Bessie had doused it all in salad cream. Suddenly I felt terribly sick. I pushed the salad away. Inexplicably my whole, perfect outing had been spoiled. When Peter and I walked home I didn't feel like talking.

Despite Peter's gifts and cuddles, life at home continued to be chaotic and I suppose it wasn't surprising that my anxieties about home bled into my behaviour at school and led to many tellings-off from teachers. I fought with both boys and girls but I never picked fights mindlessly. I didn't know what morality was, but I fought on the basis of my own brand of justice.

I may have been tiny but I was tough and strong. When I was about nine, there was a girl called Sarah who was even smaller than me and terribly timid. She wore her blonde hair in two neat plaits and looked a lot more genteel, and so more vulnerable, than the rest of us. The bullies sniffed out her weakness immediately and positioned themselves to swoop.

'Come over 'ere, stuck-up Sarah,' Janet, the lead bully, shouted. She was a tall girl with small, sludgy, no-colour eyes and a smaller, sneery mouth. 'We're going to mess up those prissy, perfect plaits of yours. Only idiots come to school with plaits in their hair.'

She moved forward to grab at the plaits, flanked by a group of admiring followers who I nicknamed her ladies-in-waiting. I was watching carefully from the corner of the playground and, when I saw the bullies strike, something snapped inside me. I couldn't understand why plaits were forbidden. They looked plump and glossy to me, and an object of admiration rather than humiliation. As far as I was concerned, Sarah and her plaits were innocent.

A surge of electric rage struck me at the same moment that the bullies struck Sarah. I sprinted forward and jumped on to Janet's back to try and drag her away from Sarah. 'You're a bloody 'orrible bully, Janet. Leave Sarah alone.'

The ladies-in-waiting looked stunned that someone as tiny and unpopular as me would dare to take on a queen bee like Janet. I wasn't strong enough to drag her away but, because I was so wiry, I managed to wrap my arms and legs around her so that she appeared to be giving me an extremely reluctant piggyback. The shock of having me on her made her let go of Sarah's slim arms momentarily. 'Run, Sarah, run!' I shouted. She did.

Janet complained to our class teacher, Miss Hill, that I'd attacked her while she'd been minding her own business and I was banned from playtime for the rest of the day. 'I wish you wouldn't court trouble all the time, Clare. You really don't help yourself and you're an extremely naughty girl,' Miss Hill said. I didn't know what 'court' meant but thought it was not a good moment to request an explanation or to explain to Miss Hill the true sequence of events.

The more troublesome I became the less nice the teachers were to me. I always came bottom of the lowest stream at school. I scribbled on the pictures of other children because I was jealous that their pictures were put up on the wall while mine never were. Because I was a 'bad' child the teachers referred to me by both my first name and my surname. The good children's surnames were never mentioned aloud. I was sent to the headmistress's office almost every day for chastisement and hated everything about school apart from PE. I did try to be good but, when I was, nobody noticed or commented. I decided that I might as well stay bad because at least then I wasn't ignored.

My mother was at home increasingly rarely and Mary often stayed at Marie's house. My oldest brother, Damian, frequently accompanied my mother when she went out so I became the unofficial head of the household by the time I was five and took on responsibility for the younger ones. Not that I had much idea of how to bring children up with my mostly absent mother and invisible father as role models. The extent of my mother's parental guidance was to say to me: 'Go to the shops and "rob" a loaf of bread, our Clare. Then pinch a couple of bottles of milk from people's doorsteps to go with it.'

As soon as I was able to climb on a chair to reach the cooker I would make pobs, a mixture of hot milk and sugar and bits of bread, for the younger ones. We had free school meals and without them I think all of us would have suffered from malnutrition. I didn't feel stigmatised for this at school because most of the children had free meals and, even if we had been in a minority, I wouldn't have cared. Hunger eliminates pride.

From the moment in Marie's Ajax bath that I had realised that I was irreversibly darker and different from everyone else in the neighbourhood, I hated my colour. I spent one Christmas as a child with foster parents. I shared a single bed with Mary and our foster mother left us both a bag of presents, one at each side of the bed. We never got Christmas presents at home so this should have been a really thrilling moment. I was so excited about the sack of presents lying at the bottom of our bed on Christmas Eve that I waited until Mary was asleep and peeked inside. I was overjoyed when I saw crayons and colouring books, but it was spoiled because of something else in the bag. We both had a doll – hers white and mine black. I recoiled from the black doll and coveted the Aryan version, which was everything I yearned to be. Surreptitiously I switched the two dolls but, when I woke up on Christmas morning, the black doll had been restored to my bag – Mary had woken up after me, had sneaked a look as I had and, equally unimpressed by the black doll, had reclaimed the white one. When I saw what she had done I was so furious that I started fighting her to get the white doll back. In the end my foster mother took the dolls away from both of us.

'It's all your fault, Mary, you shouldn't have switched the dolls,' I shouted at her.

'No, it's not. It's your stupid fault,' she yelled back. 'You're black. You should be happy to have a doll that looks like you.'

We spent most of Christmas Day in our bedroom sulking at each other and dreaming of being the sole owner of the white doll.

At the Queen's Head pub close to where we lived a man used to give me money for doing handstands against the wall. I thought he was paying me because he considered me to be a great gymnast in the making, when he was probably just getting a kick out of seeing my skirt drop over my head and of getting a view of me either with or without knickers on, depending on whether I had wet myself that day or not. Another man offered to pay me money for taking my knickers off, lifting my dress and sitting in the middle of a field. The field had very green grass stretching endlessly. There was a block of toilets in the field and I saw he had something small in his hand. Although I had no idea that such things existed at the time, it was probably a camera, which he was using to film me out of the small toilet window. As far as I was concerned, getting paid for lifting my dress up, pulling my knickers down and sitting in a field while some stranger watched from a distance was a very good deal. It was much easier than running errands for the neighbours to earn sixpence. I waited patiently for him to finish whatever it was he was doing, clutched the two shillings he pressed into my hand and scampered off gratefully.

My mother was never around to witness any of these incidents. And when she was at home she seemed to be getting angrier, especially with me. My mother often smacked me and the others across the head. The frequency of the violence made it almost banal. Her oft-repeated words to get out of her sight, and to 'Shut up crying' still ring in my ears.

Until the day she died I never really understood my mother. Mainly she was vague and distant and absent. Even when she was at home chastising us there was a faraway look in her eyes, as if she was just passing through our home and our world on her way to somewhere she hankered after. Although she yelled at us I didn't feel she hated us, just that we were another chaotic inconvenience, tripping her up on her way through her already messy life. She seemed to prefer the pubs and the men to us but, even with a glass of whisky in her hand and a man pawing her, part of her was a long way away.

I don't think she ever found the peace and contentment she pined for. Perhaps, in death, she found what had eluded her in life.

CHAPTER FOUR

As soon as I started school, nits became constant companions. Miss Hill, my class teacher, explained that they sucked the blood out of our scalps and I felt cheated. I wanted to keep all my blood for myself and I thought that, if I didn't have the nits constantly guzzling at my expense, I would be far less hungry.

Mary and I had a mission to seek out each other's nits and pull them out of our hair. We didn't want to kill them though. We developed a technique of trapping them between the nails of our thumb and first finger and then sliding them off a piece of hair without squashing them. We stored them as carefully as gems in my mother's discarded matchboxes. I can't remember why, but we thought the nits were precious and desired once they were no longer attached to our scalps. Perhaps it was the fascination of watching them flounder like fish on the shore and the control over life and death they gave us. They didn't survive long without our blood, however, and we tipped the dead ones into the bin to make way for the endless supply of blood-fattened ones that we plucked from our heads every day. When Mary wasn't looking I pinched her nits, because I wanted more for my matchbox.

At school we received regular visits from the nit nurse, visits I dreaded because it meant humiliation for me. She wore a white overall so starched it would put the fear of God into any nit, and parted my hair in a tokenistic way. She knew the nits were there.

'Dear, dear, Clare, what are we going to do about those pesky little nits? You don't seem to be able to get shot of them do you?' All the other children who'd been pronounced nit-free whispered and giggled. 'Take this letter home to your mother. She really must sort you out.' She handed me a white envelope as stiff and disinfected as her overall. I hung my head and quickly stuffed it into the waistband of my skirt in the hope that the other children wouldn't see it.

My mother was furious that the school had shown her (not me) up in this way, and angrily took the scissors to my hair, chopping at it vengefully. When she had finished cutting I was too scared to look at what she'd done but, before I could risk a glance in the mirror, she had picked up a razor and was shaving off the remaining tufts, which fluttered, silently reproachful, to the floor. I could see the nits jumping perplexedly from abandoned strand to abandoned strand.

The nits had left me with sores where they had sucked into my scalp. My mother made no comment about them, briskly scooping up the pile of hair and newly homeless nits from the floor and throwing them on to the fire before I could rescue them for my matchbox. She handed me an ugly red and yellow bobble hat and told me to wear it until my hair had grown back. I suffered badly at school for that, with the other children shouting 'baldy' at me and pulling my hat off so they could have a good laugh.

'Ugly baldy with an 'orrible 'at,' they taunted me. They found my tears hilarious.

Through blurred eyes I punched the children who tossed back their glossy heads of hair and called me names. My teacher saw what had happened to my hair and asked me gently, 'Who did this to you?'

'Me mum,' I cried, with my chin pushed down into my chest. The teacher shook her head from side to side and touched my arm. She didn't say anything more. I endured the other children's taunts until my hair grew back. The nits moved back in immediately.

I was never sure why I felt like an outsider at school. I was the only non-white child there and got used to the regular taunts of 'Paki, go back to your country.'

I always retorted indignantly, 'I'm not a Paki, I'm English!'

I fought better and more aggressively than most of the other children, and maybe they resented me for that, or perhaps they smelled my poverty and recoiled from it. When we were fostered and changed schools I tried my best to hide the fact from the other children. If they found out that I was being fostered they often taunted me with cries of 'You've got no mum or dad, ner, ner, ner, ner, ner. You're a sad orphan, so there!' Usually I punched them when they made remarks like that because I felt too angry to speak.

The teachers at whatever school I happened to be attending, sometimes with my sisters and brothers, sometimes without, didn't always show much sensitivity about my fractured home life. I struggled to understand all the subjects I was taught but, for me, maths was the most impenetrable. Cheating seemed the only solution and, whenever possible, I manoeuvred myself into the seat next to one of the cleverer girls in the class.

One day the maths teacher, Miss West, had set us some work that involved putting a series of missing numbers into vertical and horizontal boxes. The numbers on the page were a sea of confusion to me, bobbing up and down and swirling past my eyes. Sarah, the girl with the plaits, was very stoical about my constant copying and didn't give the game away to the teacher. She seemed to think that allowing me to cheat was fair recompense for me defending her against the bullies. But that day Miss West spotted what I was doing and summoned me to her desk angrily.

'Have you been copying, Clare?' she asked sternly.

'No, miss,' I mumbled. I didn't sound convincing and I knew that Miss West would make me sit by her desk and would watch me working on the sums. I had been found out and I was about to be shamed and humiliated again.

'Write down the answers,' she said curtly, jabbing her finger against the sums I hadn't yet copied from Sarah. Miss West knew I wouldn't be able to manage any of them but she made no attempt to explain the work to me. She simply sent me back to my desk with an angry red cross through the sums I had guessed at. To make things worse I couldn't go back to copying from Sarah because she had handed her paper in by this time. I never discovered how to do those sums.

Although life at school, at home or with foster parents was often wretched, there were also moments of pure joy. I wished that one of the dinner ladies, Mrs Abbott, could be my mother. She was wonderfully warm to me and knew without asking me any questions that life at home was hard. She was a slight, optimistic woman with hair streaked seven or eight different shades of grey, who always wore a pink twinset with razor-sharp ironing creases down the sleeves, and a sensible black skirt.

One day she appeared by my side as I was scraping the last few remaining streaks of custard from the side of my bowl. None of us had eaten since the previous lunchtime. The cupboards at home were empty and my mother hadn't been home that night.

'How would you like to come back to my house for tea one day after school, Clare?' she asked, beaming.

My mouth dropped open and I looked carefully at her in case she was teasing me. 'Oh, yes, I'd be made up. Yes, please,' I replied.

'Good,' she said. 'I'll write a note for your mum and, if she gives her permission, you can come after school tomorrow. I'll wait in the playground for you. I only live round the corner from here.'

I raced home, praying my mother would be there to give her permission. She was at home, half sitting, half lying on the sofa I was born on, with her eyes shut and her brow wrinkled.

'Mum, Mum, I've been invited round to one of the dinner ladies' houses for tea tomorrow. Please, please, please say I can go.'

'Don't shout like that, Clare, I've got a terrible headache. Yes, you can go, but leave me in peace now. Get out the way.' She made a shooing gesture with her hand and I raced upstairs and lay down on the bed, for once not noticing the scratchy blankets.

I was overjoyed that my mother had given her permission but I wasn't even sure that she had properly heard what I was asking her. I started to fantasise about what Mrs Abbott's house would be like and what food she'd give me to eat. I hoped she'd have some sherbet fountains and liquorice Allsorts in her cupboard.

The following day at school I spent even more time than usual with my mind elsewhere. At 3.30 p.m. I sprinted out and, as she'd promised, Mrs Abbott was waiting for me. I felt extremely proud walking down the road with her. A privilege had been bestowed on me which none of the other children in my school had been offered.

Mrs Abbott's house was immaculately tidy and full of comfortable chairs and peaceful pictures on the walls. She had made a huge pile of egg sandwiches cut into neat little triangles with the crusts off, and a plate of dainty fairy cakes with pale lemon and pink icing and a little Parma violet in the middle.

'Oh, Mrs Abbott, these are so yummy.' My hand instinctively stretched out to grab a second cake but I suddenly pulled it back on to my lap, not wanting to be considered rude or greedy.

'Go ahead, Clare, you can take another one. I made them especially for you. There's only me rattling around in this old house and I certainly won't be able to eat them all. Whatever's left over after tea you can take home with you and share with your brothers and sisters.'

I was floating on Mrs Abbott's kindness and the sugary fullness in my stomach. For her, the act of inviting me back for tea was, I suppose, a small one, but, for me, it was as big as the world. Regular sprinklings of the gentle goodness of Mrs Abbott and her kind would equip me to stride through life shaking off slaps from my mother and harsh words from my teachers like a handful of raindrops on a hot summer's day. Briefly I felt loved and powerful and fired up by the possibilities which life offered.

Mrs Abbott gave me fruit and sweets to take home as well as the fairy cakes, which I shared with my sisters and brothers. I couldn't believe my good fortune. She gently put her arms round me. I hugged her hard, screwing my eyes tight shut to better pretend that she was my mother.

'You look after yourself, Clare. Now off you go home.'

I raced home, fired with anticipation at handing out the goodies to my siblings. Arriving home with something infinitely superior to a stolen bottle of milk and loaf of bread would, I hoped, raise my standing among them. Starving and unrestrained, they filled their mouths. Mary cheered. She had given Tom most of her helping of bread and milk because there hadn't been enough to go round.

'You're an angel, Clare, for bringing back all this lovely grub,' she said, panting slightly because she was swallowing so fast.

Apart from the rare excursions with Peter or to Mrs Abbott's, however, our lives were hungry. Like a tortoise I was always mentally preparing myself for hibernation and tried to fill my stomach whenever an opportunity presented itself.

When I was eight, Tom and I saw Mrs Bennett, the lady who lived next-door-but-one to us, go out. That hot, still afternoon we crept into her back garden and found she had left the back door open. We did a quick visual inventory to see what food was lying around and spotted five perfect apple pies, still warm, sitting on a shelf. Tom sat on the floor while I climbed up to reach the pies. I decided that it would look too obvious to cut into one of the pies or to steal a whole one so I burrowed carefully under the piecrust and excavated all the apple filling, which I shared with Tom. The apple tasted like heaven – hot and sweet and tangy and forbidden, and I ended up finger-vacuuming every single bit of apple out of every single pie, scooping bits into Tom's hands, which he lapped up with his tongue.

We ran back to our house as soon as the deed was done, bellies comfortably bulging, and weren't surprised to hear an angry knock at the door a few hours later. I never spent much time thinking about consequences as a child, only about survival. Gazing at her with a wide-eyed innocence that could have competed with Tatum O'Neal in *Paper Moon* for an Oscar, we shook our heads blankly when a furious Mrs Bennett accused us of stealing the apple out of her pies. She marched off, convinced that we were the culprits but unable to prove it. I can still remember how luscious that apple tasted and how jubilant we felt as she walked back to her house because we'd got away with it.

Food and fibs often went together during my childhood. Because I was perpetually hungry I used to try and get two dinners at school. After I'd finished my first meal or my first pudding, almost always something with thick yellow custard perfumed with fake vanilla, I'd lick my plate clean so that I could go up for a second portion, pretending that I had just walked up to the dining room and been given a clean plate to collect my meal first time round.

Whether the dinner ladies knew what I was up to and let it pass or simply didn't notice I don't know. Occasionally one said, 'Haven't you been up already?' And then I adopted that same wide-eyed look I used with Mrs Bennett and her hollow pies, shake my head, look baffled at such a suggestion and then shuffle off. As soon as my back was turned from them, with the precious extra portion winking up at me from the plate, a huge grin would spread across my face.

It was my job to take my little brother John to nursery school but he was often reluctant to go. One morning I had to literally drag him along the street and decided that the only way to make him move by himself was a spot of bribery. I had a shiny sixpence in my pocket, which I had earned from running an errand for a neighbour and was saving it for a chocolate feast after I had dropped him off. I weighed up the pros and cons of losing my hard-earned sixpence to John or continuing to drag him along the street, and opted to lose the sixpence.

'I'll buy you a Bounty bar if you walk along nicely,' I wheedled. John instantly brightened up and straightened his spine. I bought him the chocolate from the mobile shop and he stopped crying.

'I'll put your chocolate in your pump bag so it'll be there for later,' I said when we arrived at nursery. He still seemed a bit upset but agreed that I could do that, and then went off with one of the nursery teachers. That bar of chocolate sitting in John's pump bag swam into my mind, swelling until there was no space for anything else. The justifications bounced in and out of my brain: he'll forget; I earned the sixpence; he had had breakfast and I hadn't. I convinced myself that stealing John's Bounty bar was not a matter of consequence. I sneaked back to where his peg was and snatched it out. On my way home I stuffed it into my mouth and demolished it in two or three guilty bites.

Luckily John had forgotten about the chocolate by the end of the day, but I felt uneasy about it for years. Eventually, when he was much older, I confessed my crime to him and belatedly handed over a Bounty bar. He shrugged and grinned and I felt absolved.

There was a lady who lived in our street who, according to a rumour spread by the children of the neighbourhood, was a witch. She had horrible teeth, hunched over her walking stick and was a voracious knitter. For some reason the combination of those factors led to the witch theory. Nobody ever went and knocked on her door because they thought she would put a spell on them. The children dared me to go instead. They were too cowardly to go themselves but I agreed to do it. I had no fear of that kind of situation and, more than that, thought it might boost my standing among my peers.

I banged hard on her doorknocker, which looked exactly the same as our doorknocker.

'Er, hello. I was wondering if you needed any errands running or wanted anything from the shop?' I asked uncertainly.

The lady smiled broadly; she must have been very lonely.

'I think I'm all right for shopping today, my dear, but do come in. I'll teach you how to knit if you like.' Her voice was sweet and soft. It seemed odd that a voice so pure could pass through her blackened, rotten teeth intact. 'But first you must wash your hands,' she said. She took out a flannel to wash my hands with, something I had never seen before.

'What's your name, dear?'

'Clare.'

'Oh, what a lovely name. I knew another little girl called Clare. At a girls' boarding school before I got old and wrinkly.' She laughed at her infirmity. 'Now, dear, when you knit, you increase whatever you're making by a stitch at a time.' She started winding wool around one of her steel knitting needles and moving the stitches row by row from one needle to the next. 'It's in, round, through, off,' she kept repeating, soothingly. 'That's all there is to it. You can make yourself a nice woolly scarf for winter once you get the hang of this.'

Once I'd clumsily got the hang of the sequencing, she sent me on my way with a biscuit and told me to pop back whenever I fancied a spot of knitting and a biscuit. I walked out, munching triumphantly.

'She's not a witch after all, you bunch of wallies,' I said smugly, lingering over every mouthful of my biscuit to underline my bravery. Everyone gaped at me in admiring silence.

The old lady's name was Elizabeth and I visited her a few more times despite raised eyebrows from the other children in the street. I got halfway through knitting a scarf at Elizabeth's house, then social services fostered us again and my connection with her was broken. I tried to knit again a couple of years later but I couldn't remember the sequence of moves and gave up impatiently.

Another old lady who showed me kindness was Minnie. She was slight and frail and smiley. I used to run up to her house, which was a bit further down our road.

'D'you want any messages, Minnie?' I'd call through the letterbox.

She would send me running down the street to buy her a bag of sugar, or ask me to polish her step, which to me always seemed perfectly clean in the first place. And then came the moment of pure pleasure. Minnie shakily climbed up on to a chair to reach the top shelf of a glass cabinet in her living room. With so much fumbling, I was always anxiously convinced that she would topple to the ground before I got my reward. Then, slower than a snail, she would pull out a tin covered in silver foil, fumble some more, and then hand me a shiny new sixpence.

'There you are, love.' She smiled, making her wrinkles deepen so much I thought her skin was going to crack.

I whispered my thanks and bolted off down the street to spend my earnings on sweets from the mobile shop.

Minnie always seemed pleased to see me and I responded to her warmth. With Minnie I wasn't the bad girl I was at home but the good girl who could help a dear old lady by eagerly running a few errands for her.

I found more comfort at the local police station than in the family home. When I got lost at the age of five I was taken there and given milk and biscuits by kind officers. So I thought that the police station was the place where you went to get milk and biscuits. The following day I managed to find my way back there and knocked on the door. An enormous, jolly looking police officer with very red cheeks was behind the counter. Standing on tiptoe I could just see over it.

'Now, what can I do for you, young lady? Where's your mother?'

'Please, mister, I was here yesterday when I got lost. I'm not lost now but can I please have some more milk and biscuits?'

The officer shook his head, beamed at me and told me to hurry home to my mother. If only he knew that my mother was very unlikely to be waiting and wondering about me at home.

The kindness of strangers, neighbours and acquaintances played a major role in helping me through my childhood. From them I learned that being nice to grown-ups often did pay off, even though it failed with my mother. Because we all tried to spend as much time as possible away from our comfortless home these moments of happiness with other adults filled much of the void and I became reliant on them for my survival.

Some of my happiest times were spent with Marie. We dared each other to do things and, one day, she said to me that she would give me some bubble gum – one of my favourite sweets – if I went to Holy Communion with her.

At first I was reluctant to go centre stage to take the communion wafer on my tongue but then, like John's Bounty bar, the bubble gum, in all its fruity, flavoursome glory moved into my brain. I plucked up the courage and stood behind the last person in line. I kneeled down, said 'Amen', and stuck my tongue out for the wafer. Then I turned away giggling and went back to Marie expectantly.

An old lady told us off for laughing at Holy Communion and made me sip a cup of holy water. 'You're a naughty girl,' she said. 'Repeat after me: "In the name of the Father and of the Son and of the Holy Ghost. Amen." '

We chanted dutifully then left the church in fits of giggles. Marie pulled a piece of warm, pink bubble gum out of her pocket. The heat from her body had stuck the wrapper to the gum but I expertly separated the two, like a poacher skinning a rabbit, and popped it into my mouth. It tasted a whole lot nicer than the bland communion wafer.

In those days I was willing to do pretty much anything that anyone dared me to do, particularly if sweets were dangled. Showing I wasn't a 'scaredy cat' was my second priority after finding enough food to fill my belly. I believed that, if I showed myself to be tough, nobody would bully me and I would be able to walk down the street encased in a protective bubble.

One time some of the children in our street dared me to lie down in the road in a game called True Dare, Command or Promise, to see if a car would run me over. Eager to please and reckless about my life, I agreed. I didn't even notice that, while the others were egging me on, they showed no signs of joining in with this kamikaze act. As I lay down blithely, not even considering what it might feel like to have a car roll its tyres over my body, a car approached and screeched to a halt a few inches away from me.

Miss Blake, one of my teachers from school, got out. 'What on earth do you think you're doing lying down in the middle of the road like that? Get up at once,' she shouted. I think she was shouting in shock and relief that she hadn't killed me rather than in anger.

From the age of four I had realised that being helpful to neighbours could generate income and, by the age of eight, I had diversified from my basic services of polishing steps and running errands to car watching, child watching (for ten minutes while mothers popped down to the shops) and hanging out washing for neighbours.

The stability and relative affluence in Marie's home translated into a kind of film-star glamour for me. Her family had some regular visitors who drove up in a dazzling, shiny, pink car. I had never seen a car like that before; most of the cars in our neighbourhood were dull, battered and second-hand. It was a rare glimpse of a different, elegant and more exciting world beyond the one I knew. It was a world I yearned to inhabit and, remembering Peter's words that I could really be something, one I vowed I would become a part of when I grew up.

I offered to stand guard over the pink car for a penny while they visited Marie's family to make sure that none of the other children scratched it. I earned my money too. If a child approached to try and touch the car I gave them a good punch, bouncer-style, and sent them away. I was discreet about my jobs and kept all my sixpences and shillings to myself. I was terrified that my mother might find out about my moneymaking schemes and demand her cut, but she never did.

My mother often talked about how the money the 'social' gave her was never enough to feed our perpetually open mouths. 'You're too expensive for me you children,' she said whenever the cupboards were bare and we wandered into the kitchen peering into them in the hope that food had miraculously appeared since we last checked five minutes before.

If the men she spent nights with on the ships or in her bedroom gave her money she never seemed to share it with us. For as long as we lived with her my mother described herself as 'dirt poor' and bought all our clothes at jumble sales or received free hand-me-downs from the neighbours.

While most of the children at school invited friends back to their homes from time to time I was never allowed to. And, to be honest, nobody really wanted to come back to our scruffy, unwelcoming house that never had the kind of treats in the kitchen cupboards that children liked to eat.

One friend called Susan did seem keen to come and play with me, though, and when we arrived home I assumed my mother wouldn't be there. I had been wondering whether we had any bits of bread left so that I could make Susan some pobs. But my mother was at home and she was leaning over a pot on the stove. She had made some oxtail soup, which we all loved but were rarely given. When she saw me appear with Susan she looked a bit put out. I couldn't tell if it was because she was ashamed of anyone from outside the family seeing our shabby home or because she just didn't want Susan around. Whatever her motive she decided on segregated dining and sat Susan down on our front step with a plastic cup of soup and chunk of bread, while the rest of us had ours inside.

Afterwards Susan and I played chase in the street with all the other children from the neighbourhood. I felt it had all gone very well, but as soon as I had waved Susan goodbye my mother appeared at my side.

'Don't you ever bring anyone into this house ever again,' she said, her top teeth mashing against the bottom ones in an attempt to control her rage. And, with no further explanation, she turned and walked off down the street.

I was aware from a very young age that I had good in me as well as bad. But I didn't seem to have much control over either, or any way of making sense of why I did certain things at certain times. I always wanted to help out my sisters and brothers, particularly the little ones, and sharing sweets and being kind made me feel warm inside, but my frustration at being black, academically incompetent and impoverished sometimes got the better of me. So many people had told me that I was a bad girl that redemption seemed impossible.

I used to bunk off school quite regularly because my failure to achieve academically quickly became a gigantic, vicious circle. I was walking down the street one lunchtime when I spotted a tin of black paint that a workman had left unattended next to a shed. Without any sort of thought process at all I grabbed the paint tin and the paintbrush lying next to it and wrote 'fuk of' on the white wall of the shed. Too late I realised that a policeman had been watching me. I threw the paintbrush to the ground and ran as fast as I could. I dodged in and out of back alleys and eventually found myself back at home. I had hoped to run into the house and hide. The door was usually unlocked whether my mother was in or out, because we had absolutely nothing worth stealing, but today she had gone out and decided to lock it. I looked around to see if there was anywhere to run to. There was nowhere.

As I sat panting on my front step, the policeman appeared. I pressed my bottom hard into the step in the vain hope that I might melt into the stone. I looked at the policeman towering above me in his black uniform with shiny buttons and was overwhelmed with fear. I thought he would probably take me away and lock me up, that my mother would be furious and that there would be nobody around the house to make sure Tom and John got to nursery in the mornings. Suddenly the hardships of Morgans Road felt enormously appealing.

'Don't be writing any more words on walls. Now go on home,' was all he said. He sounded stern but not angry.

I couldn't believe I'd got away with it, but I remembered his kindness. My mother never did find out what I'd done and so I avoided a beating.

Like social services, who removed us from home temporarily and regularly at my mother's behest, the policeman asked no questions about why an eight-year-old girl wearing a mud-stained white blouse, ragged flowery skirt and shoes with holes in the soles, was sitting all alone on the front step of a house.

It was remarkable that we weren't permanently removed from home earlier. It would have been hard for us to have looked any needier. The neglect of all of us was palpable. Our stained, smelly clothes, our matted hair, our perpetual hunger and the way we ran wild in the streets, usually without any sort of parental supervision, surely should have set alarm bells ringing at social services much earlier. But somehow everyone in authority turned a blind eye until the day came when they could ignore our plight no longer. When our removal finally did come it was swift and unexpected.

CHAPTER FIVE

We all knew about social workers because we were so often placed with temporary foster parents when my mother was ill. But the social workers who lifted us out of Morgans Road always seemed unconcerned about our circumstances when they returned us to the bare squalor of our house. When my mother called on them they appeared, and when she didn't they stayed away. We never encountered the same social worker twice. It felt as if the entire Liverpool social services department danced to the tune of my mother's childcare needs. At that time children's feelings were rarely taken into account and their opinions rarely canvassed, particularly by statutory bodies like social services departments. Social workers may well have asked my mother questions about our welfare but they never probed us directly.

It was about 9 p.m. on a particularly dark February night when everything changed. I was nine years old. I'd made pobs when we got home from school but our stomachs emptied quickly; there was no food left in the house.

Tom always asked me to lay my ear against his stomach to listen to the rumbles when he was hungry. It seemed to comfort him that someone was prepared to gather evidence of his hunger so directly.

'Can you hear the bubbles popping, Clare?' he asked as I rested my head against his concave belly.

'Yes, Tom, I can, but don't you worry. We're going to fill your tummy up to the top with yummy sweets and crisps in a few minutes.'

He beamed. He trusted me implicitly.

We had some empty glass bottles to take back to the local shop, which we could exchange for a few precious pennies. Some of the street lamps weren't working and it was pouring with rain. We were scared of going out into the dark wetness but we were all starving. Tom and I started walking down the road. Neither of us had a raincoat, and by the time we had reached Mrs Bryant's house, which was only a few doors away from ours, the rain was dripping off our noses and woollen sweaters.

I grabbed Tom's hand.

'Just imagine if every raindrop was worth the price of a diamond, Tom. Then we could sell these raindrops and buy mountains of food.'

He looked doubtful, puzzling over how raindrops could become diamonds.

We arrived at the local shop, which was attached to the Queen's Head pub, and stood outside it until a man who looked kind came along. The shop sold sweets and crisps and lemonade.

Whenever I met older people I checked the direction of the lines on their face in a bid to decipher their characters. If the lines around their eyes and mouths crinkled upwards I trusted them; if they hung downwards like Sam's lines had, I tried to keep away from them. This man was all upward creases.

'Please, mister, would you take these bottles in for us and get our pennies back on them?' I asked in the purest voice I could.

He looked at us, obviously wondering why two such young children were out by themselves so late at night.

'OK, kids,' he said, without asking any awkward questions. Some adults did ask us uncomfortable questions about where our parents were if they spotted us out alone. Although I was nine I was very small for my age and easily passed for six. Tom was just four and also small for his age, so the bedraggled pair of us could well have aroused suspicion. 'I'll be out in two ticks,' was all he said.

He came out almost immediately and tipped the pennies into my hands. Joyfully, we bought some nuts and crisps and started stuffing them into our mouths. I was chewing so hard I could hear my teeth grinding the fatty, salty food into a pulp. I couldn't chew and swallow fast enough to fill the urgent hole.

The food warmed me and I suddenly felt tired.

'Let's get the bus back, Tom, it's so cold out here and we've still got a couple of pennies left.'

Because it was so dark and because I was so tired I missed our stop and we got off at the stop past ours. As I peered up and down the street trying to get my bearings, a lady jumped out of a car.

'Are you lost children, where do you live?'

'Morgans Road, miss,' I said quickly, trying to sound confident and not lost.

'Well, why don't you both hop in and I'll drop you off home. I'm going that way.' We didn't hesitate; we were both soaked and Tom looked exhausted.

'Are you all alone?' she asked as she took us into our house.

The house was in complete darkness because the money in the electricity meter had been used up. We were always trying to scrounge money to put in the meter but that night we hadn't managed it.

'Where's your mother?' she asked, her brow folding into worry shapes.

'Me mum's out,' I said vaguely, in the hope that it would prevent her from asking more questions.

'Where's your dad?'

'We haven't got one.'

She left looking perplexed and we thought nothing more of it. We ate more of our crisps and nuts in bed. The others were asleep. We drifted off to sleep feeling blissfully full and carefree.

The lady must have reported our situation to social services because the next morning a middle-aged woman wearing glasses turned up at our house. She parked her shiny orange mini outside our front door. She had no lines on her face so I couldn't properly work out what she was like, but she wasn't smiling. We had only just woken up and gathered at the door in the crumpled clothes we'd slept in. Our ruffled hair must have looked like a collection of haystacks of different heights.

'Is your mother at home children?' she asked softly.

We all silently shook our heads, wary of divulging too much in case we got ourselves, or our mother, into trouble. Although she wasn't wearing a uniform she had a look and smell of officialdom about her. We were all used to seeing unfamiliar adults around the place but they looked nothing like her: they were usually my mother's boyfriends and they ordered us around. This polite line of questioning seemed unusual.

Our mother hadn't come home the night before and we genuinely had no idea where she was. We had thought nothing of her not being at home because her absences from Morgans Road were becoming increasingly frequent. Peter had disappeared from the scene about two years before when I was seven years old. His departure was as sudden as Sam's and again there was no explanation of why he had left my mother. She had not replaced him with any sort of permanent boyfriend and instead found her men in the pubs and docked ships.

'Very well,' she said. 'I'm afraid you can't stay here by yourselves any longer. It isn't legal for children as young as you all are to be left in a house without a responsible adult to care for you. How have you managed to keep yourselves clean and fed and get yourselves to school?'

All of us stared dolefully at her. None of us answered out of loyalty to my mother. The lady shook her head in a gesture of sadness mixed with exasperation.

'Now, children, you have five minutes to pack a few things into a suitcase and then we really must be on our way.'

We all looked questioningly at her. 'Don't worry, dears. I'm taking you to a place of safety where you won't have to worry about keeping clean and getting fed any more.'

We didn't pack any clothes but left the house in what we were standing up in. I was wearing navy blue trousers with a stirrup which went under my heels and a bright red top with white spots on it. I loathed these clothes. Mary took charge of the communal metal comb with three missing teeth. We obediently climbed into the car. Suddenly I remembered that I had left a few pennies of precious savings at Marie's house. To me it seemed like a fortune, and I jumped out of the car to reclaim my cash before the lady with glasses had turned the key in the ignition.

I knocked at Marie's door, and when she opened it I said: 'Can I have my money now because we're going in a car.'

I didn't say anything else to her and she didn't ask any questions, but she looked at the woman driving the mini and then at me and sensed that we weren't off on a brief outing to the local park. She went and fetched the pennies out of a jam jar on the kitchen shelf. Then we hugged and said goodbye solemnly and Marie touched my cheek very gently. After that I was very reluctant to get back into the car.

'Bye, Clare, let's play again soon,' she said, sounding like a wise adult.

Nothing had been explained to us and I had no idea where we were going, or whether it would be even worse than life in Morgans Road. The unnamed lady who had come to claim us ran after me, took me firmly by the hand and led me back to the car.

'Where exactly are we going?' I asked her anxiously. Although so much of our lives with our mother and her various boyfriends was hellish it was our hell and the sheer familiarity was strangely comforting now.

'We're going for a ride,' she said quietly and then squeezed her lips shut, peering anxiously into her mirror every few minutes to see five pairs of bright, questioning eyes fixed on her. As the eldest Damian was allowed to sit in the front. He too stared unblinkingly at her. I think the social services lady was terrified that tears would suddenly pour from all the eyes trained on her but our eyes remained dry. Although we had no idea what was going to happen to us, we all sensed that we needed to stay strong.

CHAPTER SIX

After fifteen minutes driving through the back streets of Liverpool the lady parked her mini in a side street darkened with thick, leafless trees. She ushered us out of the car and led us up a long, sweeping driveway, at least ten times bigger than our front path, to an enormous house. It had turrets rising from the roof and was painted in all different shades of green with a big tower in the centre pointing skywards. I thought we were moving to a palace in a fairy tale.

The lady knocked on the thick, wide door and a woman dressed in a long black gown with an enormous white collar and a black and white headdress appeared. I thought she was a magical angel from the fairy-tale palace, which I decided must be a kind of pre-heaven, a rehearsal for the real thing and a reward for our years of hardship with my mother.

However, I thought angels were supposed to be smiley and kind, and she seemed stern and unfriendly. I had never seen a nun in my life before and it was only later that I discovered that that was what she was.

'Come along,' she said briskly, after looking us up and down as we stared and stared at her on the doorstep.

I wonder what she thought of us all, a bedraggled, dirty bunch of children unaware of what lay ahead. The sense of walking into a fairy tale fell away. I felt as if we were cattle being herded into a pasture.

It would be impossible to find a greater contrast between the home we had just left and the one we now entered. In Morgans Road all was chaos and dirt, with an absence of Christian morality. Our new home adhered to a rigid routine, an unnatural cleanliness and a morality buttoned into a straitjacket. I was nine and a half years old and I was to spend the next five years of my life here.

I found out after a few days that the name of the place was Park Hall Children's Home, an establishment run by an order of Irish nuns. We were ushered into a tiny room, which had two sinks in it, a toilet and lots of hooks for clothes. There was a clean but unpleasant smell in the room. I discovered later it was the rough, bleach-based disinfectant that the nuns favoured.

We huddled together. I was sobbing and Tom, who often took his lead from me, joined in. When I realised this, I tried to control my own tears and hush him in case we got into trouble for making such a noise. As we sat and waited I spotted lots of children filing out of another room. The girls were wearing long black net dresses with veils over their heads. They seemed very subdued. They had just been to chapel to pray, I discovered later.

The nuns saw it as their job to disinfect our bodies and our souls. Our bodies were easier to put in order. The boys were marched off in one direction for baths and us girls in another. We were put into a white, gleaming bathtub. It was even more pristine than Marie's. One of the nuns, Sister Joanna, picked up a slab of soap and started scrubbing at us. She pummelled enthusiastically, starting between our toes and moving systematically right up to our infested hair. A glistening moustache of sweat formed between the top of her lips and the bottom of her nose. Swirls of grey broke up the layer of white soap scum resting on top of the bath water.

She wrinkled her nose up at the smell of us.

'My goodness, you certainly need a good clean up,' she said tetchily. None of us liked being scrubbed so hard by Sister Joanna and one by one we all started to cry, our fat tears splashing into the dirty water.

Our clothes were crawling with fleas. They were briskly removed and were later burnt in the incinerator, although I didn't discover this until much later. Sister Joanna picked up the biggest pair of scissors I had ever seen.

'All of you are crawling with nits. I'm going to have to cut your hair extremely short to get rid of them.'

Memories of my mother's abrupt cropping came flooding back and more tears came to my eyes.

'Oh, please don't,' I whispered, expecting her to produce a bobble hat at any moment. She ignored me and pulled a nit comb through our stubbly hair, squashing each wriggling nit with malicious pleasure against the teeth of the comb.

We were given some clean clothes, starched as hard as cardboard, to wear. We girls had grey flannel skirts and scratchy navy blue sweaters while the boys were given grey flannel shorts and pale blue T-shirts. I had never felt so clean or seen my sisters and brothers looking so scrubbed. In Morgans Road, on the rare occasions when we did have a bath we always put our dirty clothes back on again afterwards, so we never looked particularly fresh.

One of the nuns rustled her way into what I assumed was a dining room and signalled to us to follow her. She put two plates of banana sandwiches down on one of the tables.

'Sit down and eat, children, you must be hungry,' she said without smiling. I brightened up at the prospect of food. As usual we were all starving and we wolfed down every sandwich at top speed, just in case the nuns had any plans to remove them before we could finish them off. None of us said a word to each other. We were all dazed by our surroundings and anxious about what these strange women in long black dresses might do to us. All our energy was focused on watching the nuns who, in turn, watched us as we gobbled our sandwiches. We had no idea whether this strange, ordered place was merely a staging post on our journey or the end of the line. Nothing was explained to us, which was something all of us were used to from life in Morgans Road.

Next we were taken down to the basement where we met the other children. I still had no idea at this point that we were in a children's home. I wondered if it was some kind of hospital because of the cleanliness and the black and white uniforms. It was peculiar to see everything gleaming and ordered after the dull squalor of home. It was nothing like the cosiness of Marie's house and I had no idea that people lived in places that looked so surgical.

'Welcome to the orphanage,' grinned one girl with even darker skin than mine. 'My name's Margaret. What's yours? We're the unwanteds and this is the rubbish bin the adults who want to get shot of us put us into. Watch out for Sister Maria, she's the cruellest, and just try and shut your ears off when they start droning on about God.'

She spoke fast and I couldn't absorb much of what she was saying, except for the bit about being 'unwanteds'. I had a sensation of my blood draining away. I didn't want to listen to any more but I was drawn to her skin. I felt comfortable and unobtrusive for the first time in my life as I put my head close to Margaret's to listen to her depressing advice.

'There's no way to get the better of the nuns. All we can all do is try to survive while we're here,' she concluded. 'None of us have any other options.'

How could my mother have allowed this to happen to us? The deprived chaos of Morgans Road seemed almost appealing compared with the united granite front presented to us by the nuns. Never again would I have the freedom to run down the road to the mobile sweet van at the bottom of the road, clutching my pennies, or to giggle with Marie and cuddle Tom when he whimpered at night. Tears began to roll down my cheeks. While we lived in Morgans Road it had never occurred to me that there was anything pleasant about it, but being airlifted into this chilly place made me realise for the first time in my life that things can always get worse. Margaret offered me a crumpled handkerchief and said pragmatically: 'Don't waste your tears on the nuns. Come on, let's go upstairs and I'll show you the ropes.'

Though Margaret was two years younger than me, she seemed so strong and sure of herself. I felt quite scared of her but at the same time I was drawn to her confidence and to what seemed to me to be a superior ability to survive.

Despite my initial shock at having been plucked from the barren desert of Morgans Road and plunged into the icy waters of Park Hall, I very soon adapted and memories of my pre-nun life faded fast.

There were five dormitories, with six to eight single beds in each, as well as the dining room, laundry room, chapel and two large TV rooms in the basement, one for the girls and one for the boys. The nuns slept at the top of the house, although one slept in a room close to one of the girls' dormitories, to keep what came to feel like a superhuman eye on us after lights out. All of us were split up into different dormitories, although Lucy and I were placed together. While at home we had stuck together to pool our resources when our mother was absent; we no longer did that at Park Hall. There were usually about thirty children there at any one time and one of the best things about living in an institution was having new children on tap to play with whenever we wanted. There was no longer the same urgency to find enough food to eat each day, which had also glued the six of us together when we lived with my mother. I think we were all rather relieved that we could let go of each other at last knowing that we would still be clothed and fed.

The food at Park Hall was generally unappetising, and sometimes it seemed that the nuns deliberately made it so, overboiling, overstewing and underseasoning, but on our diet of Spam, stringy meat and boiled potatoes we certainly didn't go hungry. Sometimes when I looked at the food on my plate – cabbage that had once been green but had been cooked until it was almost white, and peas that had evolved from green to grey in the oven – I felt that the nuns treated the food the same way they treated us, as something troublesome that had to be subdued.

A few days after I arrived Sister Joanna came and sat in the bathroom while I was washing myself in the bath.

'Would you like me to wash you like I did on the day you arrived?' she asked softly. It was the first time any nun had spoken to me so gently since I had arrived but her proposal sounded silly to me.

'No, of course not, I'm a big girl and I can wash myself,' I said indignantly. I was cross that she considered that a big girl of nine like me needed help with something I was proud to have mastered all by myself. After the unwashed years at Morgans Road I quickly grew to love the feeling of being clean and liked seeing the water go grey as I scrubbed myself with the carbolic soap and then rinsed it all away.

Two of the young nuns seemed uneasy in their roles. They didn't seem to gain the same sort of pleasure some of the others did from chastising us at every opportunity. Sister Patricia was the nicest. She always slipped her veil off when the other nuns weren't around and joined in with our childish jokes and giggles. She used to join in with the boys' football games, hitching up her skirt as she ran and kicked the ball.

After we had been there for a few months she mentioned vaguely that she might leave the order.

'I don't think I'm cut out for this life,' she said, smiling sadly. 'Too many rules and regulations and restrictions. I think I'd like to live a little.'

I was shocked because I had no idea that once you were a nun you could decide to stop being a nun. I looked at her wide-eyed but said nothing.

I found out later that she, along with another young nun, Sister Marie, who always had a faraway look in her eyes during Mass, had both become pregnant by one of the older boys at Park Hall.

I hardly missed my mother because she had been absent for so much of the time in Morgans Road. I did miss the anarchy of playing out whenever we wanted to, of running down to the shops to buy penny sweets and of going to bed when we pleased. But I did adjust to leading a restricted, regimented life, as distant a point on the compass from my previous life as it was possible to travel.

CHAPTER SEVEN

The absence of explanations about anything of any importance was like a cheese wire which sliced through the middle of our lives at Park Hall. A couple of months after we arrived there we were taken to an old and imposing building in Liverpool.

'Where are we going, Sister Joanna?' I asked. 'What's this building?'

'Mind your own business, you'll find out soon enough.' She sniffed at my impertinence.

The effect of never having anything about key events in my life explained was quite devastating. I had less control than most children over what happened to me from one minute to the next, and as a result I felt weightless and anchorless, like a creature in a science fiction film. Avoiding beatings from Sam and getting enough food to fill my stomach had been my priorities in Morgans Road. At Park Hall these priorities had changed to trying to beat the nuns' system without being caught out.

We climbed flight after flight of stairs, and as we panted to the top there was my mother, standing elegantly in a long brown fur coat with a neat line of red lipstick and her blonde hair woven into two French plaits crossing her forehead. Despite everything my old loyalty and instinct to protect came to surface. She was smoking a cigarette and to me she looked like a film star. I felt proud that someone so beautiful was my mother.

Not understanding what was about to happen, I shouted a cheery 'Hiya, Mum' to her. She waved feebly. Her eyes were full of tears.

'What's up, Mum?' I asked, still chirpy.

The children's home had seemed strange when we first arrived but this place was even stranger. We were taken into a room crammed with rows of dark wooden benches and lots of men and one lady wearing old-fashioned wigs and black gowns covering their clothes.

We were instructed to stand in a line and say our names. I focused on the woman in the wig and when it was my turn to speak I gave her a friendly wave and a smile, not understanding that that wasn't the way to behave here. I thought that perhaps it was some kind of dressing-up party, and that because we were poor we hadn't come along in the right outfits. Throughout the brief hearing – which turned out to be to remove us permanently from our mother and make us wards of court – my mother sat in a corner of the courtroom with her eyes fixed on the floor. As well as her pain at losing her children she was ashamed to be shown up in a court as an unfit mother. Unlike her I had no idea of the finality of the court proceedings. Because of the shifting uncertainty of family life it was just another thing that happened to us, and no one explained anything.

The men in wigs mumbled words like 'wards of court' and 'rubber stamping' while I smiled and waved. The whole process only took ten minutes. Sister Joanna had brought us to court and she hurried us out before we could go up to my mother to ask her why she was sobbing.

'Why's me mum crying, Sister Joanna? What were all those people in wigs talking about?'

'Never you mind, it's nothing that concerns you,' said Sister Joanna abruptly. 'Now let's hurry back or you'll all miss your tea.'

Nothing more was said about our day in court. We were taken back to the children's home and continued our new lives. I had no idea that our mother's parental responsibilities had been dissolved that day. Although my mother was frequently absent from our lives, the idea of some man in a wig and a gown stamping a piece of paper to make her no longer my mother would have filled me with rage. Had I known, I would have screamed in the courtroom in a bid to halt proceedings, and if that hadn't worked I would have taken Tom in the middle of the night and crept out of Park Hall, carrying him on my back, to find my mother. I was particularly attached to Tom. I had looked after him almost from birth during my mother's absences. He had a moist-eyed innocence about him that made me physically ache with love for him. It was my first experience of unconditional love and I would do anything to protect him. The others, I felt, were more able to fend for themselves, but Tom, although he was five, had the soft, downy soul of a newborn and I felt the need to keep him near me as much as I could.

But I didn't understand what had happened in court so I didn't run away with Tom. Instead I dutifully followed Sister Joanna home.

We received no tenderness from the nuns even on the day we officially lost our mother. Clinical indifference to all of us, laced with cruelty, were the hallmarks of our guardians. One nun, Sister Gertrude, used to bend her hand so that her knuckles stood out and then she jabbed the sharpened knuckles into my head or my back.

Nothing was done at Park Hall to raise my self-esteem. My opinion of myself was already so low it was like a piece of scuffed, sodden material dragged along the ground. I wet the bed, which I shared with a girl called Christine, regularly. I lied to the nuns and said Christine's bladder was to blame. I didn't understand then why I wet the bed so often but now I think it was because I was in a constant state of anxiety as a child, first with Sam and my mother, then with the foster carers, and afterwards with the nuns. Every muscle and fibre was tensed like an animal's in the forest trying to anticipate an attack from a predator. Clenching my bladder muscles along with the rest of me was just too great an effort and that was the one part of me that I let go. I wet the bed very frequently in Morgans Road and nothing that happened at Park Hall inclined my bladder to behave any differently.

Christine was younger than me and very timid, and she never spoke up to contradict me. To eliminate any margin for error the nuns smacked us both across the head whenever the sheets were soaked.

Now and again people visited the home to take a child out for the day or for the weekend. Though I saw my brothers and sisters rarely while we were still all at Park Hall as we all had our own groups of friends, we and all the other children had to line up like contestants in some perverse beauty pageant while the grown-ups looked us up and down. My sisters and brothers were picked now and again for a day trip to the seaside or a weekend away, and eventually everyone except for Mary and I was fostered permanently. My brothers and sisters were more desirable than I was. I was certain it was because their skin was lighter than mine. I looked down at my dark arms and legs and scratched my nails across my skin in fury. How could I have been so unlucky to be black when all my sisters and brothers were beautifully white? My oldest brother Damian and I had once got on a bus to go into the centre of Liverpool. He saw some of his friends lounging on the back seat.

'Pretend you don't know me,' he growled under his breath. 'I don't want them to know my sister's black.' Then he hurried away to sit with his friends. I sat at the front of the bus, staring straight ahead, determined not to cry. The nuns always said that we had to pray very, very hard for things. I screwed my eyes shut and begged God to turn me white.

If anyone looked at me with interest the nuns hissed, 'Don't take her, she's a bad girl, got bad blood in her. That dark skin has made her rebellious. She's as bold as brass and cheeky and aggressive with it.'

The parents who came to view us took the nuns' advice and I was never chosen. I felt hollow and miserable and worthless. When all the other children had been picked for outings I huddled into the corner of the settee in the girls' TV room, wetting one of the cushions with my tears. I couldn't understand why Mary was never picked though. She wasn't black and she wasn't bad like me. Everyone called her the 'goody goody'. She was helpful to the nuns and never had a bad word to say about anyone. She was tall and she was mature for her age, so maybe prospective foster parents decided she was too close to the edge of childhood to be moulded into the child they wanted.

I was cheeky to the nuns and answered them back when they told me off. I knew this would make them dislike me even more than they already did but the urge to destroy myself, which gripped me so forcefully later on, was beginning to manifest itself. I craved attention and if being bad was the only way to get it I decided that it was worth it.

The nuns always issued commands starting with the word 'get': 'Get your teeth cleaned' or 'Get to chapel' or 'Get into bed immediately'. I mimicked their tone: 'No, I don't want to do that, you can't tell me what to do.' But joking about their commands didn't dilute the corrosive effects. The nuns practised a form of counter-nurturing which damaged us all.

I often clashed with Sister Gertrude. When I defied her she said: 'Well, I'm going to report you to Mother Superior.'

'Go on then, I don't care,' I replied boldly. Calling her bluff seemed to work, as Mother Superior never picked me up on my rudeness to Sister Gertrude.

I was learning how to survive at Park Hall.

CHAPTER EIGHT

Although the morality of my mother, who served paying customers by opening her legs and the morality of the nuns, who served God by keeping their legs clamped tightly shut seemed poles apart, there were uncomfortable similarities between them. Both doled out punishments to me in a casual, careless way, neither troubled by conscience nor tempered by compassion.

Whether the children who arrived at Park Hall had any particular religion or none, the moment we crossed the threshold we all became Catholic whether we liked it or not. The nuns attended Mass twice a day and we were expected to go to the 6 p.m. service with them.

'Who made you? God made you. Why did God make you? God made you to love him and serve him in this world.'

The words, meaningless at the time, and even more puzzling now, are still branded on my memory. To my knowledge none of the children I was at Park Hall with went on to become nuns or priests; the force-feeding of religion failed us all.

Miss O'Brien, one of the kindest, gentlest women to set foot in my childhood, fostered Tom for much of the time we were at Park Hall. Tom adored her; he loved every bone in her body and from an early age knew that she had rescued him. She visited the children's home daily. She gave some of us extra help in maths and English and taught us all our catechism – the summary of the doctrine of Catholicism. She joined the ranks of Minnie and Mrs

Abbott and Marie in the gallery of people I loved inside my head. When things were bleak I visited this gallery, peering into the faces in my memory and gaining strength from them.

School was a difficult place for me to be most of the time. We had all moved schools so many times before we arrived at Park Hall, as we drifted between Morgans Road and foster carers, that I had never really settled into any of them. The nuns sent us to St Augustine's secondary school and going to the same building every day for almost five years did help.

I made more friends here than at my previous school, partly because I was always prepared to carry out pranks to endear myself to my peers. One day a few of them dared me to lock the teacher in the classroom's tiny storeroom. She went in to get some paper for us all and like lightning I jumped up, slammed the door and turned the key in the lock. My classmates laughed and clapped but the teacher forced me to open the door and sent me straight to the head teacher for a severe telling off. I didn't mind about the telling off; it was worth it for the sheer fun of outsmarting the teacher, who constantly criticised my academic performance, and for the endorsement of my classmates. These modest rebellions sustained me and made me feel more alive.

Miss O'Brien tried to look cross when she heard about it but couldn't help smiling at me. 'You're a very spirited girl, Clare, do you know that?' she said. I didn't know what spirited meant but as she was smiling I decided to take it as a compliment.

'Thank you, Miss O'Brien,' I beamed.

Most of the time at school, though, I was acutely aware of how much I differed from everyone else. The overwhelming majority of the children were white and the more time I spent with white people the more I loathed my own skin. 'Paki' was the most frequent reference to my skin colour. After a while I couldn't be bothered to say, 'I'm not Paki, I'm English', and I just shrugged and walked away.

The other children seemed to manage the schoolwork much better than I did. I had gone beyond the copying tactics I employed in primary school and had more or less given up on subjects like maths and English. I was placed in lower classes than the rest of my year in these two subjects in the hope that I'd catch up but I didn't, and after the first few years the teachers gave up with me.

Whenever I got an answer wrong in class some of the meaner pupils whispered 'Silly billy' or 'Dunce' loud enough for me to hear but too quietly for the teacher's ears. But worse than living with a skin colour I considered to be inferior, and much worse than failing academically, was the bereft feeling of being parentless. The girls I was friendly with constantly chattered about the ups and down of their home lives but I had no anecdotes to contribute about my own mother and didn't want to remind people any more than necessary that I was a cast-off child dumped with a bunch of nuns. I listened in silence to their tales and tried to smile at the right moment.

Sometimes parents met their children at the school gates and I used to go up and talk to the mother of my friend Donna. Donna's mother was tall, brown-haired and very smiley. I used to run up to her whenever I saw her at the school gates, pretending inside my head that she was my mother rather than Donna's.

One afternoon I plucked up the courage and asked, 'Can you take me home with you and foster me?'

She was almost a foot taller than me and she bent down and hugged me.

'I'm so sorry, Clare, but I can't do that, I've already got my family. I'll be coming to school again soon and I'll see you then, all right?' She gave me a little wave and walked off with Donna. I knew that I shouldn't have asked her and I knew that she couldn't possibly say yes, but all the same I felt as if I had been punched.

My biggest ambition at school was to conform, but sometimes I was prevented from doing so by the nuns. The shame of the school concert remains with me. I was fourteen and all the children at my school were taking part in it. The other girls chattered excitedly about how they were going to discard their school uniform white socks in favour of grown-up tights for the big event. Of course I wanted to wear tights too, to join in with a rite of passage because I felt excluded from so many others.

'Please, please, Sister Maria, can I have some tights like the other girls?' I begged.

But the face of Sister Maria remained as blank as rock. 'Certainly not: and look like a little floozy? No thank you very much. You'll wear your white knee socks and stop making a fuss about this frivolous nonsense.'

She pursed her lips to show me that the matter was closed and moved off in her starched black habit. I grew to hate the crispy sound the nuns' habits made as they moved.

When the day of the concert arrived I felt sick with dread and isolation. As I expected, the other girls proudly compared who had the best shade of American tan tights on as we filed in.

'Oh, I love yours Betsy, what shade are they? Did you get them at Blacklers?' said Justine, one of the most popular girls.

She glanced at my white socks, sniffed and quickly looked away. I tried to make my white legs melt into something invisible but I felt as if I had flashing neon lights strapped to my skin and presumed that everyone was looking at poor misfit Clare in her babyish socks with disgust. I was sitting on the front row so it was impossible for anyone not to see my humiliation. For once I decided that the colour of my skin might be an asset. I considered removing my socks in the hope that my brown-skinned legs would pass for American tan tights but Sister Joanna, who was sitting across the aisle from us with the other nuns, fixed me with a glare, as if she was reading my mind, so I placed my hands demurely in my lap and tried to avoid her gaze.

The nuns sat as still and stiff as dead people, their eyes blank and their wimples starched. I wanted to shout out, 'I hate you, I hate you, I hate you', but the words never got further than the inside of my head. I remained silent and to all the world looked like an obedient little girl.

My hopes were dashed again at Christmas. At home with my mother I never thought about presents because we never got any. Nor did she mark our birthdays in any way. The only time we had ever received presents prior to our arrival at Park Hall was from foster parents. But at the children's home every child received a gift of some description. At Park Hall I was even asked what I would like.

I had seen a film called *The Red Shoes* and it had made a big impression on me. More than anything else I wanted a pair of red ballet shoes like Moira Shearer had worn in the film. The way she danced represented pure freedom to me.

'Can I have a pair of red ballet shoes?' I asked earnestly.

'No, they're far too dear' came the curt reply. I felt the enquiry was only made to heighten the final letdown.

Although I knew that the red ballet shoes weren't going to materialise on Christmas Day I couldn't help holding on to a few shreds of hope that, just maybe, the nuns could see that this mattered to me more than anything else I had asked for before and would grant my wish. Or maybe they would do it to get extra brownie points with God.

John Monks, a man who lived round the corner from the children's home, always dressed up as Father Christmas to hand out our presents to us on Christmas Day. The younger children were very excited because they still believed in Father Christmas. My eyes were firmly fixed on the two sacks of presents which the nuns stood guard over, handing gifts one by one to John Monks to give to the children.

When he handed me my present I felt it carefully before I opened it. It didn't look shoe-shaped and I couldn't feel any squishy red leather. I ripped the paper off hopelessly. It was an ugly plastic brush and comb set. When the nuns weren't looking I threw it into the bin, tears stinging my cheeks. As usual, irrational hope was stronger than logic in me. I played with the other children and their equally unappetising presents, like cheap dolls and boxes of coloured pencils, and tried to blot out all thoughts of the red ballet shoes.

The nuns made us a really nice dinner on Christmas Day – turkey, roast potatoes and vegetables – and in the afternoon all the children played with their new toy. We had to have a special outfit for Christmas and mine was always a hand-me-down from one of the bigger girls because I was very small. I didn't mind about that though; it was still a new dress to me.

I didn't succeed in getting the red ballet shoes out of my mind and soon afterwards the nuns allowed sweet Miss O'Brien to take me to ballet lessons. I couldn't understand why the nuns had given their permission, but I didn't dare enquire in case they changed their minds.

'Somebody paid for your shoes and your lessons,' confided Miss O'Brien, 'but I've no idea who it is because the nuns won't tell me.'

I never got to find out who my mystery benefactor was. I suppose that in those circumstances it was impossible for the nuns to deny me my wish. I was overjoyed when I finally held the supple leather shoes in my hands. Part of the thrill was showing them off to all the girls in my class at school. Miss O'Brien sewed some ribbons on to the shoes for me, and every Saturday I went along to ballet classes. I got a medal for showing the most improvement in a short time and swelled with pride. It was one of the first times that I had ever had any recognition that I was good at something. It felt alien in the best possible way. Miss O'Brien was delighted for me about the medal.

'Well done, Clare, well done,' she said, giving me a warm squeeze around the shoulders. I was continually surprised that the nuns allowed someone so soft through the heavy front door of Park Hall.

The dancing lessons were one of the highlights of life with the nuns, or rather away from them. Gliding and pirouetting in time to *Swan Lake* and *Tales from the Vienna Woods* allowed me temporary oblivion.

One phrase that still shouts through my mind is 'bold as brass'. Bold as brass, bold as brass. I tried to delete the phrase from my memory but instead, each time it snarled out of a nun's mouth, it rang louder inside my head. The nuns' black habits rustled extra loud when they meted out criticisms as if the negativity they were dispensing was inflating their own sense of virtue before God.

As the years dragged by in the children's home my anger at my treatment there made me more daring. It was driven by frustration and lack of love rather than by the surly disobedience that the nuns believed had to be pummelled out of me. I'm amazed that I was robust enough to take them on, but whenever I felt that I or one of the younger ones who couldn't speak up for themselves had been treated particularly unjustly I couldn't stay silent.

Every morning the nuns woke us up at 6.30 a.m. We had often competed the night before to see who could stay up latest, and peeling off the blankets and springing instantly into subservient mode was horribly difficult. Out of our bedroom window we could see a tower block. It was grey and ugly and angular but, gazing out at it, it summed up freedom to me. Families I presumed were ordinary, cosy and content lived there and the test we set ourselves after the nuns thought we were all fast asleep each evening was to watch the warm yellow lights from the tower block windows go out one by one. Whoever could stay awake until the last light went out was the winner, although the award was an honorary one with no prize attached.

It was often me who managed to stay awake longest. On the nights that I won the game I went to sleep happy.

CHAPTER NINE

The nuns were extraordinarily thorough in their mission to keep our bodies, souls and surroundings permanently disinfected and docile. Any evidence of behaviour that challenged their version of events was promptly scrubbed away. Battling against the regime took courage and boundless energy. Usually there was simply no spare oxygen available for insurrection.

For the most part we obediently filed in and filed out of the right rooms at the right times and went to bed at the obscenely early hour of 8 p.m. even at the age of fourteen. In the name of God the nuns systematically stamped on our souls. The last thing we were expected to do before climbing into bed was to attend a session at the chapel, kneeling down and praying for forgiveness for any number of sins, including those we weren't aware we had committed. We had to put on black lace mantillas to pray and there were heavy penalties for anyone who dared lose hers.

One of the nuns used to come and wake us up every morning and then we were all expected to do a chore before breakfast. Mine was to buff the floor with a special machine. The nun who came to wake us would satisfy herself that we had all climbed out of bed and then return to early morning prayers in the chapel. I was forbidden from switching on the machine while the nuns were praying in the chapel but at least a couple of times a week I managed to drown out a handful of 'Hail Mary's' before an irate

Sister Maria rustled and strode towards me with the kind of twisted expression I imagined was common in Hell.

'Can't you see we're having Mass?' Her voice quivered so much I thought a yell was going to break through at any moment.

I faked a startled expression and mumbled my apologies. Sister Maria was not fooled but couldn't quite square a smack across my head with God because she couldn't prove I was deliberately being sacrilegious.

These modest acts conferred a blend of popularity and notoriety on me among the other inmates of Park Hall.

'How on earth do you get away with it?' asked Millie, one of the older girls, grinning worriedly. 'It's a wonder that the sisters haven't taken you up to the tower yet to beat you red raw for refusing to obey them and God.'

Later I would experience the horrors of the tower but for now it was just an abstract bogeyman to me. I knew that most of the other children tilted their chins down on to their chests and spent their days trying to move silently, invisibly, past the nuns, but something stopped me from exercising similar caution. I felt as if there was a glittering diamond of enthusiasm and vitality inside my head, which every so often burst out of my skull to display itself to the world. I hated lies as well, and when one of the nuns insisted that something which was clearly black was actually white I invariably piped up: 'No it isn't, Margaret never said she didn't want to go to Mass', or 'Philip didn't deliberately make a hole in his jumper. That bully Harry from Broadstairs Close picked a fight with him at school.'

Nobody thanked me for these interventions, having decided that the route to survival lay in silent agreement with everything the nuns said, however absurd. But I continued anyway. I felt that if I remained mute about everything I would sooner or later combust.

My biggest frustration with the chasm between my truth and the nuns' truth related to matters of God. The sisters were forever telling us about God's boundless goodness and kindness and yet they, who referred to themselves as the Lord's humble servants, ladled out big dollops of cruelty to us day after day. Even I, however, knew that that was a point too far to challenge the nuns on, and whenever I felt particularly indignant about something they'd done, of which I was sure God would disapprove, I copied the other children, burrowed my chin into my chest and jammed my lips tight shut.

Because of my 'bold as brass' approach to life, the nuns automatically blamed me for things I hadn't done as well as for those I had. When a child broke the Hoover – I never found out who – I was blamed. I felt such a sense of injustice at this false accusation that I decided I was going to burn the Hoover. It was just before teatime, and I placed the Hoover in the middle of the room where it was stored and surrounded it with piles of books which I was going to set alight. As I was about to strike a match Sister Maria walked in.

'What on earth are you doing?' she gasped.

'I told you it wasn't me who broke the Hoover but none of you will believe me, so I'm going to set it on fire.'

Sister Maria's lip quivered. She could hardly take in my impertinence. A stinging slap across my head released some of her anger.

'You must go and pray for your forgiveness,' she said in a more controlled tone. 'But firstly you will tidy away every bit of this horrible mess you have made and then you will go directly to the chapel. After that it's straight to bed without any tea.'

I was mortified to have done something which meant missing a meal – food being almost my main aim in life – but my friend Pauline shared my sense of being wronged, and in solidarity she sneaked an oversized jam buttie up to the dormitory for me.

'Go on, Clare, you tuck into that and enjoy it. The sisters will never know. They were all crowding round that poor little new boy, Bobby, telling him off for smearing some of his jam on the table when I sneaked out.'

The bread was very fresh and chewy and the jam was full of sickly sweet bits of strawberries. The food made me even gladder about the Hoover revolt; it tasted of triumph.

Before we were allowed to eat our breakfast the nuns ran critical fingers across the tops of our lockers and checked that the mirrors shone. If dust and sticky finger marks had been clinically banished we were allowed to go downstairs and eat our stale cornflakes.

One of my tasks was to pour cornflakes into bowls every evening ready for the following morning (which is why they were always stale). Our breakfast never varied, it was always and only cornflakes. The bowls were garish hues of plastic and the pourers were under strict instructions to tip no more than one scoop into each bowl. I thought I had beaten the system by tipping two scoops into my bowl and then rubbing a bit of margarine under it so that I would recognise it even if someone switched my bowl around. Even though I was less hungry here than I had been in Morgans Road, my instinct, to grab whatever food I could because I didn't know where the next meal was coming from, remained strong. Of course it never occurred to me that another child could simply dig their hand into my bowl and scoop out some of my excess cornflakes, leaving the margarine signpost intact, before I got to the dining room.

After breakfast we had to go down to the basement and put on our school uniforms, which were hanging up in a tiny room. We weren't allowed to wear them in the children's home and as soon as we arrived back after the day's lessons we had to remove them, hang them up in the airless basement room and then jump in the bath.

As with the cornflakes, I tried to think strategically. The same bath water was used to clean several children and I became exceptionally speedy at removing my uniform, hanging it the way the nuns expected it to be hung and then sprinting upstairs to the bathroom to secure the first bath. Lying down in clean, hot water was a sliver of luxury in the place some of us nicknamed the workhouse.

At 5 p.m. one of the children rang a hand bell and we all filed into the dining room for tea. I don't remember what we were given on weekdays, only that bread was piled high on the table with pots of jam to fill us up. On Saturday we were given lifeless Spam and sodden chips and on Sunday a roast.

Occasionally if the nuns – who ate earlier – had any leftovers from their meal, they brought them in for the 'good' children to eat. Needless to say, none of the superior, grown-up food was ever handed out to me. Excluded from this succulent, forbidden fruit, I decided that I was going to sample it with or without the nuns' blessing.

One Sunday lunchtime while the nuns sat in their dining room eating their roast, I hid behind the kitchen door and, when the coast was clear, crept into the kitchen, grabbed a handful of roast potatoes and poured some gravy over them. The soft potatoes, crisp, greasy skins and salty gravy tasted like heaven to me. Our roast on Sundays was accompanied by tasteless boiled potatoes, which disintegrated when you sank your fork into them. I never got caught – if I had I would certainly have been whacked across the head – and chalked this up as another small victory.

Although it was stealing, and I knew that stealing was wrong, I felt as if I was righting a wrong with my secret stuffing. I decided that the nuns' God of love would come down firmly on my side if Mother Superior and I ever had to stand before him in the cloud-fringed court of heaven.

The set up at the home was very much an *Upstairs Downstairs* affair. The nuns even had a separate grand staircase while we had to use the shabby back stairs.

The chore I hated most was wiggling my small fingers into the gaps where the wrought iron curled under the banisters to get the dust out. The tedium of the job made me squirm but there was no escaping the beady-eyed gaze the nuns fixed on all surfaces on which dust might dare to settle. Dust was a form of sin; it was as dissolute as a promiscuous woman and in urgent and constant need of redemption by annihilation.

On Sundays we all filed out of the children's home and walked to the church down the road. We had Sunday clothes, Sunday shoes, Sunday straw hats and Sunday pure white gloves. I hated the gloves. I was sure the nuns made us wear them as a test. Inevitably I sullied mine and got Mother Superior's bent knuckles between my shoulder blades.

This was the time when we were on display to the believers who populated the nuns' world. A crease in a blouse here or a grey smudge on a white glove there went beyond the boundaries of what was acceptable in civilised Sunday society, even though we were all energetic children.

'Clare Malone. It's bad enough that you always look dirty with that darkie skin of yours, but please do not make matters worse by turning up in church with your socks and gloves stained with mud,' said Sister Maria irritably. 'Have you been climbing trees in your Sunday best or something?'

She gave me an expert swipe to the side of the head. It was so fast and so silent that a passer-by would not have noticed that her two hands, clasped peacefully below her navel, had parted company for a second. I noticed of course, and the sharp sting of the blow brought tears to my eyes, something I did not want any nun to see.

'Sorry, sister,' I said, casting my wet eyes downwards. 'I haven't been climbing any trees. I don't know how the stains came.'

It was impossible to keep the gloves pristine. It seemed that the simple act of sliding my fingers into them made them dirty. The nuns knew most of the children would soil their gloves most of the time, and so they had a guaranteed stream of dirt-related sins to harangue us about.

One thing I did love about my Sunday outfit, though, was my pair of shoes. They were black and shiny and, I felt, infinitely superior to my ugly, sensible school shoes. One weekday I smuggled my Sunday shoes out in my school bag and as soon as I arrived at school I switched them. I felt fantastic in my shiny shoes, like a queen. But the nuns found out.

The 'You're as bold as brass' catechism followed. Sister Maria flexed her knuckles ready to bury them in my spine. She hit me across the head for good measure and I never dared wear my Sunday shoes for school again. Tears came, but this time I felt the pleasure I had gained from wearing forbidden shoes for school was worth the blow to the head and knuckle bruise against my spine.

We called the nuns by their Christian names and never knew their surnames. When I came home from school one day in a bad mood and rushed to the basement changing room to hang up my uniform, Sister Claire was there ironing. I knew that she wouldn't want me to know her full name so I tried to read the name stitched into her blouse sideways on.

'Don't be so nosy, Clare,' she said crossly.

Sister Claire was one of the nicer nuns and I don't know why but I suddenly lashed out at her, delivering a smart slap to her right cheek. The whole thing probably had nothing to do with her at all; it was cumulative frustration with all the blows I had received myself.

Sister Claire turned white with shock.

'Oh my goodness, how dare you do that!' she said, and scurried out of the room to report my sin to Mother Superior, who managed to arrive in the room less than fifteen seconds later.

'How dare you strike a nun,' she said.

A little voice inside me was screaming, 'And how dare you strike me over and over again with the smallest excuse!'

'Get into the chapel and pray for your forgiveness,' she said.

I knelt down and wasn't allowed to leave the chapel for two hours. I could hear the other nuns whispering disapprovingly about me. More than one muttered, 'Bold as brass . . .'

Although I was sorry to have hit Sister Claire – I wished I had landed a smart slap on Sister Maria's cheek instead – I still felt some kind of justification for what I'd done. The two hours I spent kneeling on the hard, polished floorboards of the chapel failed to change my mind about that. Afterwards I could still hardly believe that I had struck softly spoken Sister Claire. I was made to apologise publicly to her, but when I bumped into her in the hallway later on I apologised to her again in my own way.

'I'm sorry, Sister Claire, really I am. I don't know what came over me.'

She nodded. 'All right, Clare, off you go now; just make sure you don't do anything like that again.' I felt we'd wiped the slate clean and ran off.

The nuns were genuinely shocked, because it was the first time anyone had ever lashed out that way. Strange how behaviour that was utterly acceptable for them was such an extreme violation of justice when I copied it.

When the nuns lit the little flat candles in the chapel I always thought the flickering light from them looked soft and pretty. I decided that they'd look pretty in our dormitory, too, and sneaked a handful out of the chapel hidden in my knickers, along with a box of matches. At bedtime I handed them out to the other girls so that we could turn our drab grey dormitory into the fairy-tale palace I had thought Park Hall was for two minutes when I first arrived. I got the other girls to practise blowing their candles out very quickly so they'd know what to do if one of the nuns appeared in our room.

'Right, this is what we do,' I explained to the more timid children. 'One, two, three, blow and then we all dive down under the covers and pretend to be asleep. Got that?'

Everyone managed it during the practice but we had just relit the candles when Mother Superior appeared in the doorway.

'What's the meaning of all this?' she asked in a voice which sounded like a dead person's.

A couple of the littlest girls had dived down under the covers when she appeared but had forgotten to blow out their candles. I didn't want them to get the blame so I spoke up. 'It was me. I took the candles.'

'Oh, you.' She swung round so that she could stare into my eyes. 'You're as bold as brass,' she said, before doling out the regulation sharp slap, gathering up the candles and sweeping out of the room.

One of the biggest battles of wills between the nuns and me was over my choice of drink. At teatime we were always given cups of tea. Sister Maria brewed it in a gigantic teapot, more suited to *Gulliver's Travels*' Brobdingnag than Liverpool. Boiling water, milk, tea bags and sugar were all stewed in the pot together. Nobody ever got a choice about how they drank their tea; we were expected to sip the bland brew without complaint. I'm not sure how Sister Maria managed to lift such a huge, heavy, scalding hot pot but she did, every day. I suppose her life and that of the other nuns was just as institutionalised as mine, but I never stopped to think about that then because, for me, institutionalised meant powerless, and it never occurred to me that among those who hold the power some are also weak.

Usually we all held our bright plastic cups out while Sister Maria poured, but one day what the nuns referred to as 'the devil inside me' snaked out of my mouth and I said 'No thank you' when the pot reached me. I turned my cup over firmly so that Sister Maria couldn't pour anything into it.

'I don't take sugar in my tea,' I said airily, feeling like an Edwardian lady for a few seconds.

'Oh, don't you now?' said Sister Maria through pursed lips. Like the rest of the nuns she found challenges to the status quo deeply unpleasant and disconcerting. 'Well, we'll see about that.'

She marched off into the kitchen and I heard a fractious clattering of pans. Then she emerged carrying a small, steaming jug.

'Here you are, Madam, tea with no sugar. Drink that if you dare.'

All eyes were upon me. I wasn't sure why I had impulsively decided to make a sugar-free stand. I had a very sweet tooth and had happily drunk sweet tea all my life. There was no way out, I had to start drinking it. It tasted foul and bitter but I managed to get half a cup down my throat. When her back was turned I poured the rest into a slop bucket at the table.

I thought that I had got away with it and that I had won because Sister Maria saw me drink the tea without grimacing. But she had outsmarted me. The next day she brought me another steaming pot of tea without sugar and the same ritual ensued. This went on for weeks until I became accustomed to the flavour and to my surprise began to like it. To this day I can't bear to have sugar added to my tea.

The other children looked at me quizzically. They couldn't understand why I had chosen this particular battle to fight and didn't seem particularly impressed by the stand I was taking. 'Why would anyone prefer tea without sugar?' whispered the girl next to me. I shrugged and couldn't explain.

I suppose that Sister Maria had won, but in a way I felt that I had won too. I had no understanding of terms like free will, human rights and democracy but when I requested tea without sugar those were the principles I was fighting for.

CHAPTER TEN

My mother was a distant, uncertain presence during my years in the children's home. She visited only four or five times during our years at Park Hall, and often seemed distracted when she did turn up.

One time she arrived looking very glamorous, with her hair swept up off the back of her neck. It was Easter and she'd brought personalised chocolate eggs for us all. I had no idea that such wondrous things existed. Our names were iced on the chocolate in pink tinted sugar.

I was overjoyed and hugged her tightly around her waist. 'Thanks, Mum, that's brilliant!' I beamed.

It was one of those moments, like the time she sat up all night with me when I was burning with fever, that I glimpsed the normal pleasures of a mother's love. Whenever she showed interest and kindness I couldn't help believing that a corner had been turned and that from that moment on she would become a proper mother to me. But these glimpses of love always faded fast, like a rainbow that can be briefly admired from a distance but can never be touched or held.

'That's all right.' She smiled vaguely and then looked away. She seemed uncomfortable with my gratitude and was looking for an escape route. As ever I was left reeling with disappointment. By this time I understood that it was the nuns rather than my mother who had legal responsibility for me. But even though she stayed away for most of the time I was at Park Hall, I couldn't help longing for a mother – although often I hankered after a perfect and imaginary mother figure rather than the specific one who carried me in her womb.

The next time she came, perhaps a year later, when I was thirteen, she was very ill. She arrived in an old car with a tall, black man who, because of his colour, I was convinced was my father. He had beautiful, sparkling brown eyes, was smartly dressed in a grey suit and smiled widely at me. My mother looked too ill for me to ask her if the man really was my father so I decided to draw my own conclusions.

My mother appeared almost unaware of his presence by her side. She leaned back in the passenger seat and inhaled deeply. Her skin looked grey and her normally strident voice was faint.

'Hiya, Mum,' I said excitedly because I had had no idea that she was coming, but I could see that this wasn't going to be a cheery visit. The belief that she had my father in tow made my heart feel as if it might burst with excitement. There were so few black people in the Liverpool I knew in the early 1960s, and that made me absolutely certain that if a black man appeared attached to my mother it could only be my father.

I ran in to tell the nuns.

'Sister Maria, Sister Maria, me mum's here,' I said breathlessly. 'But she's not well.'

'Well, for goodness sake tell her to come in,' she said.

'I've got a dad, I've got a dad,' I kept saying over and over. The man stayed in the car while my mother stumbled up the steps into the children's home.

The nuns gave her some sweet tea and she revived slightly, but she left soon afterwards. I never got to find out what was wrong with her. Like so much about my mother it was unexplained and unresolved.

I whispered excitedly to Margaret: 'I've got a dad, I've got a dad and he's here, he's come to see me.'

When my mother returned to visit a few months later she arrived in a good mood. I blurted out as soon as she'd said hello, 'Mum, was that my dad who came last time?'

She smiled and shook her head.

'Oh no, Clare, your dad lives a long way from here. That man was a different man altogether, very different.'

And that was all she would say. I felt my heart deflate so far it felt like a flat, sagging apple skin with all the pulp sucked out.

When I had seen the man I decided was my father I felt a very instant and different connection to him to the one I had with my mother. My brown skin was the same shade as his and it felt good to have proof that I was made in the image of someone real at last. I was able at last to recognise a part of myself that I hadn't been able to recognise until then, having my pink-skinned mother as my sole genetic point of reference. Discovering that the unnamed man was not in fact my father made me feel worse about being black than before I set eyes on him. I had briefly tasted a sense of belonging, and being told I had wrongly identified my father made my sense of unbelonging much more acute.

My mother's erratic visits continued. One time, I remember, the nuns told me that my mother was coming to visit me the following Saturday. I kept hoping and hoping that she'd bring me a present. I ran down to the bus stop fifteen minutes before she was due to arrive and sat down on the bench.

As each bus stopped I scoured the faces of the passengers who were getting off but none of them was my mother. Two blonde women in dark-coloured coats looked like her through the distorted shadows of the bus window, but when I pressed my nose against the window while the bus was stopped I could see that they looked nothing like her. After the fifth bus had passed with no sign of her I walked home, scuffing my shoes against the pavement: she'd hurt me so I was going to hurt the pavement and my shoes. I don't know whether I loved my mother or not but she always had the power to wound me like no one else.

The utter predictability and lack of prospect for change at the children's home dulled the stinging pain of mother-related disappointments. Periodically people arrived at Park Hall and selected children for adoption or fostering. A few months after we arrived at Park Hall, before John, Damian, Lucy and Tom were fostered, my mother appeared with all her brothers and sisters. Her sisters had her smooth blonde hair and wore elegant, long coats like hers. I hardly knew any of them but it was thrilling to have so many visitors, particularly visitors who were freely handing out pennies to us. As they looked us up and down, the way so many of the prospective adopters did, I fervently prayed that they would take us away with them, one each. To me they represented liberation and a happy-ever-after ending.

'Oh, haven't you grown,' exclaimed one uncle in the way adults who don't know how to talk to children talk.

'You're a bonny lass,' said one of my aunts to my older sister. 'You'll grow up to be as beautiful as your mother.'

They glanced quickly at my brown skin and dark hair and said nothing. It turned out that they hadn't come to foster us but merely to view us in our new home. After half an hour they left, exhorting us to be good girls and boys for the nuns.

Because of the shame my mother obviously felt about having a black child, inferiority based on the colour of my skin had been drummed into me from an early age. My self-esteem wasn't boosted by life in the children's home and by the age of thirteen I began to doubt whether I belonged to my mother's family at all.

I was sitting on my bed talking to Mary when Sister Maria walked in. I'd been telling her my theory about my origins, which was that I'd been abandoned by or stolen from a black family and somehow ended up in Morgans Road. I was rather hazy on the detail of this belief though.

'Mary, how can I be from the same family as you? I don't look anything like the rest of you. I think I'm from a black family. Maybe they lost me when I was a baby and my mother found me and took me in. What do you think?'

'Don't be so daft, Clare,' said Mary. 'You're as much a Malone as the rest of us are. I was in the room when you were born, before Marie's gran quickly shooed me out. Our mum is your mum.'

But I wasn't convinced. Sister Maria was listening carefully and in a reckless moment that I would pay for later I blurted out, 'I shouldn't have the same surname as them because I'm not from the same family.' I sounded brash but it was the only way I knew to try and conceal the hurt I felt.

Sister Maria lifted her eyebrows right into one of the arc lines on her forehead but said nothing. The following day Mother Superior came to find me.

'Your mother is here to see you,' she said curtly.

As usual I was delighted at the unexpected interest in me. I was shown into the room with the stripy curtains and maroon sofas where my mother was waiting. She looked well and glamorous and had her trademark hard line of bright red lipstick across her full mouth.

'Oh, hiya, Mum,' I said breezily. 'I didn't know you were coming.'

She didn't even bother to say hello. The nuns had told her what I'd said about not being part of the family.

'How dare you go around saying you're not part of our family,' she said, furiously. 'Haven't you brought enough disgrace on this family without going around telling nasty lies to the nuns. I won't stand for that sort of behaviour, Clare, really I won't. If I've told you once I've told you a hundred times. You're a Malone and that's final.'

Trembling with rage she slapped me across the face and swept out of the room.

I cried more out of hurt that she had dismissed my fears about not belonging than because of the stinging blow. Sister Maria looked triumphant, as if she had righted an important wrong.

'Off you go and do your homework now,' she said. 'We'll hear no more about this nonsense.'

I never mentioned my doubts about my origins again, although from time to time they dominated my thoughts. I didn't understand why I had said something so wrong. All the evidence pointed to me being different from my sisters and brothers; I was treated differently so surely I had come from somewhere different. The term 'mixed race' was not used when I was growing up and I couldn't understand that I could have a white mother yet end up black. If only I could meet my father I was sure that my yearning to belong would be over at last.

CHAPTER ELEVEN

For most girls, their prime source of information about all the strange things that start to happen to their bodies when puberty invades childhood is their mother. But my mother had neither the presence in my life nor the inclination to unwrap the mysteries of breasts which suddenly took off from the chest wall, bras which banished their natural wobbliness and, most of all, periods. I had no idea about these changes and felt frightened and repulsed by what was happening to me. The sex education I received from the other girls in the school playground did nothing to clear the fog, and the nuns refused to divulge anything about these mysterious changes.

When I was twelve, Ann, one of the older girls, kept dropping the word 'red' into the conversation in a way that didn't make sense, and gave knowing looks to Mary, another of the girls.

'That red toast was horrible and as for that red window –' All the girls started giggling.

I looked from one to another, feeling about five years old. 'What does red mean?' I asked irritably.

'Ah, we'll tell you when you're thirteen; you're too young to know now.'

I begged them to tell me; withholding the information was a form of bullying and I felt sick in my stomach.

'You'll have to wait till you're thirteen,' they mocked my naivety.

I was dying to know what red was code for, and as soon as I was thirteen pleaded with them to tell me. 'I'm thirteen now, tell me what red is,' I said. But they laughed and wouldn't share it with me.

When I was thirteen and a half I found blood in my knickers. I burst into tears and ran to tell the nuns.

'Sister Maria, Sister Maria, I think I'm bleeding to death,' I gasped, clutching at a nearby stair rail at the thought of my imminent demise.

Sister Maria looked impassively at my tear-stained face and silently led me to a huge cupboard between the two girls' dormitories. She handed me a thick, cotton wool pad and said coldly, 'Whenever you get blood in your knickers use one of these.' Then she glided off silently.

When the nuns didn't want to continue a conversation because they found the subject matter distasteful, or because there was no logical justification for the harsh position they were taking, they would hurry off. Because their feet never showed under their long habits this swift, smooth movement made them look as if they had wheels on their heels.

I wanted to ask Sister Maria how long I was supposed to use a pad for, how often I'd get the blood and when would it stop, but she was gone and the matter was never mentioned again. Once I was in the 'red' club at school the other girls explained a bit more to me, but I didn't really understand what periods meant or why I bled.

My developing breasts were greeted with an equally blank response by the nuns. As I took off my school shirt one afternoon in the poky basement changing room, one of the nuns appeared at the door and threw a bright yellow cotton bra across the room at me. 'Here, wear this,' said Sister Isobel. She turned on her wheel heels and rustled off, not wanting to engage with my bewilderment and embarrassment.

'What is this, how do I put it on?' I asked one of the older girls. She showed me in a matter-of-fact way how to slip my arms through the straps and fasten the hooks against my backbone.

'It's so you don't, you know, jiggle around,' she said when I continued to look blank.

'What's wrong with jiggling?' I asked.

'Well, it's just not . . .' she seemed to be wondering herself, 'ladylike.' She finished her sentence proudly.

I hated the feel of having this restrictive thing strapped around my chest. At least before my body had felt fairly free but it was just one more children's home rule that ultimately I had to buckle down and accept. Because I found out that all the older girls at school were wearing them I assumed there was no choice in the matter and that it was something all girls just had to do once their breasts started to show through their clothes.

From the moment I had come out of my mother's womb the wrong colour everything that happened to me had been beyond my control. I was scared of my changing body. It felt as though some force separate from me was doing something I didn't like to me. I longed to return to early childhood, where breasts and periods didn't exist, and then I could curl up and protect myself from the world.

Sister Claire was a large, plump nun. Her pillowy girth reminded me of a Teddy bear and I longed to cuddle up against her and rest against the soft folds of her skin. One day she was talking quietly to me, no one else was in the room, and I walked up to her and threw my arms as far around her waist as they would reach.

'Oh my goodness,' she said. 'You mustn't do that, that's wrong.' She pushed me away sharply.

So I was left unhugged, as usual. Sister Claire had said it was wrong so I knew it must be, but all the same every fibre of my body yearned to be gently, physically enveloped by someone older who could dissolve my fears.

The nuns were no better at meeting our physical needs than our emotional needs. One time I had a blister on my fourth finger, which putrefied to a hard greenish-yellow bubble. It was violently painful, especially if I accidentally knocked it against something. It looked up at me, a translucent, malevolent eye. Sister Maria noticed it one morning while I was cleaning the nuns' bathroom. She said nothing but went to fetch Mother Superior. Neither one expressed any sympathy for the pain I was in.

'Come along now,' said Mother Superior harshly. Of all the nuns I decided that she was the cruellest. Framed by her wimple her face was almost entirely drained of colour – dull grey eyes, pallid skin and thin lips with all the redness squeezed out. The other nuns followed her lead, and perhaps had they had a more benign boss guiding them they might have been kinder to us. She grasped my hand roughly, seeming irritated by the inconvenience

I was causing her. She examined my septic blister and then picked up a big needle. Without any explanation she plunged the needle deep into the blister.

The intense pain as she dug the needle in bounced off every cell of my body. I watched the greeny-yellow slime spurt out and suddenly I was spinning in the stuff, faster and faster until blackness blotted out the colour.

I woke up to find myself propped up between the freezer and a cupboard in the kitchen. I was very cold and conscious of sticky crumbs grinding into my legs. I wondered how such an oasis of dirt had escaped the nuns' continuous purge. I could hear the strains of Mass coming from the chapel and closed my eyes, glad to be away from it all. One of the nuns had put a bandage round my finger while I was unconscious.

I didn't feel abandoned slumped against the freezer awaiting instructions, just numb. We had been conditioned to expect no warmth and no humanity from the nuns so I wasn't expecting any of them to suddenly become caring. However, logic and emotions didn't always match up inside my head. As I rested against the unwelcoming freezer I squeezed my eyes tight shut. I could just about visualise a female figure, without defined facial features – neither my mother, nor one of the nuns or anyone else I recognised – who was coming towards me with sympathetic, outstretched arms to make everything better. Although I had no experience to speak of, of a loving mother figure or mother substitute, the desire to be loved and nurtured, was as basic to me as the need to eat, sleep and keep warm.

After Mass Sister Maria appeared, hoisted me to my feet and sent me on my way, without enquiring how I was feeling. The vision of the woman with outstretched arms faded fast.

The strictness of the nuns made it hard to step out of line but we did manage it from time to time, and the triumphs always tasted sweet. The nuns' daily struggle, their fulfilment of God's will on earth as they saw it, was to beat and purge the sin out of us until we were as flat and subdued as a cartoon character left squashed after a steamroller has ironed it into the ground. My daily struggle was to remain vertical and three-dimensional and to keep on looking the nuns in the eye. I knew that once I bowed my head in their presence I'd never lift it again.

When I was fourteen I was egged on by some of the older girls to go on a jaunt into the centre of town with them. Once we started secondary school at the age of eleven we were allowed to go into the town centre unaccompanied at weekends. We jumped on the number 17 bus, which stopped close to Blacklers, an Aladdin's cave of a department store in the centre of Liverpool that no longer exists. Inside that shop was everything we could ever imagine, including clothes of many hues, thin tights, thick tights, sparkly make-up, heavily perfumed pink soaps with a pretty gingham ribbon tied around them and gaudy sets of colouring pens in clear, plastic boxes shaped like cats.

As we stood outside the shop salivating at the window display one of the girls said, 'Let's steal something', in a conspiratorial whisper. Not wanting to give ourselves away by discussing the impending crime too much we all nodded our heads. Excitement at the array of goods on offer blotted out fear of getting caught and the consequences.

'Let's divide up into twos so we don't attract so much attention,' said Ann, one of the oldest girls. We paired off and sauntered in. I was with my friend Margaret. She headed for the sweets counter and cupped a packet of chocolate buttons sprinkled with hundreds and thousands behind her hand.

As this was my first shoplifting experience I decided that I wanted to take something a bit more permanent to mark the occasion. Green had always been my favourite colour and when I saw a box of pencil crayons containing both a dark green and a light green I decided it had to be mine. With one deft movement the box disappeared up my jumper. I felt extremely pleased with myself for being such a discreet shoplifter. Memories of stealing loaves of bread at my mother's bidding flooded back to me. I had never got caught when I hid loaves under my coat. Shop assistants never dreamed that a girl as young and small as I was could be up to no good. Surprisingly I hadn't forgotten my technique and with a very quick flick of the wrist had moved the pencils from my hand to under my jumper.

We met up again outside the shop and everyone had got something. It was the first time for most of us, and fear enhanced the thrill of getting something for nothing. I ran home filled with glee. I felt rich and powerful and in control. I hid my box of pencils in my locker. I was going to take my time over using them but I kept on lifting them out of the folds of my sweater where I'd hidden them in my locker, admiring them and then, even more carefully, restoring them to their new secret home.

However, my shoplifting career ended abruptly. When we arrived home from school the following day we were summoned by Mother Superior. Her mouth looked as if it had been bolted downwards and her colourless eyes glittered like ice cubes. It was a look she reserved for misbehaviour of a most serious nature.

'Now which of you girls was involved in the shoplifting incident at Blacklers yesterday?' Her voice was quiet and to the rosy-cheeked policeman sitting opposite she probably sounded quite reasonable. Only we saw the rage behind her eyes.

'I want each of you to own up to exactly what you stole.' She moved down the line of girls who hung their heads, righteous rustle, righteous rustle, righteous rustle.

The first girl confessed through tears that she had stolen a pair of knickers with pink spots on, the second a notebook and pencil. When it came to my turn I remained calm and tearless.

'I stole a packet of pencils,' I said almost cheerfully, a tone I would pay for later.

We were dispatched to our lockers to retrieve the smuggled goods. I slipped the dark green pencil out of the packet and put it back inside the sweater in my locker before I handed the box back. As it was such a wonderful colour, and as I'd gone to so much trouble stealing the pencils, I felt I should at least be able to keep a small souvenir of my expedition. After all, Margaret's chocolate buttons had been eaten within minutes of acquiring them, so if she got to enjoy her ill-gotten gains so should I.

The police officer collected up the pathetic collection of cheap merchandise, the kind of thing that ordinary teenagers would be able to buy out of their weekly pocket money with change to spare. Then he gave us a lecture about the slippery slope we had started to slither down.

'You're a bad lot and unless you take action now every last one of you is going to end up at approved schools or even in prison. I don't want to ever, ever catch any of you stealing anything ever again. Is that understood?' We dutifully nodded our heads and some of the girls started sobbing again.

'I won't be pressing charges on this occasion, Mother Superior, but if any of these girls are caught again they're looking at time behind bars. There'll be no second chances.'

'Oh, thank you officer. I do appreciate you exercising your discretion on this occasion. Truly I do.'

He tipped his helmet to Mother Superior and marched off. There was something familiar about his manner. At first I couldn't put my finger on it, and then I realised that he was peddling exactly the same self-satisfied brand of 'I've got God on my side' as the nuns.

Mother Superior peered out of the window to check his departure and when the thick, black gates clattered behind him she turned to us. All traces of calm and restraint had been erased from her voice.

'How dare you bring shame on this children's home, how dare you, what were you thinking of?' Her voice was getting louder and more agitated. 'Go to the chapel and pray for forgiveness.'

We all scurried for the door thinking we had escaped quite lightly, considering that we were sent to pray for forgiveness even when we hadn't done anything wrong. At this moment the prospect of kneeling in front of the Virgin Mary for a couple of hours seemed desperately appealing. But before we could bolt out of the door she called us back.

'But first up to the tower.'

The tower was out of bounds and none of us had ever been up there before. I had no curiosity about that tower; it reminded me of the story of Sleeping Beauty which our primary school teacher had read to us. When I first heard the story I silently willed Sleeping Beauty not to venture into such dangerous territory. Now I was facing a fate much worse than Sleeping Beauty's but, unlike her, I couldn't exercise the free will to turn around and run away from the tower.

'Line up outside,' said Mother Superior. I presumed we were all going to get some sort of beating and when the cries of the first girl pierced the heavy wood of the closed door everyone tensed. Girls came out sobbing with their hands over their face. Margaret went in before me and came out whimpering. But when she caught my eye she gave me a wink. The nun who was calling the next girl in saw Margaret's spirited gesture and called her back in for another beating. She came out trying not to cry, she was very tough.

The nuns often referred to Margaret as a 'monkey' because of the colour of her skin. Like me she wasn't always prepared to fall into line and Mother Superior made the cruellest comments to her. 'You're a wild girl, you belong in the jungle up a tree', was one of her favourites. For some reason the nuns never called me the same derogatory names relating to my skin colour.

'You're lucky they don't call you the names they call me,' said Margaret. 'It's probably because you've got straight, black, shiny hair rather than a wild Afro like mine that the nuns don't know how to manage. You're so lucky, Clare, I wish my hair was like yours.'

Through the door I could hear Mother Superior yelling a variation on her usual theme. 'You're a wicked, no good monkey, your kind should never have come out of the jungle,' she said. Through the door as she beat Margaret her cries sounded like an electric bolt of energy, as if something enormously repressed in her was finding release at last.

When it was my turn I was hysterical before I went into the room, which must have been the point in lining us all up outside the door. Mother Superior curled her lips in distaste and commanded me to be silent.

'Bend over this chair and pull your knickers down,' she said in a tight voice. I looked at the door to see if there was any chance of escape but Sister Maria was barricading it with her bulky body. I swivelled my head towards the tiny window but it had bars across it. Even if Mother Superior decided to beat me to death there was no alternative but to submit. She raised a leather strap high above my head and brought it down with such force that my flesh sizzled. She whacked and whacked for what felt like at least thirty minutes although I suppose it was only for a few seconds. I couldn't sit down for a few days after that and I never stole again, at least not from a shop. It was what the sisters called 'a really good hiding'.

While even the word shoplifting made my heart race with fear, certain kinds of stealing seemed to be more morally acceptable to me at that age. A group of us were out playing a few weeks later and were dawdling down a back alley when we saw the branches of an apple tree hanging invitingly over the fence of someone's back garden. We all agreed that those perfectly ripe, juicy apples, with just a blush of pink on the green skins, needed picking before they rotted and fell off the tree. Eager to bite into an apple I whispered excitedly, 'I'll climb the wall to get to the apples.'

Margaret gave me a leg up and I managed to clamber to the top of the wall and jump on to the lower branches of the tree. I started grabbing greedily at the apples, throwing them down for the others to catch. I felt like a bountiful Santa. The others cheered as

I rained apples into their outstretched arms and, emboldened, I started to climb higher. But the branch I eased myself on to snapped as I pressed my weight on to it. I slammed to the ground, landing on my back. The pain made my head spin and I couldn't get up off the floor. All the time threaded through the pain was the worse fear of being caught and not being able to make a run for it.

Somehow I managed to get on to my feet. The shock pain in my back was wearing off but it made me more aware of an agonising pain in my wrist. I walked home feeling too fragile to press my feet properly to the floor. I was tiptoeing lightly to avoid jolting my wrist and had started to feel terribly sick.

As we approached the familiar, hateful towers of Park Hall Children's Home (how could I ever have thought it was a fairy palace?), I started to panic. What was I going to tell the nuns? I was in agony and couldn't move my wrist, so I'd have to say something to them.

Sister Maria opened the door.

'Oh, Sister Maria, my wrist hurts.' Screwing up my face I came straight out with it.

'Whatever have you been doing?' she asked, looking concerned and suspicious at the same time.

'I was trying to climb a wall for a dare but I fell off,' I stammered, sure that she would know by the look in my eyes that in fact I had been stealing apples. However, my secret appeared to be safe. She took one look at my wrist and said it was probably broken. She didn't seem cross that I had climbed a wall for a dare, probably because she was preoccupied with what she needed to do to sort me out.

'Come along, we'll have to get you to hospital,' she said briskly.

As usual there was no acknowledgement of the physical pain I was experiencing. The sisters didn't have a car, and because Sister Maria decided the break wasn't urgent enough for an ambulance she took me to hospital on the bus. I rested my head against the window of the bus and groaned quietly. I closed my eyes and tried to stop myself from vomiting.

'Hush now,' she said through gritted teeth when my moans started to get louder.

When we arrived at the casualty department and Sister Maria explained what had happened, the nurse was very sympathetic.

'This silly young madam tumbled off a wall I'm afraid,' said Sister Maria to the nurse.

'Oh, you poor little thing,' said the nurse soothingly. She looked carefully at my wrist, barely touching it. Her hands felt soft.

'We'll have to X-ray it but it certainly looks broken. I'll have to get you undressed, lovey, and put you into a hospital gown. I'm afraid you'll have to stay in hospital for a few days with a nasty break like that.'

Gently she took off my socks and noticed that my feet were sandy. There was a sandpit at the children's home and us older children often played in the sand with the little ones, enjoying the smooth, gritty feel of the stuff just as much as they did.

'Do you like playing in the sand?' she asked kindly.

I felt my face burning with shame because I knew that really I was far too old to be doing such things. But the nurse didn't say anything like that.

My arm was X-rayed and my wrist pronounced officially broken.

'She'll have to stay in hospital for a couple of days,' the doctor confirmed to Sister Maria, addressing his remarks across the top of my head as if I didn't exist.

Rosalind, a woman who lived close to the children's home and always stopped for a chat whenever she saw any of us, came to visit. She slipped an enormous bar of chocolate out of her bag and put it on the locker by my bed. I was so pleased that someone had brought me a special present that I couldn't bear to eat it until it was almost time for me to be discharged.

Sister Maria came to visit too. She brought a bottle of sickly orange-dyed lemonade. Although I didn't particularly like the stuff I beamed with pleasure because one of the nuns had bought something especially for me, but she returned my expression with a frown.

'All the trouble you children cause us, I don't know why you do it, I really don't. Once in a while it would be nice if you could just show a little bit of gratitude to us for all the things we do for you.'

'Thank you for the pop, Sister Maria,' I said. She stayed tutting for another five minutes and then left me in peace to drink it.

My arm took a couple of months to heal and after that I became a little more cautious about taking risks. But the thefts didn't stop altogether although a particular habit I got into didn't feel like theft at all.

When I was playing out by myself I sometimes wandered into the graveyard of the church close to the children's home. It always felt very peaceful and was often deserted. I walked in there one sunny afternoon and could almost feel the collected souls taking a nap. I looked at the names on the gravestones and the dates of birth and death. A few of the inscriptions were for children and babies and I wondered how they had died. Some of the graves looked neglected with long grass growing up around them, while others were immaculate with bunches of fresh flowers. I picked a few flowers out of the generous bouquets and placed them on the graves with no flowers. The splash of colour improved their appearance no end. I spent quite a while rearranging the flowers so that everyone had at least a few stems of something pretty on their grave. Then I walked back to the children's home. Nobody had spotted me shifting the flowers and I felt good about my impromptu redistribution. I returned several times and carried out the same Robin Hood-style operation, always feeling warm and peaceful afterwards. Although I knew that stealing the flowers relatives had put on their loved ones' graves was wrong, and that if the nuns found out I would get a beating, the core of me felt as if I had done the right thing.

CHAPTER TWELVE

A bright moment during a period which was otherwise all greyness pock-marked with black was the annual children's home holiday. Each year a small group of children were taken away and when it came round to my turn I was so excited I couldn't sleep. We went to a holiday village just outside Dublin and became friendly with ordinary families. One family had six children and we got into the habit of sharing cocoa and biscuits with them every night before bedtime. Apart from the set up at Marie's house I had never seen a normal family in action before, and I was mesmerised by the way they conducted themselves. My eyes took endless photographs which my brain filed neatly away and labelled 'happiness'. The parents always seemed to be listening intently to the things their children had to say. They laughed at their jokes and – the thing that aroused most envy in me – cuddled them frequently in the easy, uninhibited manner of true love.

'What's it like having nuns for parents, Clare?' Walter, the nine-year-old boy of the family asked me one evening as we sat around cradling our cocoa, shivering slightly as the summer night chilled. As the nuns were sitting among us I was guarded.

'Well, it's all right really. It's like having lots of mums instead of just one. And when they're not looking we can slide down the banisters of this big, grand staircase we've got in the children's home.'

Walter didn't ask any awkward questions about why I had ended up in a children's home and what had become of my parents, and I was grateful for that.

The nuns seemed less stiff in the holiday environment. Their habits rustled less and the zeal in their eyes dulled a little. They were permitting themselves a brief sabbatical from God's work. They felt, as my mother did, that what went on behind closed doors was a matter for them but that it was important to put on a good, public show. Standards weren't relaxed entirely though. We were expected to keep the chalets we stayed in sparkling clean and so tidy they looked uninhabited. We won a prize for the neatest chalets, much to the delight of the nuns – it all reflected so well on them.

Sister Moira cooked sausages on a little primus stove for us. They tasted much crispier and juicier than the ones we ate at home. The escape from the Park Hall routine was a balm. I was allowed to enter a talent contest and dressed up as a little Indian girl, with a blanket round my shoulders and a red dot in the middle of my forehead. I won second prize – it was the first time that the colour of my skin had done me any favours. My prize was a delicate china doll dressed in English national costume. I was so proud of myself for winning a prize: it was only the second time I'd ever been awarded anything – the first was my progress award in ballet. It felt like a hypodermic syringe full of the purest sugar had just been shot into my veins.

'Well done, Clare,' said Margaret, squeezing my arm supportively.

Even Sister Moira congratulated me. 'Good for you, Clare,' she said. Then, pulling herself up, proceeded to reprimand: 'But you can't be walking around like a little Indian girl for ever more. Run to your room and put your day clothes back on now.'

One of the venues for the annual holiday was Blackpool. Only the older children were permitted to go, but when I turned fourteen and was eagerly anticipating my turn by the seaside the nuns announced that I wouldn't be going.

'You're too bold,' they said. 'And too cheeky!' They refused my pleas with pursed lips and repeated that a girl as bad as me couldn't possibly qualify for such a treat. But after making me utterly miserable and watching tears roll down my cheeks for the best part of a month, they relented.

I was determined to take part in absolutely everything and not to waste a moment. I loved the rough smell of the sea, the wide promenades and the glut of happy families. I went to the beach every day and revelled in the feel of the sand on my back and legs. I spent hours turning myself over and over in it like a piece of cod getting battered, and then running into the sea to wash it all off before repeating the whole cycle again.

While we played and stretched out on the beach a group of boys from Ireland a couple of years older than us approached us. I was sitting with four other girls and each of the boys targeted one of us and asked us to be their girlfriends. My instinct was to run away and shake off the boy who kept putting his hand insistently on my arm, but the other girls seemed keen on getting to know these boys better so I went along with them. The last thing I wanted to do was be different from the others. Within minutes the boys were kissing us, forcing their tongues into our mouths. I felt as if I was choking and tried to ram my lips shut, but my 'boyfriend's' tongue was still in there so it made matters worse not better. I wanted to run off along the seashore and return to that blissful state of pleasing myself but the urge to conform was stronger and in the end I allowed my mouth to droop open and let the kiss take its course.

With the nuns' blessing I entered another talent show, hosted by Bob Monkhouse. I sang 'Green Grow The Rushes-O', a song I'd learned at school. The song was very repetitive, like 'The Twelve Days Of Christmas' or 'Ten Green Bottles' and before I'd got halfway through Bob Monkhouse took out a plastic gun to pretend to shoot me in a bid to shut me up. The audience were roaring with laughter but I carried on singing steadfastly until I'd got to the end. I knew what he was doing but I pretended I hadn't noticed the gun and that I had no idea that my song was repetitive. This made the audience laugh all the more. They had to vote for their favourite act and to my amazement I got more votes than anyone else – people put two hands up for me instead of one.

I soaked up the attention and experienced an unfamiliar emotion. Fleetingly I felt I was worth something. My insides glowed with warm contentment and I got a brief glimpse of my own value. Perhaps I really could make something of my life, maybe I could even become a professional singer – my imagination started to run away very pleasantly. Clutching my prize of a compendium of games I felt suddenly different. For a few moments I was a girl who could be something better than the bad, black girl at the children's home who came from a white trash family who didn't want her.

The euphoria didn't last though. Although I was fourteen when I went to Blackpool I was still wetting the bed. Another boy of my age who went on the trip also wet the bed and the two of us had to go downstairs and present our sodden sheets to the woman who ran the guesthouse.

'We're sorry, miss, we wet our sheets,' we said in unison.

The humiliation of standing before the stern landlady, who surveyed the wet sheets with arms clamped folded and lipstick-smudged lips quivering with irritation, swiftly divested me of my fantasy that I could become a singer hobnobbing with the likes of Bob Monkhouse on a regular basis. By the time we returned to Park Hall my moment of singing glory was all but forgotten.

The school I went to tried to find jobs for us all; most of us planned to leave at the age of fifteen. I was sent along to do an interview at Littlewoods Pools and my interviewer told me I showed some aptitude with counting up the columns of figures quickly and accurately.

'Well, Clare, I'm very impressed with the way you've performed in your interview. You're obviously as bright as a button. I'd like to offer you a job here and now. I will, of course, get a letter typed up right away for you to give to your guardians.'

'That's brilliant, really brilliant,' I said.

I bounded back to Park Hall. At last I could see a way out, independence, a life of my own, a permanent escape from the nuns. But I had no idea how I would survive on a day-to-day basis without Park Hall; although I often loathed the place it had become a life-support system of sorts for me. The scent of freedom in its most abstract sense felt extremely good though.

When I showed the letter giving me a job to Sister Joanna, however, her normally immobile features came alive and she turned on me ferociously.

'I'm absolutely disgusted with you. How dare you go looking for jobs working for an organisation involved in a dissolute practice like gambling? No girl from here is going to get mixed up with that kind of thing.'

Then she ripped up the letter in front of me. I was bewildered as well as devastated. I had thought the nuns would be so pleased with me for going out and finding my own way in the world. The more the nuns undermined me, the more dependent I felt on them. Bit by bit they were excavating my personality, leaving the shell of my body intact but invisibly sucking out my emotional innards until there was nothing left inside me to sustain myself as an independent adult trying to make my own way in life. I'll never know if my life would have taken a different course if the nuns had allowed me to accept that job with their blessing.

However, after five and a half years of wearing white gloves on Sundays, eating stale cornflakes for breakfast day after day and having the message of how bad I was reinforced for me by various sets of knuckles, the nuns were preparing to spit me out. They never bothered to explain my arrival, my progression through the home, or the erratic appearances of my mother on the scene. And it did not occur to them to explain my imminent departure. We were all commodities to them, simply numbers, and when the time came to move us out of Park Hall it was done silently and without emotion.

A few days before my abrupt departure I was taken by Sister Claire into Blacklers, the department store in Liverpool which I would for ever associate with the shoplifting episode.

She picked out a black A-line skirt for me in a scratchy Crimplene material, which I longed to roll into a ball and hide in the nearest dustbin even before I tried it on. The nylon white blouse with prissy frills on the front, which she selected next, also made me recoil.

'You'll look lovely in these, Clare, very proper and grown up, now stop pulling cheeky faces at me. You should be thankful you've got somebody to buy you a whole set of new clothes.'

She picked up a new pair of pure white gloves and a burgundy coat with a peaked cap in a matching shade of sour wine. It was the same shade as the communion wine and I was sure that was no coincidence. I looked longingly at the displays of jeans with embroidered flowers on them and T-shirts with the latest designs but it was clear from the way Sister Claire quickened her pace as we approached them that these were not destined for my wardrobe.

I was deeply suspicious about Sister Claire's motive for buying me new clothes when I usually got hand-me-downs. But she refused to be drawn, replying only to my questions with, 'All will be revealed by the Good Lord soon enough.'

'But if the Good Lord has revealed it to you then surely you can tell me,' I nagged. She gave her best Mona Lisa smile and placed a single finger against her lips.

The clothes were whisked away as soon as we got back to the children's home and I almost forgot about them. Instinctively I felt they represented something unsavoury and when they disappeared I thought that maybe whatever the nuns had in store for me wasn't going to come to pass after all.

Three days later, however, when I was changing out of my school uniform in the basement, I spotted a big black suitcase which had my initials stuck on. I peeked inside and there, folded into razor creases, lay my hated new clothes. I snapped the suitcase clasp shut and wondered what use the suitcase of clothes would be put to.

Later on when there were no nuns in sight I sailed down the banister. As I reached the bottom I saw Sister Claire hurrying across the hallway. She ignored the fact that I was travelling via banister, which was unusual in itself.

'Sister Claire, I've seen a suitcase full of my new clothes in the basement. Do you know what's going to happen to me?'

She looked around to make sure none of the other sisters were heel wheeling by and leaned forwards, lowering her voice. 'Try and be good,' she said. 'They're moving you.'

I was shocked. I had assumed that I was being moved to a new school or going to visit someone important, who I needed to look smart for. It never crossed my mind that I was actually leaving the children's home.

'Where to? Will I be put in another children's home?'

She must have seen the frantic expression in my eyes. 'I'm sorry, Clare, I can't go into details at the moment.'

Like living with my mother, living at Park Hall involved plenty of misery, but at least it was familiar misery. I'd acquired a range of survival mechanisms and at least I knew how things worked. I even managed to dodge the nuns' flexed knuckles most of the time now. Mary was still at Park Hall, although she had got a job working in a department store in Liverpool and was hoping to move into a flat soon. Lucy, Damian, John and Tom had long gone to foster parents and we hadn't been allowed to keep in touch.

The thought of being plunged into the unknown once again was terrifying. That night I dreamed of my mother's old boyfriend, Peter. He was piling sweets into my lap and I was gratefully scooping them up and stuffing them into my mouth because I was terribly hungry. But then I started to feel sick and Peter just carried on shoving the sweets at me and directed me to eat them. I woke up still feeling sick and managed to run to the toilet just before I vomited.

CHAPTER THIRTEEN

The next morning it became official. The nuns announced that I was leaving.

'A lady called Mrs Christie from social services will be arriving shortly to pick you up and take you to an assessment centre, Clare,' said Sister Maria. 'Now please don't disgrace the good name of Park Hall by getting up to the sort of mischief you've been getting up to here.'

'What's an assessment centre?' I asked. I could feel the blood draining out of my face. It sounded like some kind of punishment. I knew the nuns thought I was naughty, cheeky and uncontrollable but I didn't feel like a bad person, and I hoped that whoever looked after me next would not think I was irredeemably bad.

The nuns saw no need to answer my question and didn't give me an opportunity to say goodbye to any of the other children. As the social worker led me out of Park Hall, only Sister Claire waved me off. The others seemed suddenly busy elsewhere in the house. I glanced up and saw Margaret watching me from the upstairs dormitory window. She waved and then crossed her fingers for me.

'Look after yourself, Clare,' said Sister Claire.

'You too,' I said, quavering with emotion.

As I climbed into Mrs Christie's mini – all the social workers I came into contact with in Liverpool drove minis – my mind switched to more immediate concerns than my future and the loss of my ordered life at Park Hall. As soon as Mrs Christie was out of the driveway and into the street with the dark trees, off came the loathed white gloves, followed by the prickly hat and coat. In my suitcase I had an emerald green polo neck sweater, which I adored. I clicked open the clasp on my case, shoved the rejected clothes in and pulled on the sweater. It made me feel a little bit better.

Mrs Christie kept trying to draw me into conversation but I felt too weary to talk, and just gazed out of the window without seeing anything we passed.

'We're going to Preston,' she said chattily.

I'd never heard of Preston and had no idea whether it was close by or at the other end of the country.

As my silence became more pronounced, Mrs Christie became more nervous, licking her dry pale lips and rhythmically pushing her wispy grey hair behind her ears.

'I'm sure you'll like it there.'

'Do you have any sisters and brothers?'

'What have you been doing in school this week?'

'Who's your favourite pop star?'

I could feel a knot of vomit gathering in the centre of my stomach. 'I think I'm going to be sick,' I said quietly.

She glanced at me and decided that I looked as if I really was going to be sick. She took a sharp left turn and we found ourselves in a quiet residential neighbourhood.

'I'll take you to my house and give you something to stop you feeling so sick,' she smiled.

When she stopped the car I felt a bit better and she took me inside her house, which surprised me because everything in it was frayed and shabby. I had always assumed that social workers inhabited a perfect universe where poverty and disorder were entirely absent. Otherwise how else could they determine the best course of action for messed up families like mine?

She rummaged in one of her kitchen cupboards and eventually produced a dark bottle of pills with a yellowing label. She passed me a glass of water and tipped two little white pills into her hand.

'Here, take these,' she said softly. I looked from the pills to her suspiciously. 'Don't worry. I'm not trying to poison you,' she smiled.

I decided to take my chances and swallowed the pills. Almost immediately I started to feel better and we got back into the car. I rested my head against the sticky plastic seat and closed my eyes.

I felt as if we'd been travelling for hours but in fact the journey took less than an hour. When we arrived in Preston she had to stop and ask a couple of people where the road was where she was taking me. Eventually we arrived at a large building of sand-coloured bricks surrounded by a fence.

A man answered the door and said a very cheery hello to us both. I had initially wondered if this place too would be run by nuns but, having seen him, I assumed not.

'Come in, come in,' he beamed.

Then he started to rattle through a speech he had obviously made many times before about the rules and regulations of the place. I couldn't take any of it in and burst into tears. The thought of unlearning the nuns' rules and learning completely different ones was overwhelming.

The social worker who had delivered me to the assessment centre disappeared into the man's office and the door was pulled smartly shut. The no-nonsense clang of the door made me feel very excluded. It was obvious the two of them were talking about me. I thought I heard the words 'difficult to place' drifting under the door but I couldn't be sure. I was left standing in the hallway; I was nothing. The social worker came out after ten minutes and said briskly, 'I'm going now, I'll leave you to it', and hurried away.

The manager patted my arm. He ushered me into his office, which had a large chart on the wall with lots of names on it with various coloured beads alongside. I found out later that the names belonged to the other children and the beads signified the various services involved in their care, such as psychiatry, psychology, probation and so on.

He showed me to my bedroom and gave me a large locker to put my clothes in.

'Don't worry, Clare, the other children will be home from school soon and then you'll have some chums to chat to,' he said.

I had recently left school for good and didn't know how I'd be expected to spend my days while the others were in their lessons.

Towards four o'clock the silence of the assessment centre was shattered as everyone arrived home. The centre housed teenagers between the ages of thirteen and seventeen. I discovered later that it was a kind of staging post between institutions, an opportunity for the professionals to pause for breath before deciding what to do with hard to place children like me.

The other children raced up the stairs when they heard that someone new had arrived. 'What are you in for, what are you in for?' they shouted, without bothering to tell me their names or ask mine. Finding out about a new crime was one of the highlights of living there.

'I don't know,' I stammered. I did a quick inventory of wrongdoings in my head but nothing really seemed to fit the bill. The shoplifting was a couple of years ago and the nuns never got to find out about stealing the apples or rearranging the flowers on the gravestones.

All the others were in there for committing crimes like setting fire to cars and sticking knives into people's bellies. I didn't consider myself to be part of that world, so I began to believe that the nuns must have sent me there because I was innately bad. When the children found out that I had never committed any crime apart from the lone theft of the coloured pencils from Blacklers, which they dismissed scornfully as a kiddie's prank, they lost interest in me.

'Is that all you've done?' said one small girl with mousy hair and narrowed eyes. 'I'm sure we'll be able to show you a thing or two. Nicking cars is easy peasy and when you whizz down the road in some bloke's posh car it's the best feeling in the world.'

Yet again I was flooded with the sensation of having been placed in the wrong life box. Everything that happened to me felt like a clash between me and circumstances, as if I was walking along a bumpy road wearing my left shoe on my right foot and my right on my left.

The shock of having my 'badness' made official turned me suddenly silent. The cheekiness and the swearing vanished and were replaced by a deathly hush. While both states were responses to my circumstances, I had always felt that if I'd been given the space to be whatever I wanted to be as a child that I would always be a joker, getting up to mischief and giggling about pranks I had got up to with friends. When I had arrived at Park Hall I was too young to understand that we had been brought there because our mother had effectively abandoned us.

During our time with the nuns, Damian, Lucy, Tom and John were selected by foster parents who rescued them from the children's home. As I sat forlornly on the bed that had been allocated to me but which did not belong to me, the accumulated rejection from my mother and all the prospective foster parents who never chose me, washed over me. Everyone wants to be selected and loved. Being dumped at the assessment centre felt a hundred times worse than being shunned by my classmates or criticised by the nuns. This really was the end of the line, the ultimate rubbish bin. For those who come from secure, loving families and embark on an independent life at the end of their teenage years with a sense of self-belief, my feelings of utter worthlessness may be hard to comprehend. Knowing that nobody in the world wanted me, much less loved me, induced a kind of paralysis. I didn't want to try and do anything because I would inevitably fail and, on top of the failures the nuns had spent years pointing out to me, it was simply too much to bear.

The small girl with the mousy hair was standing over me. I was so deep in thought that I hadn't realised she was talking to me.

'Are you deaf or what? We're off to have some fun down the shops. Coming?'

I shook my head, immediately understanding the kind of fun she had in mind. She shrugged and walked away, calling to the other teenagers, 'Hurry up or there'll be nothing left to nick.'

I lay back on my bed, which was covered with a musty candlewick bedspread in a shade of orange that made me feel nauseous. I assessed my situation: fifteen years old, unwanted, unloved, unskilled. The energy I had always had to take on the nuns had gone; I could feel it fizzing out of my bones on to the bedspread, where it evaporated. From now on I was going to give in and let whichever institution I happened to land in take the lead with my life. I drifted off to sleep feeling extremely sorry for myself.

A man in a trilby hat and shabby overcoat arrived the following morning and gave me some sort of test. Like the nuns he didn't explain why I had to do the test or what it was for. I had to copy pictures of different coloured blocks, which I found very difficult and various number tests, which I couldn't do.

I overheard one of the staff saying, 'William Pickles did above average in the test but Clare's performance was below average.' To me she sounded as if she was taking pleasure in my failure.

It didn't surprise me, and I retreated further into myself.

Children were only expected to stay at the centre for six weeks but I ended up staying seven months. Many children were fostered from there but again, I was never chosen.

One of the staff confided, pityingly, that I wasn't chosen because of the colour of my skin. Racism was so intrinsic to daily life in the white Liverpool of my childhood that I never thought to question it. At school and at Park Hall the white children sang rhymes like 'nigger, nigger pull the trigger' and 'what do you want for breakfast? Coonflakes. What do you want for dinner? Coon beef.' A black school friend of mine used to put talcum powder on her face to make her skin look lighter and she bought a straight hair wig to conceal her natural hair. I don't remember any black child I came across feeling comfortable in their skin. Like me, all yearned for the pasty, white skin of the majority.

For those who have never had to undergo the beauty contest that is fostering it's hard to convey the pain and rejection connected with never being picked. I was never chosen at the children's home, nor was I chosen here. My skin colour was part of my inferiority complex but there were other inadequacies too: my lack of family, which would have accorded some kind of status, my lack of academic ability and my hopeless fashion sense – the clothes the nuns bought for what must have appeared to others as a deliberate effort to look as unappealing as possible.

My mother came to visit me twice while I was at the assessment centre. I didn't know it at the time but she was working close by as a bus conductress in Preston. She appeared one day with a child's knitting set which she handed over unceremoniously. She seemed neither happy nor unhappy to see me and after a minute or two said, 'I'll have to go now, I've got the bus stopped right outside.'

I glanced out of the window and reminding me of a surreal still from a Beatles photo shoot was the red bus parked at the bus stop with rows of people on seats with their necks craned backwards to see where my mother had gone. They all looked too startled to be cross with her. And my mother, who was never one to observe rules, appeared unconcerned about the temporary abandonment of her passengers.

The next time she visited she was cross with me. 'What have you done wrong to put people off from fostering you?' she snapped after nodding a silent hello to me.

I had continued at the assessment centre as I arrived. Quiet as a mouse and never getting into trouble the way I had at Park Hall. I didn't challenge any rules or anyone's authority, I never asserted myself and I barely spoke to the other children.

'Nothing,' I replied, staring into her cold eyes.

She looked at me sternly with a trace of chilly pity shot through, like the veins in a Stilton cheese.

'Well, I've had to sort something out for you because you can't stay here for ever. Remember the man I was with that day when I visited you? His name's Anwar Ahmed and he's married to a white woman called Jenny. They're a lovely couple and they've said they'll take you. You can move in with them on Sunday so you better start packing your bags.'

I did so joyfully. Walking away from the assessment centre was an enormous relief. At last somebody wanted me.

CLARE AHMED 1970–1971

My foster father was called Anwar Ahmed. I adopted his surname

CHAPTER FOURTEEN

Familiarity with the mechanics of being selected, or in my case passed over for adoption or fostering over the years didn't make the hurt any duller. What was most painful about the process was the naked honesty of it all. Nobody would take on a child just to avoid offending that child's sensibilities. It all boiled down to looks – I looked different from the other children; all the potential foster parents were white and they didn't want to take a chance with a girl with the wrong colour skin. When my mother told me that at last a couple had agreed to take me, I decided that all my troubles were over and that, finally, I would belong somewhere.

The first time I met Jenny and Anwar Ahmed they were charming to me. Anwar Ahmed came from Pakistan; he spoke halting, heavily accented English. He was tall and slim with very short hair greying at the temples. I never discovered his age but decided he was probably in his early forties. He dressed smartly in a shirt and trousers and worked as a driving instructor. Previously he had worked as a driver on the Ribble buses, which was where I suppose he met my mother when she was working there as a conductress.

Jenny introduced herself to me with a formal handshake. She was a sensual looking woman with dyed black hair and a large mouth covered with lipstick so thickly, ferociously red it looked as if it had been smacked on. She was dressed in a lilac shirt made of some sort of shiny material, which was stretched a little too tightly across her breasts and a black skirt, which stretched equally tightly across her hips and bottom.

'Hello, Clare, nice to meet you.' Her hand was soft and I envied her red, polished nails. There was something about her that I found absolutely hypnotic. She had left her husband and two sons, then aged three and four, more than a decade ago to go and live with Mr Anwar. Social services knew nothing of the family she had put behind her when they approved her and Mr Anwar as foster parents.

Mr Anwar nodded at me and stared hard. My gratitude at being chosen blunted my instinct to be wary.

'Come and sit down next to me, Clare love,' said Jenny. She patted the beige leather sofa and I did as I was told.

She did all the talking while Mr Anwar folded his long limbs into an armchair and carried on staring at me.

'Now you'll have to tell me what you like to eat and what your favourite things are.' She rubbed the bottom of my black cotton shirt critically between her thumb and forefinger. 'And we'll go out and buy you some nice new stuff to wear, all right, Clare?'

I just nodded. The air felt heady, her voice was making me feel drunk. Nobody had ever showed this much interest in me before. Her questions kept winding around me like a drug I knew I shouldn't be inhaling but which was too enjoyable to turn away from.

'Got a boyfriend have you lovey? No, well I'm sure we can sort that out in a jiffy. I've got a lovely young man who would suit you down to the ground.' The lovely young man she turned out to have in mind was her son Brian from her first marriage, although she didn't elaborate on this at our first meeting.

Mr Anwar remained silent, although one eyebrow arched a couple of millimetres upwards when she mentioned fixing me up with a boyfriend.

'Right then, I'd best show you to your room. Me and Ahmed are delighted to have you here, aren't we Ahmed?'

He grinned at me: 'Yes, we're really delighted.'

I settled quickly into life with Jenny and Mr Anwar. Thanks to my years with the nuns following orders was horribly, meticulously embroidered in to my DNA.

Jenny helped me to find a job as a filing clerk working for Peter Craig, the catalogue company. I loved the work: it wasn't too hard for me as most things at school had been, and those above me treated me in a kindly, paternal way and told me I was doing well. All the money I earned was handed straight over to Jenny every Friday. It never occurred to me that it was mine.

She did buy me the clothes she promised me, but with the income they received from social services and my modest wage they must have made a reasonable profit out of me. My mission throughout my childhood to acquire enough money to buy sweets remained strong but beyond that I had very little interest in spending money. Having Jenny take control of my finances was no different from the way things had worked at the children's home and the assessment centre and I accepted it unquestioningly.

Mr Anwar took to calling me Dolly. He thought he was being very clever, comparing the mixed colour of my mother's and father's skins to dolly mixtures, and chuckled to himself at his pun every time he used it: 'Make me a cup of tea, Dolly', 'Can you take the dog out, Dolly?'

My obedience continued. After living with them for three months they decided they no longer needed to be on their best behaviour with me. The syrupy period was over and as their criticisms of me increased, familiar feelings of worthlessness resurfaced.

I left Park Hall with no knowledge of simple things like how to boil an egg or use a washing machine. I put a pile of my clothes in the washing machine one day but had no clue about where to put the soap powder or how to turn the dial to get the thing started. Jenny came into the kitchen and saw me hovering uncertainly over the machine.

'Are you thick or what?' she said, exasperatedly. Without explaining to me what to do so that I would know for next time, she spun the dial and walked out. She reminded me of the maths teacher I'd had at school who told me off for copying but then didn't explain to me how to do the sums. I decided that people like Jenny and that teacher enjoyed watching people like me squirm powerlessly and didn't want to spoil that enjoyment by removing our ignorance.

Jenny offered to teach me to drive but when I struggled to master the controls of the car and confused left and right in the first few lessons, she gave up on me.

'You're impossible to teach,' she said. I felt more of a failure than I did before I embarked on the lessons with her.

Jenny asked me to do more and more of the household chores. She was very proud of their immaculate bungalow and worked hard on cleaning and polishing it herself, but expected me to work alongside her in the shadow of her mop. Her initial softness fell away and she showed herself to have a soul with spikes. I grew to fear her sharp tongue.

'She's a witch, your mother,' she said whenever I mentioned her. Although I was under no illusions about my mother's shortcomings as a parent I felt distressed and protective when others maligned her.

'She's always done her best,' I said weakly.

But, as with the instructions to clean the house and hand over my entire pay packet, there was something about Jenny that compelled me to do whatever she asked. I felt that I was sleepwalking through my time with her, dangling on the end of a marionette string with which she directed me across the events of her life.

One evening about six months after I arrived at Jenny and Mr Anwar's, my mother appeared at the door to take me out to a club, something she did very infrequently, but which she and I had arranged over the phone a couple of days before. I had just turned sixteen and was legally allowed into these places. This was probably the most stable period in my mother's life and the time I saw most of her and got along best with her. She had a fairly steady job as a bus conductress with Ribble Buses, didn't appear to have any violent or otherwise unsuitable men in her life and even seemed to be drinking moderately.

'Now that you've turned sixteen, Clare, how would you like to go out to a club for the evening with me? I know you like dancing. We can have some fun,' she'd said. I'd agreed eagerly. If my mother was showing interest in me I wanted to do everything possible to encourage it.

She appeared on Jenny and Mr Anwar's doorstep in a smart blouse and skirt. 'Are you all ready to go then, Clare?' she said, when I answered the door. Jenny immediately appeared behind me.

'Go where?' she said suspiciously.

'I've arranged to go to a club with me mum,' I said brightly.

'You'll do no such thing young lady,' said Jenny, fixing my mother with a hard stare. 'Don't forget, we're her legal guardians now,' she said, cruelly, to my mother. 'I don't think a girl of sixteen should be hanging around in those sorts of places. In any case Ahmed and I have arranged to take her to the cinema.'

My mother shrank on the doorstep. It reminded me of those sci-fi movies where the enemy is eliminated into a pile of mush by one zap of a lethal futuristic gun. Jenny hadn't mentioned anything to me about going to the cinema.

My mother spoke very quietly in a strangled voice. She lowered her eyes and lifted them only briefly to look into mine. 'I'll be in touch, Clare.'

She turned and walked down the path, gingerly putting one foot in front of the other as if she was in physical pain. For the first time I noticed that my mother, who had always represented physical perfection to me, was starting to look old and frayed, like a leaf at the very beginning of autumn. I had rarely seen her so cowed in connection with any of her children. It was a moment, like the one in court where we were forcibly removed from her, where the alcohol fumes cleared and she saw how completely she had lost her children. She was ashamed.

Even before my mother had turned the corner of the street Jenny had frogmarched me to the car. Mr Anwar swung into the driving seat and we roared off. My mother turned her head slightly at the noise and Jenny raised her hand in a smug, malevolent wave as my mother looked helplessly inside the car.

'I think you were bit hard on Dolly's mum,' said Mr Anwar.

'Hard, what do you mean hard?' said Jenny sharply. 'The old cow doesn't have the first clue about bringing up children and look at all those men she carries on with.'

'You know what, Jenny, sometimes you can be a really cruel bitch.'

The argument escalated in both vitriol and decibels and after a few minutes Mr Anwar, who could never win an argument against Jenny's more cunning logic, screeched the car to a halt at a phone box and jumped out.

'Wait here. I've got to make a phone call.'

Jenny bounded out after him like a lion with the taste of flesh between its teeth and squeezed herself into the phone box with him, where the row continued. I couldn't hear much of it but the words 'bitch' and 'bastard' drifted across to me. Finally they burnt out their bile and got back into the car. We were half an hour late for the film.

Although I was naive and gullible when I arrived, Jenny's treatment of my mother that evening and her screaming match with Mr Anwar left me in no doubt that the show they staged for me when I first arrived at their home was phoney. I was beginning to understand the real Jenny and Mr Anwar.

Jenny's moods were hugely changeable, yet there was something about her that continued to suck me into her irrational whims.

I had begun to get used to their Alsatian dog, Ted. Initially I was so scared of him that I was going to refuse to go and live with them. But gradually I realised that he was the only straightforward, dependable living thing in the household. I was never rude or cheeky to either Jenny or Mr Anwar. However, both of them started to find more and more fault with the way I looked, the way I behaved around the house and the things I said.

One of the girls at work asked me to go to a club with her and I rushed home to tell Jenny, thrilled to be asked. I was always amazed when I managed to pass off as a 'normal' teenager. I felt that it would be obvious to all the people who came from stable, sturdy homes what my upbringing had been. I expected to be shunned.

'Jenny, Mandy from work's asked me to go to that big club in town with her tomorrow night. Can I go? Please say I can.'

I looked up at her the way I had looked when I wanted the nuns to let me wear American tan tights instead of the white socks for the school concert, physically willing her to give permission. Jenny looked hard at me, considering her options. Then her face slammed shut. She had made her decision.

'You'll be doing no such thing, Clare. There's all sorts goes on at those clubs, they're not a place for innocent young girls like you. You'll have to tell Mandy you can't go. You should be grateful that you've got a responsible parent in charge of your welfare now. More than can be said for your mother.' She sniffed haughtily as if to clear the bad smell of my mother from her nostrils.

This time I couldn't absorb the insult quietly. I started screaming: 'Don't you dare talk about my mother like that, I hate you, I hate you, you're mean and cruel and you don't let me do what other teenagers are allowed to do.' My voice was rising to a high-pitched wail and I realised my protest sounded clumsy.

Jenny's face darkened. She raised her hand above her head, poised to rain down a slap or two, and then whacked me across the shoulder. It unbalanced me so completely that I went spinning across the room, landing with my head jammed against the beige leather sofa.

I never asked her permission again and I never tried to go out in the evenings with friends again either. I always followed Jenny's orders. The more she criticised me the more I tried to be good enough to win a few grudging words of praise from her. Now and again it worked. If she was in a good mood she might remark, 'Your hair looks lovely and shiny today, Clare', or 'You've done a nice job on polishing the bath.' When she handed out these crumbs I felt very proud.

The rules Jenny imposed seemed unnecessarily restrictive to me. I was banned from bringing anyone back to the house although no justification or explanation was ever given. They decided who did and did not cross the threshold. I had no visitation rights to hand out to others.

Soon after the cinema incident with my mother they invited her to visit. It wasn't a gesture of reconciliation but an exercise in grinding her underfoot. They strutted round the house peacock-style when she arrived, reeling off the number of bedrooms they had as if each one held the status of a university degree. They chatted about how they had travelled all the way to Kendall's, a large, plush Manchester department store, to purchase a top-of-the range sofa.

They knew that my mother was in a constant state of hand-to-mouth poverty and both seemed to take pleasure in stuffing the inventory of their home into her ears. She looked tired and drawn when she arrived and not particularly impressed by the relative abundance of riches. Her glossy, blonde hair was heavily streaked with grey. Usually she dyed it but she had obviously given up on doing that. She was wearing the same brown fur coat she had worn the day she signed away her parental rights to us in court. The colour had evolved to a sticky, shiny orange where the top layer of the material had rubbed away and there were a few cigarette burns near the buttonholes.

As Mr Anwar walked into the living room he spoke slowly and deliberately into my mother's left ear.

'And this is the lounge, we wanted something spacious and comfortable, you see.' He flashed her a smug, oily smile.

My mother looked uncomfortable. She had greeted me in the vague, offhand way devoid of warmth I was used to, but when I saw Mr Anwar doing his best to make her wince my usual instinct rose up through my throat although no words came out. It was as if I was my mother's mother and she was my particularly vulnerable child. Suddenly I was back in the family home watching Sam beat her with his fists and offering her my little umbrella for protection. I couldn't think of anything to say that wouldn't anger Mr Anwar and wouldn't have dared anyway, just as I didn't dare stand up to Sam directly when I was a child. My mother stiffened her spine but said nothing.

Jenny walked in at that moment and the oil of Mr Anwar's smile dispersed across the room. She too was keen to impress my mother and had used the best china teacups and a silver-plated tray which rarely saw daylight. Even the biscuits were an upmarket brand of Dutch shortcake instead of the McVitie's we usually ate. Both of them seemed keen to show that they were providing me with a better home than my mother ever had or could. It was obvious that my mother wasn't welcome beyond the show visit the two of them had choreographed.

'As you can see Mrs Malone, we're providing your Clare with a stable, secure home here.' Jenny's reddened mouth split open like a trodden on tomato.

My mother nodded and looked more uncomfortable.

'Thanks to both of you for taking in our Clare,' she said. 'Well I'd best be getting back.'

She nodded a goodbye to me and then hurried off down the path. This time she didn't look broken, just relieved to be making a quick getaway. As she watched her go Jenny said in a satisfied, disapproving tone, 'She was looking at her watch the whole time she was here.'

It felt even more wounding than Mr Anwar's regular comments, entirely devoid of irony, that nobody wanted me because I was black. Even my mother supposedly didn't want me.

My mother and I didn't stay in regular contact while I was with Jenny and Mr Anwar but a few months later I bumped into her in the centre of Preston.

I never knew what she was thinking and she never asked many questions about how I was getting on, but this time she seemed almost pleased to see me. Emboldened by her smile I said, 'Do you fancy coming back to mine for a cuppa?'

She thought for a minute and then said, 'OK, why not, as long as you're sure those snooty foster parents of yours aren't around.' We both laughed and walked back to their house.

I couldn't imagine what could be wrong with having my own mother visit me for a cup of tea. She didn't stay long and she didn't spill tea or flick ash on their precious sofa but somehow Jenny and Mr Anwar got to find out about the visit and both of them went wild.

'What are you doing having her round here without our permission? We don't want her to have contact with you,' said Mr Anwar.

'She never wanted you,' said Jenny, narrowing her eyes in exactly the way I remembered girls at primary school doing when they judged me for looking scruffier and poorer than they did. Her voice turned deadly, 'Because of your colour, of course. I can tell you, Clare, there aren't many foster parents who'd want to take on a black child. You've no idea how lucky you are to have us.'

I didn't feel remotely lucky and became increasingly disenchanted with life at my foster parents' home.

I started to assert myself more and more and we argued over the pettiest things. Each time, despite my lack of self-belief, I felt certain that I wasn't in the wrong. I began to realise that I was at an age where, for the first time, I had some choices, albeit limited ones. At least I knew I could earn money and support myself. All the months I had dutifully handed my wages over to Jenny it hadn't occurred to me that that money could be a way out for me.

'You might as well go back to the assessment centre,' said Jenny after one row. She had been nagging me as usual to get a boyfriend.

'Please, Jenny, leave it. I'm not interested in boys, I've got plenty of time for that later on.'

The only relationship I yearned for was one with a mother who would love me, cuddle me and fight my corner the way I had seen lionesses do with their young in a film we were shown at school once. Despite the glut of evidence to the contrary I kept hoping that Jenny would give me that love.

'You're such a baby, Clare. All you like doing is drinking milk just like a baby.'

Actually I loathed milk and other white creamy foods like yoghurt and salad cream, although I wasn't quite sure why. Something about the texture reminded me of something but I could never remember exactly what. Jenny knew I loathed these foods. I think it enhanced the taunts for her.

CHAPTER FIFTEEN

The most warped aspect of my time with Jenny was her peculiar longing to grab the baby she was plotting for me to conceive with her son Brian.

'I've always been dying to have a little girl, Clare, a cute little thing I could dress up in pink frilly dresses and booties. If you could just get pregnant with a lovely little girl I'd bring her up as my own.'

She never asked me about my childbearing intentions. Her eyes shone when she talked about this little girl who she said would bring her so much happiness.

Brian had been to visit a few times with his younger brother and he seemed like a nice boy. He had an open, handsome face, very different from Jenny's. He was in his early twenties and married, although I never met his wife. His intentions were written across his features in bold capital letters, in contrast to the hieroglyphics that obscured the way Jenny's mind worked.

One afternoon when he was due to come over and visit, Jenny pushed twenty pounds into my stiff palm.

'Go on take it,' she urged as I gawped at this large sum of money. 'You and Brian go and get yourselves a nice room in a hotel and make that lovely little girl for me.'

I nodded. Though I had become bolder, ultimately Jenny still controlled me. Whether it was cleaning the floor, Hoovering, arriving back from work on the dot of six or having sex with her son to please her, all orders were carried out with soulless, mechanical precision. Although the nuns had frequently criticised me for challenging their authority and not doing as I was told, more of their disciplinarian ways had rubbed off on me than they realised. It had taken a while for the subservience they craved to take effect in me but now that it had I wasn't sure I'd ever challenge anyone about anything ever again.

Brian had obviously been briefed by Jenny and he arrived smiling; I suppose he must have been her robot too. He had a car and we drove off together. Neither of us knew what to say. Jenny hadn't specified. In the silence of the car I felt terribly awkward but knowing that he was as much at Jenny's mercy as I was made me feel slightly better.

We arrived at a small hotel in the centre of Liverpool, locked the door behind us and started to undress. I felt as if both our minds had become detached from our bodies and were floating elsewhere. Only our skin, our bones and our organs were left in the hotel room. I could hear the gulls whining across the Mersey.

'Don't!' They seemed to be shrieking.

I just lay there naked, cringing at the sight of the soft flesh around my stomach and thighs, while Brian did all the work. He didn't seem to notice my physical imperfections; in fact, he didn't seem to notice me at all. I had sometimes wondered what it would feel like to have sex, although I had no desire to find out. I was scared as he eased himself inside me but only in an abstract sort of way. I briefly considered jumping off the bed, grabbing my clothes and running out of the room but somehow I didn't have the energy, and the thought of defying Jenny made me feel terribly weary. I submitted. It was rather painful yet boring at the same time. I knew I wanted Brian to get off me so that I could have my body to myself again, but the dreamlike state I was in glued me lethargically to the bed. I found the experience neither distressing nor illuminating, just odd. Afterwards we shyly got dressed, he dropped me off home and I never saw him again. We said as little in the car going home as we had on the way to the hotel.

Jenny, thankfully, asked for no details. Two weeks later my period arrived and the matter was dropped.

The blood between my legs made me feel powerful. My body had defied Jenny. It awakened me from the trancelike state I had been in with her. I decided that life would be better anywhere apart from with Jenny and Mr Anwar. I threw a few clothes and a toothbrush into a bag and ran away while they were both at work.

I imagined that they'd be as glad to see the back of me as I was of them, and felt pleased with myself for taking decisive action which would be to everyone's benefit. I'd tried to run away a couple of times before but Jenny had always come after me in the car, often alerted by the dog's barking that I was fleeing, and brought me straight back home.

'Now, now, Clare, there's no need to be a silly girl, is there?' She would say in a fake soothing tone. 'I haven't got time for all this nonsense. Just come home and try and be a good girl will you?'

I never had the power to resist her and always climbed into the back of the car, slammed the door shut and slumped against it until we got home. Then it was as if it had never happened and my life with them resumed at the precise point I had tried to snap it off at.

However, this time my escape worked. I decided to go back to the assessment centre. The sun was shining when I left and I felt I was really going to have a new start. Jenny sometimes stood at the upstairs window watching me when I left the house and I was certain that she was watching me now, sauntering off down the road with my little brown suitcase. I was tempted to turn round but managed not to. I jumped on a bus I thought would take me to the assessment centre but got off at the wrong stop and walked down several wrong streets before I found it. By this time it had started to pour with rain. I was wet and cold and no longer felt optimistic about the prospect of a life without Jenny and Mr Anwar. When a member of staff I didn't recognise opened the door they found me dishevelled with tears streaming down my face. I even felt disappointed that Jenny had not pursued me as she usually did. Obviously my departure hadn't even mattered enough to her to make her angry.

When I left Jenny and Mr Anwar the thought of using my wages at Peter Craig to rent a little flat for myself and become independent at last never occurred to me. All I knew was life in an institution and, as far as I was concerned, because my foster placement hadn't worked out my only option was to return to an institution. I knew that I was unlikely to find a new foster placement and hoped that somehow the assessment centre could wave a magic wand over my life and sort things out.

'Please, please take me back. I hate it with Jenny and Mr Anwar. I'm always in trouble there.' I could barely get the words out and felt extremely sorry for myself. The member of staff looked rather surprised but ushered me inside. The manager, whom I had got along with reasonably well the last time I was there, agreed to take me in for a few days until something more permanent could be arranged.

'You can't really stay here for too long because you've already been assessed,' he said. 'But don't take your situation with your foster parents too much to heart. Things can get a bit tricky with these arrangements.'

It felt an enormous relief to be back in an institution. I didn't need to get too close to anyone and I understood the rules better.

After a few days Jenny called and asked to speak to me.

'Are you all right, Clare? I really am sorry about the way things worked out. Mr Anwar and I have missed you. We know we've said a few things out of turn but would you forgive us and give things another try?'

My instincts screamed 'NO' but I knew that the alternatives open to me were non-existent. I wasn't capable of living on my own, and, even if my mother was prepared to take me in, I didn't want to go back to the unpredictability of life with her.

'OK,' I said in a very small voice, too choked to say more. I returned to them the next day, feeling young and stupid and utterly powerless.

At first things were better. They made me my favourite meal, steak and chips, to welcome me home and the criticisms abated. However, my loathing of Mr Anwar increased because he kept trying to kiss me whenever Jenny wasn't around. He used to lie on the floor watching TV and beckon me to him with a glint in his eye, which I failed to interpret correctly.

'I've got some loose change in my pocket, Clare,' he said wheedlingly to me whenever the coast was clear. 'If you put your hand in my pocket and can find it it's yours.'

I sensed but didn't fully understand that my pecuniary gropings were exciting for him and went ahead exploring the insides of his very deep pockets, feeling a lumpiness in his groin which made me feel nauseous. But I'd done plenty of things to survive before now and the instinct to accumulate cash to protect myself persisted.

I triumphantly fished out a handful of small change and expertly darted out of the way as he tried to lean over and snatch a kiss from me. I was expected to make him a cup of coffee every morning, and when I handed it to him he always leaned forward and tried to steal a kiss from me.

I was able to be firmer with him than I could be with Jenny; he didn't seem to have the same hold over me: 'Don't do that, you're supposed to be a dad to me, dads don't go around kissing their daughters on the lips. Please stop it.' He would temporarily back off, but was always back for more the following day.

While Mr Anwar seemed keen to have me for himself, Jenny, to my horror, was urgently seeking a boyfriend for me more permanent than her son Brian. Neither the teenage boys I knew nor any of the young men she proposed remotely appealed to me.

One morning Jenny narrowed her eyes and gave me a circling, critical look.

'Even though you're small, you're not a bad looking girl you know,' she said to me. It was typical of the grudging, half compliments she paid to me. 'It's high time we found you a boyfriend. I don't know why you haven't showed any interest in the opposite sex. I think we'll make an appointment to see the doctor just to make sure there's nothing wrong with you.'

'Oh, Jenny, don't be daft, I don't need to see a doctor, I'm only sixteen. I want to wait until I'm a bit older before I get involved with boys.'

I trembled whenever a man got too close to me, whether it was Mr Anwar or Jenny's son, or the boys we met on the beach in Blackpool on holiday with the nuns. I wanted to lock myself away from any sort of sexual contact with both men and women, although I continued to crave the motherly hugs I had been starved of.

Jenny had to pull me along the street to the doctor's surgery and we went in to see Dr Roberts.

'I think there's something wrong with her doctor. She seems cold as a fridge if a boy goes near her. Are there any pills you could give her to warm her up a bit, make a bit of excitement flow through those chilly veins of hers?'

I hung my head and started to wrap my fingers rhythmically around each other, twisting and turning to try and block out the room and Jenny and the doctor. Dr Roberts seemed to be squirming too. Only Jenny seemed perfectly at ease, on her mission to make my apparently dormant sexuality bloom. Jenny seemed terribly puzzled by my lack of interest in the opposite sex. She considered it to all be terribly straightforward, as if my sexuality was a five-pound note I had inadvertently dropped which needed to be picked up and popped back into my pocket.

'I don't think you need to worry about that right now, Jenny,' the doctor said, looking around for some diplomatic words. 'She's had a lot of upheaval in her life. Let her settle a while.'

Jenny looked disappointed, as if she'd been cheated of a part of me she considered to be rightfully hers.

I had led a very sheltered life with the nuns, leaving me naive about all matters sexual. Perhaps they thought that if they never mentioned sex they would successfully obliterate all our natural sexual instincts. At sixteen I probably had less understanding of sex than an average twelve-year-old. The nuns' extreme efforts to censor sexual knowledge appeared as a series of scorched patches across our childhoods. Apart from the absence of information about periods, bras and the like, sex wasn't even explained as a form of sin or as a cold, mechanical baby-making process.

Any child who ever asked anything remotely connected with sex would routinely be told by any or all the nuns: 'You should be washing out your mouth for speaking filth like that, hush now.'

Because of this naivety it took me a long time to work out that Jenny was having affairs with five different men and that she was using me as cover for them. She never said very much but one time, when we were off for the third time that week to 'visit Jenny's mother', she looked at me conspiratorially and said softly, 'You must never say anything about the fact that we're not really going to see my mother to Ahmed.'

I didn't know exactly what she was doing. She would park the car in various different anonymous roads around Preston, glance furtively around her and then dart off.

'Sit tight, I'll be back soon,' she said. She seemed more animated when we went on these outings than she did at home. She was usually gone for around an hour and returned beaming, with a shiny line of sweat glittering between her nostrils and her top lip.

She always carried a big red bag with a red clasp and one day at home I saw what I thought was a white tissue poking out of the bag. I went to stuff it back in and it turned out to be a brand-new pair of white knickers, next to a big pile of tissues.

When I did finally realise what she was doing she revealed that several of her lovers were pillars of the establishment – a solicitor, a bank manager and a policeman. One man worked in a chip shop and another came from nearby Fleetwood but she never said what he did. I never met or even glimpsed any of them. I suppose the liaisons were extremely discreet and to me her lovers remained a shadowy composite figure of Jenny's 'lover'. As I sat in the car waiting for her I used to wonder about the mechanics of it all. How could Jenny enjoy sex so much? After my experience with Brian I couldn't imagine ever leaping joyfully naked into a man's arms.

She showed me a vibrator she'd bought and explained how it worked.

'Ahmed thinks it's for stirring the tea with!' She laughed deep inside her throat and a snort escaped from her upturned nose.

On more than one occasion Jenny hissed as she got out of the car, 'If you tell Ahmed I'll break your legs!'

I never revealed anything to Mr Anwar, partly because I disliked him so much, and partly because it was ingrained in me from early childhood to keep secrets. Sex always seemed to me to be a very secret kind of activity and not something that should ever be discussed openly. Perhaps that view came from too many years spent with the nuns. They considered such conversations ungodly and although I'm sure they knew exactly what sex entailed, they weren't prepared to discuss it.

Mr Anwar asked me quite detailed questions about what I had done at Grandma's whenever Jenny and I returned from one of her liaisons, and I would force myself to answer. While some lying felt right to me – lying to protect myself or others from danger, or lying to save hurting someone's feelings – this lying felt wrong. Every cell in my body arched away from these untruths but, obediently, I repeated them.

'What did you have for tea there? Are you still hungry?' he asked as he made himself a sandwich.

Because I was supposed to have had a slap-up meal of egg and chips, according to Jenny's pre-lover briefing with me, I replied, 'No, thank you, Mr Anwar, I've already eaten and I couldn't eat another thing.' (I kept a stash of sweets and chocolates in my bedroom for these times because otherwise I would have gone to bed hungry.)

But Jenny wasn't the only one who sought out extra-marital thrills. I imagine that Mr Anwar had lots of scope to slide his hands over the bodies of the nervous young women he taught to drive as he tried to do with me. Jenny caught him once having sex with a pupil on the linoleum floor in the bathroom in their bungalow. She went wild, overlooking her own string of carnal adventures as she screamed obscenities at him.

In general Jenny's policy seemed to be to manipulate me into submission with a combination of kindness and cruelty. At times she would cuddle me and offer me the motherly love I craved, but she also delivered stinging barbs most days and often withheld cuddles precisely because she knew how much I loved them.

'Nobody wants you because you're black' was the phrase she repeated most; 'You know it wasn't me who wanted to take you, it was Ahmed.' And whenever we had a row she would shout: 'Why don't you just go back to the children's home?' She reminded me of the rhyme about the little girl with a curl right in the middle of her forehead. When she was good she was very, very good, and when she was bad she was horrid.

Her cruel streak extended beyond me. Two thirteen-year-old girls who lived in our road used to sit chatting on the front step of the bungalow. The invasion of her space irked Jenny and one day she spread bleach across the step so that the girls' dresses would be ruined. She laughed in the same dirty, gleeful way that she had over the vibrator as she watched the girls sit down chatting blithely.

All my life I've been prone to eczema and when Jenny spotted it on my leg one time she got a determined glint in her eye.

'We can scrub that off in no time at all.'

She got a scrubbing brush and dunked it in carbolic soap and water, and then scratched it up and down my inflamed skin. Of course it made my eczema far angrier and I've still got a scar on my leg where Jenny scraped off the top layer of skin. I remembered Marie trying to scrub my brown skin off so many years before, but her scrubbing was motivated by kindness and innocent curiosity; Jenny's was motivated by malice.

Jenny and Mr Anwar were always coming up with schemes – ways to beat the system, get rich quick, or avoid paying tax wherever possible. One of these plans was to marry me off to one of Mr Anwar's cousins who was living in Pakistan, in order to secure a UK passport for him.

'He's ever so nice,' said Jenny, wheedlingly. 'He's called Mustapha, he's very handsome and you are coming up seventeen. In Pakistan most girls of your age are settling down and getting married now.'

I shook my head. The thought of marrying any man, let alone one I'd never met, made me recoil. Jenny could see my lack of enthusiasm.

'Look, if you meet him and you don't like him, you won't have to live with him,' she coaxed.

I brightened a little. I didn't mind doing someone a favour to get them into the country as long as I wasn't expected to be joined at the hip to them. We exchanged a couple of letters describing ourselves and our interests. Jenny told me what to write for the most part but I did insist on a few personal touches, including a detailed description of all the dolls I collected – dolls in national costumes, dolls which looked like real live babies and the doll with only one set of eyelashes which I'd bought at a jumble sale because I felt sorry for her. But writing a couple of letters didn't seem to appease Jenny and Mr Anwar. They kept trying to put more and more pressure on me to meet Mustapha, who was due to visit England in a few weeks time. I was terrified that they were going to go ahead and marry me off to a strange man despite my opposition. I decided that I had to leave Jenny and Mr Anwar's and that I had to leave immediately, before I woke up one morning with a wedding ring on my finger.

CHAPTER SIXTEEN

I knew that my most obvious escape route from my stifling life with Jenny and Mr Anwar and the marriage they were plotting for me was through my social worker. I had previously had a male social worker who showed little interest in my progress, but I had recently been assigned a new one called Sally, a young woman with a fresh, honest smile and light brown freckles across her nose. She seemed interested in my future and I made an urgent appointment to see her.

I thought it better not to mention precisely why I needed to get away from Jenny and Mr Anwar. I never gave away secrets and I decided that Jenny and Mr Anwar's planned nuptials for me would fall into the category of something which should never be disclosed. Part of me felt reluctant to leave Jenny and Mr Anwar, because I knew it was unlikely that any other foster parents would take me in and I was used to putting up with less-than-perfect situations, but the thought of being forced into marriage gave me the courage to try and escape. The plans to marry me off to Mustapha were not mentioned again after the few letters we exchanged.

'I'd like to spread my wings a bit and go out into the world now I'm seventeen,' I said, trying to sound casual.

'That's fine, I can understand that you want to make your own way in the world,' said Sally, squeezing my arm supportively. 'What we need to do is find a job for you that you enjoy, perhaps something with accommodation attached so you don't need to worry about that side of things. What would you like to do most of all in the world, Clare?' she asked me.

Without hesitation I replied, 'Look after children.' It was something that after years of caring for my younger siblings I felt came naturally to me. At Park Hall I had always tried to look out for the younger children and to protect them from the sharpened knuckles and tongues of the nuns.

The thought of having a boyfriend made me shudder but I longed to have children of my own. I fantasised about having a baby all to myself, who would have everything I didn't have and nothing that I did have as a child. This seemed the logical way to break the cycle of lovelessness and cruelty which characterised my own childhood. I had always wanted to be loved and although that hadn't happened, I felt that giving love was still an option open to me.

Sally found me a job at a little private school in St Annes on Sea. It took day pupils as well as a handful of boarders and was run by a lovely woman in her early seventies called Mrs Dawson. Her daughter helped with much of the day-to-day running of the place.

I was expected to live at the school, which suited me perfectly. And no qualifications were required. I was told I'd be in charge of the pre-school children who were four years old. In the mornings I had to teach them their letters and numbers and in the afternoon we could play with jigsaws and Plasticine. I was delighted to be offered what appeared to be a perfect way out. Apart from my marriage anxieties I was getting more and more fed up with lying to Mr Anwar about my secret role as decoy for Jenny's affairs, and more and more uneasy with Mr Anwar's increasingly predatory attitude towards me. He walked around the house in his socks and trod quietly. Often he would come up behind me before I had even realised he was in the room and try to kiss me.

'Get off, get off, you're supposed to be like a father to me, not a lover,' I said, but he just grinned undeterred. He would withdraw temporarily, but he was like one of those sturdy summer flies that, no matter how many times you try and swat, never settle in one place long enough to be dispatched and keep returning to buzz around your brain in the hope of driving you insane.

My feelings towards Jenny were much more complex and something held me to her. Although she was never explicit to me about the goings on with her lovers I think being able to share her secret with someone relieved the stress of her secret life. Also, despite her sharp tongue and her sometimes cruel remarks, I did feel that there was something about me she genuinely liked.

She wrapped me in a big, generous hug when I left. ''Bye love, make sure you come back and visit us really often. St Annes is more or less round the corner from here isn't it?'

Whenever Jenny showed kindness and affection towards me I forgave her every barbed syllable she had uttered. For a few seconds I felt like changing my mind and staying with her. Then Mr Anwar lined up for his farewell cuddle and I became resolute about leaving once again. With Jenny standing there I didn't see how it could be avoided. As he too enveloped me in a bear hug I tried to lean away from him so that our bodies weren't actually touching.

'I better go or I'll miss the bus,' I said lamely, and walked off down the path with my suitcase.

At the children's boarding school I was given a tiny little attic room to sleep in, with miniature windows. There was only enough space to squeeze a bed in and my wardrobe was outside in the corridor. I felt as if I'd swallowed *Alice In Wonderland*'s potion and stepped into a secret, miniature world, one that I found delicious rather than claustrophobic.

'I'm terribly sorry that it's such a small room,' said Mrs Dawson. She had a way of tilting her head to one side and giving broad, sympathetic smiles, which I liked. Her wrinkles all pointed in the right, upwards, smiley direction.

But the size made me feel very secure – like a womb. I wondered if I had even felt secure in my mother's womb or if her anxiety about who my father was had passed through the umbilical cord, unnerving me from the moment of conception. Although I'd had my own room at Jenny and Mr Anwar's it always felt like their room rather than mine. This one definitely felt like my own.

There were twelve pre-school children in my care and all were pleasant and co-operative. I adored being with them. Although I wasn't a trained teacher and had struggled with reading and writing at school, I was praised by the other teachers there for the way I taught the children. Perhaps because I had struggled myself with the basics of literacy I could explain things to the children clearly and simply. One little boy, called Peter, had a hole in his heart. I felt terribly sorry for him and used to sit him on my knee and read him extra stories that were especially for him. Stuart, another pupil of mine, was extremely bright and whenever Mrs Dawson showed prospective parents around the school she proudly used Stuart's exercise book to demonstrate the exceptional learning ability of her pupils.

Working at the boarding school was a tranquil oasis for me. It proved to be the most peaceful and successful period of my life so far. Without exception the staff were kind, the children responsive and the parents approving. I was intermittently in contact with my brothers and sisters, but at times I was no longer sure if the events which preceded my life there had really happened to me or if they belonged inside the life of another human being entirely. It was a time of healing for me and the shrivelled core of my self-esteem strengthened slowly and sturdily.

Many of the children were day pupils, returning to their parents each afternoon, but five were boarders, mostly the children of a family who ran a travelling circus. After the school day had ended I played with the boarder children and helped the school's live-in matron to look after them until they went to bed. I only saw love and kindness towards the children at the school from their parents. They cuddled them, told them they were little princes and princesses and showered them with the latest toys. I babysat for them sometimes and saw their perfect lives at close range – comfortable homes which smelled of freshly cut roses and recently washed floors, inhabited by parents who always seemed to have time to listen to their children and to squat down on the floor playing trains or dolls with them.

I felt terribly envious of all these four-year-olds who had someone to come and take them home from school every day. I wished and wished that some golden person would turn up on the doorstep and take me home. Obviously it would not be my mother, but perhaps one day my father Jorges would turn up on the doorstep and whisk me away like Rhett Butler did to Scarlet O'Hara, without the kissing of course. As time went by and nobody appeared, I yearned more and more for the kind of family life I was seeing and realising that I had missed out on. I had glimpsed scenes from 'happy, family life' at my friend Marie's house in Morgans Road, but nothing more in my first seventeen years. Now I truly understood what it meant to be loved and nurtured by parents. I wished I could be a little girl again with a brand new set of perfect parents to care for me. I was sure that with the upbringing the children I taught had, my life would have turned out very differently

As I lay in my little room at night I asked the low, sloping ceiling, 'Why have I missed out on my chance of being a child and having someone to love me?'

Of course, I never dared utter these words in front of another human being and I'm sure I was universally viewed by staff at the boarding school as jolly, helpful and uncomplicated. On winter afternoons, when it was dark by 5 p.m., I walked down the nearby streets sometimes, looking through the windows of comfortable homes after they had switched on their lights but before they had drawn their curtains on the world. Seeing the outline of restful pictures on clean, white walls and soft sofas all bathed in yellow light made me feel homesick for the things I had never had. It reminded me of the times as a child when I would knock on the doors of people who lived in nice houses asking for a glass of water or whether they needed any jobs or errands doing. I was keen to get my pennies for sweets but I was more interested in seeing what their houses looked like so that I had a physical picture to carry in my head when I returned to my own four walls, which felt like nothing more than a bundle of bricks.

After a couple of blissful years at the boarding school, the mother of a little girl I had become particularly close to, called Sara-Jane, asked me if I would be interested in going to work for her full-time as her daughter's live-in nanny. Although I was very happy in my job I adored Sara-Jane, a pretty china-doll child who seemed to have an infinite capacity for giving and receiving love, and I was keen to take up the new job.

It was not onerous. I liked and got along well with Sara-Jane's mother, a woman called Ann Ewell. She lived in a beautiful bungalow in Preston, which had been furnished according to a luxurious, comfortable and hygienic set of homemaking standards. I looked after Sara-Jane before and after school, and tidied up the house in between. I was in a protected environment almost entirely devoid of stress and once again I was content. Sara-Jane's parents were separated and both lived with new partners.

Several months after I had settled into this undemanding daily routine, Ann said, out of the blue, that Sara-Jane was moving to Inglestadt in Germany.

'Her father and I have decided that it will be best for everyone if she moves to Germany. This will mean the end of your work here, Clare. I am sorry. You've been a great asset and absolutely indispensable to Sara-Jane.'

She could see my mouth drooping. I was very attached to Sara-Jane. Her contentment with everything around her and her trusting straightforwardness acted as a balm for all the scars from my own childhood.

'Sara-Jane is going to be looked after by her father and his partner Ursula, but we were all wondering if you'd be able to go with her to Germany just for the first six months, to help her settle down and make the transition?'

As far as I was concerned there was nothing to consider. I wanted to carry on working and I didn't want to be parted from Sara-Jane. I had met Sara-Jane's father a few times when he had visited her and Ann. He worked as a senior test flight engineer for Lufthansa and seemed to be a perfectly nice man and a loving father to Sara-Jane.

'Yes, I'll go,' I said immediately. Living in another country for a while appealed to me even though I couldn't speak a word of German. Not having to start from scratch and make a new set of decisions about my life appealed most of all.

We moved a couple of weeks later. Sara-Jane seemed apprehensive about her new life and cried bitterly when she had to part from her mother.

Ann didn't hang around at the airport.

'Don't worry, darling, you'll be coming home to visit me very soon. I love you, be a good girl for Clare and daddy and Ursula.'

Then she turned to me and hugged me too. 'Thanks for everything, Clare, you're a wonder with Sara-Jane.'

Then she quickly hurried out of the terminal building. Her eyes were wet as she left and I could see from the back that her hand kept going up to her face. I remembered my own frequent abandonments by my mother as a child but I didn't feel that Sara-Jane was in quite the same predicament as me. I had met her father's new partner Ursula, who seemed very kind, and knew that her father was absolutely devoted to her.

Ann had never told me the circumstances which led to the decision for Sara-Jane to separate from her to move to Germany and I remained puzzled as to why she didn't remain with her mother. During the wretched years with my mother I thought that the reason for all our problems was that we were so poor and that acquiring a nice house full of lavish possessions would smooth out the tangled, coarse fibres of our lives. But Sara-Jane lived in a beautiful home and her mother was kind to her and yet she was still being uprooted and removed from her mother.

I found the journey by plane thrilling. Neither Sara-Jane nor I had any sense of the risks attached to travelling by air and I gained as much childlike pleasure from bouncing through the clouds as she did.

The months in Germany passed quickly and without incident. Sara-Jane learned German at school and she came home every day and tried to teach me the language. She was a poor teacher and I was a poor student and we didn't make much progress. I got along very well with Ursula, a plain-speaking, kind woman who noiselessly began to fill the space left by Ann.

I celebrated my twenty-first birthday with them and they took me out for the day to visit a beautiful forest close to where we lived. It was only the second time in my life that my birthday had been marked in any way. The first time was when I was seventeen and living with Jenny and Mr Anwar. I had begged them to allow me to have a party and they had agreed to hire a room above a pub for me and invite friends and relatives. I had only a handful of friends to invite and after previous bad experiences with my mother and my foster parents I had decided not to invite her. I was very excited about the party and had invited a few of my friends along, but it ended in disaster when Mr Anwar accused me of spending too much of my time talking to Jenny's relatives and not enough time speaking to the guests he had invited.

'You're an ungrateful girl to ignore the people who matter to me,' he'd said. 'You're only ever interested in Jenny and people who are connected to her.'

I had had no intention of being partisan at my birthday party and fled into the toilets crying.

The stroll in the woods with Sara-Jane, her father and Ursula was a much more successful, if rather quieter celebration.

From the start of my time with Sara-Jane in Germany I knew that I was only going to be there for a short time, but when the six months was up I found it very difficult to say goodbye. Sara-Jane had just begun to settle into school properly and could now speak German quite well. She looked disorientated when I left, as if she couldn't quite trust adults to arrange her life the way she wanted it. We hugged each other hard and promised to keep in touch. I felt bereft but I knew she would be all right. She was a naturally bright and popular child and was very loved at home.

The wrench was far harder for me than for her. I was returning to a void in England. I signed on with a nanny agency, which recruited nannies to travel around the world with families. I had excellent references from Sara-Jane's parents and travelled to Jersey, Malta and Canada with different families for the next few years. Often I was employed on a short-term basis when families went on holiday. Some were kind and decent; others treated me like a servant, an inferior being who was there to do their bidding because they were giving me cash.

When I was twenty-five a Ukrainian family employed me to go and work for them in Canada. They treated me worse than any family I had worked for previously. They lived in Vancouver but I might just as well have been in Morgans Road for all the Canada I saw. They wouldn't let me out of the house and expected me to scurry around serving them all day long. As soon as I arrived I knew I'd made a terrible mistake.

By the third day I had perfected my escape-plan. I came down to breakfast red-eyed. The mother of the three children was called Anna.

'Oh, Anna, I've just had some terrible news. My older sister Mary has died suddenly, they think it was her heart. I must get back to England immediately for her funeral.'

Anna looked crestfallen at the prospect of losing her skivvy so soon but there wasn't much she could say.

Rubbing my eyes hard to keep them reddened I bid the family a hasty farewell and, as soon as I jumped into the taxi which was taking me to the airport I couldn't stop myself from crying out 'Hooray, hooray.'

After that I stayed closer to home. I tried to opt for placements with babies rather than with older children. The younger they were the closer they seemed to the state of total innocence which I aspired to return to.

I continued doing this job for the next three years. I saw little of my mother or my siblings and forgot all about Morgans Road, Sam, Peter, the nuns, Mrs Dawson and my beloved Sara-Jane. Those years were like a peaceful, dreamless sleep.

CHAPTER SEVENTEEN

I did keep in touch with Jenny and Mr Anwar, however. We hadn't communicated much while I was travelling the world but when I got back to Liverpool I called them. I felt a tie with Jenny that I couldn't explain. Although everything about her repelled me I felt myself sleepwalking back towards her. The couple had moved to a less genteel part of Preston and had opened a Spar shop, which was open all hours.

'You're thick you are, you'll never amount to much,' Mr Anwar used to say when I lived with him and Jenny. 'You'll never even be able to pass your driving test because you don't know your left from your right.'

Part of me wanted to go back to crow about the triumphs I had accumulated since I'd left them – my globetrotting jobs, my glowing references and, most of all, the fact that I'd passed my driving test. I savoured the announcement.

'Oh, by the way, I passed my test quite a while ago,' I told them on my first visit back when I was twenty-seven. My plan had been to casually drop the information into the conversation after an hour or so. Instead I blurted it out immediately after saying hello. Mr Anwar raised his eyebrows but said nothing.

I began staying with them at weekends, helping out in the shop and sometimes even taking their two dogs, Ted and Papoose, for a walk.

The balance of power in my relationship with Jenny and Mr Anwar had swung a little away from them towards me. They were no longer my foster parents and I was no longer dependent on them for a roof over my head. I had stopped nannying because I felt like a change and had got myself a well-paid job assembling electrical components at the engineering firm Plessey's. Whenever I visited I chatted to Jenny about my work in the factory, the different families I had worked for, their foibles and the things I loved about their children. Jenny had bought herself a push bike in a bid to get fit and lose some weight, and she bought one for me too so that we could ride around the park together.

After I had been visiting them at weekends for several months it emerged that Jenny had been diagnosed with breast cancer. Mr Anwar seemed unperturbed and Jenny made light of it.

'Oh, it's just a tiny lump, they think they've caught it early enough. I'm going to be fine. I've got a good few years ahead of me serving in the Spar shop yet.' She laughed hollowly, not because she thought she was going to die but because, for the first time, she was aware that her life had flashed by in what felt like a matter of moments. Although she had never discussed her life ambitions with me, I imagined that taking money for pork pies and toilet rolls was perhaps not top of her list of ambitions to be achieved.

And she was wrong about the cancer. It turned out to be invincible. Arriving secretly and silently as if clad in slippers to avoid detection, and then creeping through her breast and then further and further. The seed turned into a beanstalk that blocked out the light for her cells and gobbled up their life as efficiently as the Nazi's final solution. I felt devastated when it became clear that she was going to die. Since I had returned to her and Mr Anwar she had been much kinder to me, and it made me forget about all the times in the past that she had been cruel. As she got sicker I began to spend more time with her, taking over the jobs she had become too weak to do, like cleaning, cooking and walking the dogs.

Around this time my mother died suddenly of a heart attack at only 49. I felt numb when I heard the news. I saw my mother very infrequently and didn't feel close to her. I didn't feel that I wanted to cry about her death and I haven't felt the need since. My mother continued drinking until the moment she died, and there was a glass of unfinished whisky on the mantelpiece when she collapsed. I'm sure she would have been furious to have died before she had finished her drink. She lived alone at the end of her life. Maybe her many sexual partners were part of a hunt for love that she never found. Perhaps her childhood had been as loveless as mine and she had adopted a different approach to fill the void. The possessions she had accumulated over a lifetime only filled three black bin liners. Damian, Mary, Lucy, John, Tom and I got together to arrange her funeral. We had to sell her threadbare possessions, mainly faded clothes and cheap costume jewellery, to raise enough money to pay for her funeral. We didn't have enough left over to pay for a gravestone so we had her cremated.

I continued to feel no emotion at my mother's funeral but I did feel a void, as if someone had scooped out part of my intestines leaving the remainder of my insides exposed to cold winds. I had been working at Plessey's when my mother died but I didn't feel confident enough to carry on. I handed in my notice and went back to live with Jenny and Mr Anwar full time.

While Jenny was in hospital I spent more time working in the shop. Mr Anwar still seemed unaffected by Jenny's physical disintegration and was tireless in his efforts to coax me into his bed.

'Come and keep me company, Dolly, I'm cold all alone in that big bed.' He would run his finger down my spine in a pathetic attempt at seduction. It felt as if he had left a greasy trail behind, sticking my shirt to my skin. 'Come on dolly mixture,' he would whisper, the least erotic thing he could possibly have said to me. I kept on rebuffing him and thankfully he never pushed things any further.

Jenny came home from hospital because they had run out of treatment options. I kept her clean, took her to the toilet and fed her sips of morphine.

It was obvious that death was close and the combination of her pain and suffering and Mr Anwar's oily ways made me feel as if I was inside a coffin with the lid only open enough to allow through atom-sized crumbs of light and oxygen. I couldn't believe that I had allowed myself to be wrapped into such sticky bonds.

I hoped that Jenny's death would be speedy because she was in agony and unable to do anything for herself. Just before Jenny got seriously ill Mr Anwar had sold the shop and was working again as a driving teacher. He seemed to have barely any contact with Jenny. She, in turn, seemed unaware of his existence as the cancer gripped her tighter. She mumbled incoherently about her sons and her first husband and constantly asked for water, but it was as if all of her life with Mr Anwar had been erased. She had moved back to her previous life, maybe that was the only one that meant something to her now. As Mr Anwar retreated further and further from her so she retreated from him. She seemed unaware that he was living in the house.

I went up to her room at 10 a.m. one morning and her breathing seemed particularly laboured. It became fainter and fainter and I thought maybe she had died. Then a groan came out of the middle of her throat and everything stopped. The death Mr Anwar had been anticipating for weeks had at last occurred.

There was a moment of intense stillness as Jenny died, but within minutes it was replaced by bustling business. Mr Anwar returned home from his driving lessons two hours later.

'She's gone,' I said with tears streaming down my face. I hadn't felt like crying at the moment of her passing but speaking the news to someone else made the emotion spurt out. I didn't feel the relief I expected to feel, only a heavy, limb-numbing sadness that made me want to sleep for a very long time. Mr Anwar seemed energised, however. He bounded upstairs, held her limp, still-warm hand briefly, then he took the thick gold cross from round her neck and the gold wedding ring from her finger and slipped them into his pocket.

'She'll have a Muslim burial and I need to get it arranged,' he said. 'We bury our dead quickly. We don't like to leave them rotting above the earth for days on end the way you Christians do.'

I had never seen Jenny practise any tenets of Islam and I knew that she wouldn't have wanted a Muslim burial. When her brother, Mike, and sister, Martha, arrived the following day they tried to dissuade him from giving her a Muslim burial. I spoke out too.

'You should respect Jenny's wishes, Mr Anwar, she wasn't interested in Islam, it wasn't her religion, it's not the way she'd have wanted her time on earth to end.'

He hit me across the head before I could say any more. 'Shut up, I don't want to hear what you've got to say.'

'What do you think you're doing?' exclaimed Mike. He looked more shocked than I did.

The slap woke me up. I didn't need to stay another minute now Jenny was dead. I phoned my younger brother Tom – I'd always been closest to him – and asked him to come and pick me up as immediately as he could. As we drove off I felt an enormous relief and a sense of resolution.

'I'm glad that's all over with, Tom. I'm sick and tired of getting tangled up in situations I don't want to be in. I think it's time I did something I want to do with my life for once.'

He agreed. 'You should, Clare, you shouldn't keep on letting people push you around.'

I did return one more time for Jenny's funeral, which was a Muslim one. There were only a handful of people there. No one who could have been one of Jenny's lovers, just Jenny's sister, brother and two sons, and some Muslim men whom I presumed were friends of Mr Anwar. I expressed my condolences to Jenny's family. Her son Brian looked blank, and I wondered if he remembered our bizarre sexual encounter a decade before. Jenny's first husband was not there, although as far as I knew he was still alive. The Muslim men took charge of proceedings at the graveside. Women were not allowed to go that close so I and a couple of women I didn't know hung around at the edge of the cemetery, screwing our eyes up to try and see what was going on. Mr Anwar had the same inscrutable expression on his face as he had when he was serving a customer in the Spar shop.

Once again my life had ground to a halt and I had to find a way to earn some money. I decided to go back to looking after children, something I loved and had proved myself at. I enrolled at Joseph Archer College in Liverpool on a two-year NNEB nursing course. I had no idea that this course was going to put an end to my years of walking in the dark and would catapult me into a dazzling, unforgiving light with the force of a cannonball.

CLARE MALONE 1971–1990

I changed my surname back to Malone to obliterate the memory of my foster parents

CHAPTER EIGHTEEN

Everything about Joseph Archer college was pleasant and unthreatening. It was an old building set in carefully tended grounds with clipped lawns framed with shady weeping willow trees. In the summer students sat under the trees and bent their heads over books. I began to study there in September 1984. I was thirty years old and living in a rented flat. I'd spent most of my twenties nannying and then almost three years at Plessey's, followed by the employment gap when I was nursing Jenny. I hoped that the course would provide me with qualifications which would lead to solid and permanent employment for the future.

The students were predominantly women who were studying health-related subjects, and a spirit of co-operation prevailed in the classes. The other girls appeared to like me. No one knew anything about my past and, unlike schools in the past, reinventing myself seemed effortless. I was no longer a dirty, neglected little girl scavenging on neighbours' doorsteps for bottles of milk, no longer the angry, cheeky child constantly shielding my spirit against the nuns' efforts to beat it to a pulp, no longer the meek, unloved teenager unchosen by foster parents at the assessment centre. I was clean, well-dressed Clare; I'd tidied up the rougher edges of my Liverpudlian accent and was friendly and helpful to the other girls.

From when I was a little girl I had always looked young for my age. Most of the girls at the college were in their late teens and I decided to knock ten years off my age so that I would blend in better. It was a habit that I continued to adopt until I started to write this book, when I knew that I had to be honest about my true age. In all the years that I lied about my age no one ever questioned the younger age I gave myself, thanks partly to my unlined face and also perhaps to the childlike quality people tell me I have retained, even though I am now in my early fifties.

Because I had more experience of looking after children than most of the other students did, I felt for the first time in my life as if I had some status. In keeping with my suddenly younger age I told the other girls that I'd had a couple of years' experience working as a nanny, and they started asking me all kinds of things about childcare. They asked my opinion about the best way to settle a baby to sleep after its feed when we were taught various different options, or about the pros and cons of a strict routine or one which was more relaxed. In fact, my standing was such that I was voted head girl in our year by the other girls in my class. It was a massive thrill. No one had ever chosen me – especially above others – before, and to receive such an endorsement was an intense pleasure. Although I felt joy, however, I was anxious that I might do something foolish or unworthy and have the head girl title pulled from under me at any moment.

Although things externally had never been better, something was swirling blackly through my happiness. It wasn't anything I could describe or even understand enough to think about inside the privacy of my own head, but knots of something bad were multiplying in the pit of my stomach. Looking back, I think the demands made on me in college were too great. A healthy person could cope perfectly well with the academic and the social side of college life but, although I didn't know it, I was in a perilously fragile mental state and it was all too much for me. The more strain I was under the more I put on a brave and jolly face at college, and the worse I felt the greater the effort involved in doing that. I was living two lives – my public, uncomplicated college life and a secret, shameful life at home that was beyond my understanding.

This splintering of my self came at a time when I was able, for the first time, to live rather than just survive; I was emotionally off my guard, something alien to my usual watchful state. Something, silently buried, moved in to make what had relaxed taut. Being popular didn't diminish my self-loathing in any way.

I looked down at my brown arms and chest and hated them more than I ever had before. I always raced home from college to a small housing association flat I was renting and bolted the door behind me. Knowing I had locked the world out brought me some relief, but not enough.

I sat in the sole armchair in the flat one evening examining the smooth, brown skin on my arms. Even more hatred than usual welled up inside me and I decided that I wanted to make my skin look uglier than it was already. I walked into the bathroom and found the razor I used to shave my legs and armpits. In a dreamlike state I laid the razor softly on my left forearm and dug it in until blood spurted. I had expected it to hurt and hoped that it would because I wanted to cause myself pain, but, surprisingly, it didn't hurt at all. Feeling the blood gush out felt absolutely wonderful, almost like holding on to a full bladder and at last reaching a toilet and being able to empty it. It was an added bonus that I hadn't anticipated at all. I mopped carefully at the blood with a tissue and hoped the scar would be ugly. After that first pleasurable experience I began cutting myself almost every day.

I wrapped the razor reverently in white tissue paper like a delicate, fragile piece of china. My love and my hatred for that blade were evenly weighted like an hourglass with the sand run halfway down. I graduated from my first timid slices into my forearms to long, bold, diagonal lines across my upper arms and chest. As soon as the lines gushed red the tension drained away. I lay back on my bed feeling light-headed and mildly euphoric as I dabbed away the rivulets of blood before they could stain my sheets.

I had begun to adopt peculiar eating habits too. I stuffed myself with the sweetest, fattiest cakes, chocolates and biscuits that I could find and then, as my disgust at myself and the horrible sickly feeling in my overstretched stomach became too intense to bear, I shoved my fingers down my throat and allowed the food, still identifiable in little lumps because I'd eaten it so quickly, to surge up through my mouth. In time I became so precise and deft at the finger sticking part of the ritual that I felt better equipped than any ear, nose and throat surgeon to navigate the innermost spaces of my throat.

When I discovered that the cutting and the puking were common confessional currency on the psychiatrist's couch I was dumbfounded. Discovering much later that thousands of other wretched people were doing exactly what I was doing and feeling at least something like I was feeling made me believe I belonged in the world a little bit more. But at the time the worst part for me was my belief that I was the only person in the world behaving in this disgusting way. My actions shocked me, and the shock added to the self-loathing which triggered the whole cycle again.

Depression drove the self-harm and the bulimia but at that time I did not properly know what depression was nor what it felt like, but, undoubtedly, that was what I had. It was a low, sinking feeling that started in my brain and settled somewhere at the bottom of my stomach, leaving me with a dragging sensation that drained my energy.

None of my college friends had any idea about my secret slashing and stuffing life beyond the classroom. I was appalled about what I was doing and decided that it was extremely abnormal. I knew from early childhood that anything abnormal had to be concealed from view, and I was terrified that if any of my new friends found out they would shun me. Concealing my habits from them became a large preoccupation. I was also terrified that if anyone found out what I got up to in my flat that I would be summarily stripped of my head girl title, something I wanted to hold on to at all costs.

Somehow I managed to giggle my way through with my friend, Sue Barlow. She was a very kind, soft person and I instinctively moved towards that. I was at last learning to keep away from characters like my mother, most of the nuns and Jenny. I didn't want to be with people who were complicated and changeable. I sought out those, like Sue, who were anchored to one solid spot and smiled in the same way one day as they did the next.

We had a series of speakers who came in on Wednesdays to explain various aspects of childcare to us. They had more specialised knowledge of their chosen topics than our college teachers. One Wednesday, a few months into the second year of our two-year course, our teacher introduced a couple of guest speakers. Both wore glasses and looked sombre, as if they were on their way to or from a funeral.

I felt particularly relaxed that day. Sue and I had arranged to go into town after lectures to buy a birthday present for another girl in our class, Mary. She was well liked and everyone had put some money into a kitty for her. We planned to go to the Coffee

Cup first, a fashionable student cafe, to drink big milky chocolaty coffees, and then we were going to take our time browsing around Blacklers, examining every item carefully before making our choice. I wanted to buy a bath-and-body-lotion set and Sue wanted to get some silver earrings.

I remember the beginning of the talk clearly. The man and the woman used a flip chart to illustrate their talk. The woman stood to the side of the flip chart, which was pinned to an easel, and tossed the pages backwards whenever the man nodded to her. He did all the talking; she had wavy brown hair and honey-coloured eyes. She looked as if she adored him but he seemed unaware and fixed himself stiffly yet passionately to his subject matter. He started with an outpouring of statistics. Everyone was calmly taking notes.

I found I couldn't concentrate and began to hear a sound of rushing water inside my head, as if I'd spent years wearing earplugs and somebody had abruptly removed them. I swallowed hard to try and quieten the rushing water.

The noise inside my head had become overpowering. It felt as if it was going to split both eardrums open. I could no longer hear what the man was saying.

'Stop, stop,' I screamed. I saw an empty chair on the other side of the classroom and decided I would have to throw it at the man with cold eyes and the woman with warm eyes at the front of the classroom. There seemed to be no other way to stop them spilling out even more words.

'Shut up, shut up, shut up, why are you saying these things to the whole class?'

All the students and the guests were looking at me open-mouthed. No more clean, respectable, fun Clare. I was out of control and now it was displayed in neon. Deep down I had known that I wouldn't be able to sustain the palatable version of myself for too long but I felt bereaved all the same. Since I walked through the doors of Joseph Archer College for the first time all my energy had been directed towards creating a normal template of myself. I had succeeded so well for a while but now I had, in a few moments, thrown it all away.

I had expected to be found out if fellow students happened to meet members of my family or nuns from the children's home, but I had hoped and prayed that the edifice I had constructed would come tumbling down this way. I had utterly disgraced myself in front of everybody yet I couldn't even understand what was happening to me, or why I was behaving this way.

I could hear Mother Superior in my head saying to the potential foster parents who inspected us as we lined up, 'Oh, she's as bold as brass that girl, it's not going to end well.'

Even in my agitated state I was aware that my outburst was deeply baffling to everyone in the room, but something inside me was more powerful than my urge to conform and appear normal.

I didn't actually throw the chair I'd gripped tightly in both hands and raised above my head. Instead I banged it down on the floor and ran out of the classroom screaming. Sue followed me and led me gently into the ladies' toilets. Up until that point it's all very clear but I don't remember much of what happened next. I suppose when pain becomes too much to bear the body's natural anaesthesia kicks in.

Later, Sue told me that I was rhythmically banging my head against the mirror, but I felt no pain on my forehead. I was experiencing a breakdown in the most literal sense of the word and no part of my brain was functioning properly.

Sue took me to the medical room and the nurse kept asking over and over again, 'Can we call someone to take you home?' My head was bowed so low it hurt my neck and I kept whimpering, 'No, there's no one.'

CHAPTER NINETEEN

I was taken home in a taxi and given an emergency appointment with my GP, who talked about depression and medication and resting. None of this seemed relevant to me; I could only feel grief and continuing confusion. Nobody talked to me about why I had had a breakdown. Nobody tried to unpick the sense of loss I felt but couldn't explain.

I sat at home in my little flat in the dark. I managed to do some things like shopping for food and washing my clothes every now and again on automatic pilot. But the fog had descended. The anti-depressant pills the doctor gave me did take the edge off the emotional pain but they didn't really seem to make much difference. I couldn't imagine how a few tiny pills could dissipate all the heaviness in me and make me feel light inside. I decided to stop taking the pills. Already a plan was forming in my mind. I managed to stir myself from the armchair in my flat where I had taken to sitting through the day and most of the night. I stared listlessly out of the window but saw nothing. Sitting very still gave me some sort of comfort, moving felt threatening. I did manage to get back into college three weeks later for a meeting with the principal. I scrubbed myself in the bath, put clean clothes on and washed my hair so that it bounced, shining, around my head.

The principal was attractive, with red hair and green eyes. She was a kind woman but there was a distance so wide between her and me that it made me shiver and button up my cardigan. I was bothered by the amount of brown in the room. Brown linoleum floor, gloomy brown desk, brown tree trunk visible out of the window, brown shoes. I wanted something light and translucent to come and lift the room but the heaviness of the colour battered me around the head.

'I think you'd benefit from taking a few weeks off,' she said kindly. She pointedly avoided talking about the scene in the classroom and the events which had preceded it, and I was too ashamed to refer to it. I also felt overwhelmingly tired, as if I had to clamber up through cotton wool or quicksand to reach her. It was more restful to sit and nod and try to filter out the brown.

Only now, decades later, do I realise how damaging this prescription for enforced rest was. What I needed the moment I broke down was instant and intensive resuscitation and rehabilitation – a 999-call for the soul. Joseph Archer College was the first place where I had truly been successful and I think that allowing me to go back with some kind of support in place would have been the best possible therapy for me. They say you should get straight back on to a horse after you've taken a tumble and start riding again, and going back to a place where I was doing well and had friends, would, I'm sure, have been helpful to me. What I needed first, though, was intensive, kind support from someone who could help me to talk about why I had broken down so suddenly and dramatically, about what had triggered it and how to heal. But that didn't happen.

Love can solve many problems and I craved it more than ever. Being loved could have provided me with some sort of validation of myself, but no love was offered to me. Instead I was left to deal with the fallout from my breakdown alone.

The events of that day in the classroom were the equivalent of a sudden and simultaneous shattering of every bone in my body. Unbeknown to me these 'bones' had been brittle and flimsy and seconds away from snapping for years. But, when they finally did, instead of setting them straight, tending them with love and care so that I would once again be able to walk upright, repaired, I was abandoned. When they did finally knit together, unsupported by plaster or splint, they set at peculiar angles so that nothing aligned again.

Nobody wanted to conduct a forensic investigation into the mess inside my head – perhaps they were fearful of what they might find – so they all left the mind bones in pieces. Pills to deaden and jargon to hide behind were easier to administer than looking me in the eye and getting dazzled by my pain.

So, when the principal advised time off, I nodded blankly. I was in no position to raise my head against anyone and fight. I knew that a year of nothingness was not what I wanted or needed, but I didn't know why I knew or how to convey this knowledge. The brief flirtation with power and control over my own being that I'd tasted at the beginning of college had evaporated. The passive obedience the nuns had drummed into me had returned. All I was able to do in the principal's office was slump and take orders.

The anti-depressants I had decided to stop taking were gathering into quite a substantial pile in a dusty drawer beside my bed. I felt entirely dislocated from the college life I had fitted into so perfectly just months before. As I sat alone in my armchair, seeing only blurred shapes of people purposefully bustling to and from work, I began to think seriously about ending my life. Death seemed to beckon like a warm, comforting coat. I had heard stories of people who had nearly died of hypothermia in snowdrifts. They spoke of an overwhelming warmth urging them to lie down and allow themselves to be embraced by the snow, a gentle lover who would bring no harm or violence to their bodies. I knew how they felt. Everything was icy and I wanted to be warm. I hated having a body that I had to drag around and wash and feed every day. It caused me too much pain. Death would lighten me, relieve me of all burdens, physical and emotional, and finish something that had become exceedingly dreary.

Nobody stepped into the circumference of the circle that surrounded me to put forward arguments in defence of living. I felt that I had been abandoned to my decision and was relieved to be left in peace. I was living alone in a small, lifeless flat and barely spoke to anyone. Throughout my twenties I had seen my sisters and brothers spasmodically, drifting in and out of contact with them depending on where I and they were living at the time. But I found it quite easy to slide out of sight when it suited me, as it did now. I felt far too ashamed of what had happened to me to face them and I made no attempts to contact friends. For the most part I was left alone, managing to sound cheerful on the rare occasions that I did see people.

The pills the doctor gave me seemed to have no effect at all on my state of mind when I took them as prescribed. I wondered whether if I took sixty all at once I would experience one almighty surge of joy before I died. Once I'd made my decision I became pragmatic about the whole thing, uplifted almost, because I had found a solution. I continued saving my pills until I had a two-month high pile of them, and kept all my appointments with my GP.

'How are you feeling, Clare, are you taking your pills regularly? Good, excellent. See you in two weeks' time. I'm pleased with your progress.' She made no eye contact with me. I suppose she was afraid of having her platitudes exposed. In her I saw what I encountered in so many health professionals over the years – a reluctance to engage, a relief at hearing the quick, tidy answer rather than the long, tousled one, even though they possibly knew it was a lie. In fairness to my GP, I did my very best to put her off the scent. I concealed my inner turmoil well with my bright and coherent answers to her questions and it would have taken a psychic to diagnose how I really felt.

The last time I saw my GP before I swallowed the pills I'd stockpiled my smile exuded wellbeing, because at last I had a plan.

'You seem so much better, Clare, soon you'll be able to think about returning to college,' she said.

'Yes, I think so,' I replied, sounding surprisingly assertive because I was giggling inside at having tricked her. Having made the decision to die I felt powerful, in control for the first time since my breakdown. At last I was untouchable, pain was something I was about to part from forever.

CHAPTER TWENTY

I planned everything meticulously. The principal had suggested I see a counsellor at college and put me in touch with a woman called Sandra whom I saw every other Wednesday. She was a lovely person. It wasn't simply a cry for help but, as a novice at suicide, I didn't fancy dying alone and she was the only person I could think of to be with when I died. I suppose I was instinctively seeking out a mother figure.

I decided there was no point in postponing my solution. I had an appointment with her the following day at 12 noon and set my alarm for 9 a.m. Usually I found it hard to rise groggily at 10 a.m. but that day I felt as if my body was made of air and I glided out of bed in a heightened state of alertness. I looked at the few possessions I had accumulated – a shelf-full of cuddly toys which I had bought because I'd never had any as a child, my collection of dolls in national costumes which I had begun collecting some years before, and a few baggy clothes which concealed my skinny frame, or so I thought. I didn't feel sad about the things I would leave behind.

I scribbled a note to Sandra, which said:

Dear Sandra.
I'm very sorry for causing everyone trouble by dying. I would like to leave my body to medical science and if my organs are of any use to anyone they're welcome to them. Thanks for being kind to me.
Love from Clare.

I popped the letter into my pocket ready for posting and started gulping the pills down. I thought she would receive it the day after I died and that would be time enough for an explanation. The pills were red and black capsules, which shone when they caught the light. It took a long time to get them all swallowed and by the end I had started to think they were little ladybirds flying down my throat.

I was disappointed that I didn't feel chemically cheerful and decided I better get on the bus quickly in case I suddenly collapsed before I got to Sandra's office. I closed the front door behind me. The lock was slightly loose and usually I closed it gently to avoid damaging it further. That day I gave the door an almighty slam. The lock could drop off there and then for all I cared.

I dropped the letter to Sandra into the post box and then walked to the bus stop. A bus came along as soon as I arrived there. Everything was going like clockwork, which made me feel as if I was in a film. In real life I usually stood at the bus stop for twenty minutes waiting for a bus to appear but not today. My plan was going ahead without any hitches, just like in a film.

I looked around carefully at the other passengers. Most were gazing out of the window or chatting about their children. Living looked so mundane. I stared hard at a woman in her fifties wearing a headscarf and a pale green raincoat. She had sharp eyes, which darted around the bus, and a nose chiselled into a pointed peak. Her eyes appeared to be conducting a rapid audit of the other passengers and it didn't appear to be a particularly charitable one. I had a strange sensation of peeling back the layers of skin and bone encasing her brain and eavesdropping on her buzzing mind.

'The woman in the red coat looks as if her husband beats her, probably lives on an estate, the teenager with the dyed blonde hair is bound to have gone all the way with her boyfriend, that man in the buttoned-up raincoat with a crisp white shirt collar looks mean, bet he doesn't give his wife enough housekeeping money.' Her silent voice sounded harsh like her features, or maybe I was starting to muddle the insides and outsides of things. She gave a morally superior sniff, bustled into her shopping bag on wheels and pulled out some knitting. I watched as she self-righteously clicked the needles. In my mind they started to stick together as they touched each other, stick, click, stick, click, as if the wool was filling up with tacky blood.

I stepped off the bus right outside the college and walked unsteadily towards Sandra's office. I told her secretary I had arrived and she gestured to an armchair polka-dotted with cigarette burns for me to sit and wait in. Everything was becoming warm and deliciously numb. Now I had arrived at my destination I felt I had permission to let go. I sat down in the armchair, rested my head against the palm of my hand and oblivion came sweetly and softly. It curled around my feet first and then moved up through my body, a voracious yet gentle fire. It wiped out everything in its path, leaving me with no body, no mind, no pain, just the heavy black of nothingness.

CHAPTER TWENTY-ONE

I couldn't tell if it was a few years or a few seconds later when I opened my eyes but I did have the sensation of having travelled a long way. In the corner of the room, nestled between the ceiling and the wall, was a strong, bright light. Although it was dazzling I didn't need to squint to look it in the eye. As I gazed at it I felt peace wash through my insides, irrigating a lifetime of wounds. This was the kind of effect I'd hoped the prescribed anti-depressants would have on me, taking one a day the way the doctor had prescribed them. Maybe they were working at last. I felt myself rising towards the light. If I could just get inside it I was certain my troubles would be over.

I glanced around the room and saw myself lying, pewter grey, on a hospital table with a yellowed plastic tube hanging out of my mouth. I was surrounded by doctors and nurses and I felt momentarily flattered at being the centre of attention. I couldn't recall any other occasion where so many people were solicitously gathered around me, absorbed in what was happening to me. I heard them calling, 'Come on, come on, there's a good girl', then they and the white light faded and sleep came.

I woke up in a bed. Sandra was by my side.

'Welcome back to the world.' She smiled broadly and seemed genuinely pleased to see me.

I looked down at her feet and could see transparent objects jumping up from the floor, like creatures in a futuristic cartoon.

'What are those things coming up out of the floor?' I asked her.

She glanced down and, seeing nothing, summoned the nearest nurse.

'Nurse,' she lowered her voice and turned away from me. 'She's seeing things that aren't there on the floor. Is she going to be OK?'

The nurse wasn't having any confidential asides. 'You all right there, Clare?' she boomed. 'You took a lot of pills but we pumped your stomach and you're in hospital now. Seeing things on the floor are you? Don't worry, lovey; it's just the effects of all those pills you took working their way out of your system.'

Until the nurse spoke I wasn't entirely sure whether I was dead or alive. Now I knew for sure I was alive and I could feel a purple rage spreading through my veins. I had failed to take control of my destiny. I had failed at everything and I couldn't even manage to carry out a simple procedure like swallowing a few handfuls of pills properly.

After a few days my anger subsided. I didn't feel exactly grateful to have bungled my attempt at dying but I didn't mind being alive too much. I lay in the hospital bed deciding that I would try and get myself a job as a nanny and make a new start as soon as the doctor gave me permission to go home.

The doctor who had pumped my stomach came to see me in the afternoon. He glanced at my chart, took my pulse and told me I was doing well.

'You're a very lucky young lady,' he said in five-year-old speak. He looked uncomfortable and I assume he didn't want to get into a discussion about motives. He was wearing an over-tight pinstriped suit, which made his stomach bulge and the stripes go wavy. His hard, sugary voice and his outfit made me feel nauseous and I turned my head away.

He was a doctor for bodies rather than minds and seemed reluctant to discuss the cause of my pain. Perhaps all the others lost in despair like me received identikit, vague responses too. A touch of pneumonia that could be proved beyond reasonable doubt by taking an X-ray was so much more reassuring than the troubling uncertainties of a mind in turmoil.

What I didn't know as I lay supine on my hospital bed was that I was about to enter the psychiatric system. At this point I had no idea that huge, secretive, rabbit warren hospitals existed on the edge of towns and cities, dedicated to encasing and managing people I had always referred to as 'nutters'.

As the period of time I later spent in the psychiatric system extended – the expected weeks rolled into months and then years – I gained an insight into the shifting shades of grey inside my head and became more honest about myself. In the eyes of society I had fallen from grace so there was no longer any point in me pretending to be something I wasn't, or in playing elaborate games to hide my real self from others.

Mental illness is not really a topic for polite conversation. Some people consider it to be infectious and that getting too close to a person with a mental health problem will contaminate them in some way. Even some of the doctors seemed to think that way. For most of them their job was simply to refer people like me on to someone more specialised, and this seemed to be an enormous relief to them.

'I'll send the psychiatrist down to have a chat with you,' said the stomach pumper, and walked off with a curt, uncomfortable nod of the head. I'd been placed on a general medical ward and he looked noticeably brighter when he arrived at the bedside of his next patient, who was recovering well from a serious asthma attack.

The psychiatrist didn't share the stomach pump doctor's opinion that I was doing well. In fact he told me I was doing so badly that he was going to send me to a Victorian mental institution just outside Liverpool, called Grove House.

'It will just be for a little while, until you're more stable. We can't have you going home and taking another lot of pills now, can we?' he said unsmilingly. He too seemed reluctant to go into details about the chain of events leading up to my overdose and any possible explanations for it. Much safer to stick to recent events and treatment for those.

'Why did you take the overdose, Clare?' The question was so bloody obvious and so was the answer. I thought I'd do a much better job at being a psychiatrist than him.

'Because I wanted to die,' I said flatly. He scribbled in his notes with a satisfied look on his face. I'd given the right answer for a period of incarceration. I decided to try and backtrack.

'I won't do anything like this again. I'm fine now; it's brought me to my senses. I'm going to get a job and paint my flat and start eating better.' And indeed that was my plan. 'I don't want to go to Grove House, that's where they put all the nutters –' My words were running away and he didn't seem to hear them.

He tried to mirror the sad look on my face but ended up I felt looking smug.

'No, I'm afraid Grove House it is,' he said, signing my notes with a flourish.

I felt too weak to run out of the hospital so I lay in bed crying with the covers pulled tightly over my head. I'd taken the pills to try and get some control over my life and now I had less control than I'd ever had before.

CHAPTER TWENTY-TWO

The following morning a nurse helped me get dressed and walked me to a waiting ambulance. Her face was expressionless and she said nothing to me apart from, 'Chilly this morning isn't it?' Like the others, she seemed to feel that my removal from general to psychiatric hospital was a perfectly normal course of events, the logical consequence of taking an overdose.

Grove House Psychiatric Hospital was enormous. It was built in sewage-coloured brick and had lots of square windows with bars across them. The windows looked like half shut eyes providing surveillance for the doctors and nurses I imagined were bustling around outside. As the ambulance pulled into the long, sweeping drive I considered trying to make a run for it. The place looked so vast I thought I would be gobbled up inside it and never seen again. My eyes kept flitting from the building to the end of the driveway as I assessed my chances of escape. In the end I decided that in my weakened state I'd never make it and I sat stiffly in my seat waiting to be led inside this terrifying building. It was January 1985 and I was thirty years old. I knew that that was the age life was supposed to begin at; it was too much to bear that my life seemed to be closing in on me more than it ever had before because I had survived a suicide attempt.

A starched nurse appeared at the back door of the ambulance. She nodded to the driver and took hold of my upper arm too firmly, as if anticipating my getaway plan. She walked me down the longest polished corridor I had ever seen. I remembered the floors we had to polish to an obsessive compulsive shine at Park Hall and wondered if the patients here were expected to do the same. There was no sign of any enforced industry though as there had been there. Patients were sitting on the floor, rocking, moaning and asking over and over again: 'Have you got a ciggie?' I was shown to a bed, given a locker and told that the TV was on in the day room.

Twice a day I was handed pills. I had been diagnosed (wrongly it turned out) with bipolar disorder and was given Lithium.

'Swallow yer pills now,' chanted the nurses over and over to all of us. I didn't know what they were, or what they were supposed to do for me and, as at Park Hall, no explanation was ever given.

A record of the pills I was given was noted down in a black book. They had various different coloured books and I was annoyed that they hadn't chosen the book in my favourite shade of green to write about me in. The lithium made it difficult for me to move my legs and I began hoarding the pills in my drawer rather than taking them, not because I planned to use them to overdose but because they made me feel so unwell.

'What are these actually for?' I asked each time a different nurse handed the pills out, hoping that one might give out more information than another. But the response was always the same.

'Swallow them down quick, they'll make you feel better.'

One day a nurse watched me close my fist over the pill. 'Let me have a look in your hand, Clare,' she said sternly. I uncurled my fingers and then opened my bedside drawer and showed her another twenty pills there.

'Nurse, my legs go numb a few minutes after I take these,' I said, searching her face for a crumb of sympathy.

I found none. However, she did say, 'Righty oh, I'll tell doctor.' She swept the pills out of the drawer and the plastic cup out of my hand. The next day the pills were changed to something else – they never said what – and this time when I took them my legs felt perfectly normal. My mood felt exactly the same though. I still felt very low and unconvinced of the point of being alive. I couldn't understand what the purpose of placing me in a psychiatric hospital was because apart from handing pills out to me, which worked no better than the ones the GP had given me, I wasn't receiving any treatment. Indeed, my depression became more intense because now I had being locked up to deal with as well as everything else. I had seen a doctor on the day I arrived and he confirmed what the psychiatrist who referred me had said.

'You're suffering from depression, young lady, but it's nothing that a period of rest and medication won't sort out.'

Days passed but nobody paid any attention to me. If my treatment was supposed to consist of resting entirely by myself, why wouldn't they send me home? I asked a nurse about this and she tutted.

'You're in the best possible place to get treatment, now be a good girl and be quiet.'

I felt that I had dropped off the edge of the earth. I was certain that rather than healing people's tangled minds, the rundown, gloomy interiors of Grove House and all the locked doors made everyone forced to reside there feel much worse than they did before they arrived. Plaster peeled off walls, and everything was painted in a variety of sludge-coloured pastels. Although the place wasn't actually dirty, the lack of maintenance made it feel perpetually grubby and grimmer than it needed to be.

There were plenty of people in hospital because they had schizophrenia. I'd never heard of the condition before and felt scared of those who suffered from it. I knew they heard voices and wondered what the voices were saying to them. Bad things, I imagined, planting whispers of nonsense to dement them. I supposed their minds were conspiring against them, which was what I sometimes felt about my own mind although no malevolent voice had taken up residence inside my head.

One woman used to walk around with a pillow bunched under her shirt.

'My baby is due soon,' she told us all excitedly. Looking at her waddling up and down with her pretend pregnancy made me feel very sad. Perhaps she had lost a baby and it had sent her mad with grief.

Another woman sat next to the phone and chattered endlessly into the silent receiver.

'Hurry up, Liz, I need to make a phone call,' I said to her.

'I won't be a minute,' she replied irritably, as if I was interrupting a high-powered business meeting. I decided that however miserable I felt my problems were not as severe as those around me. I felt as if I was standing in the middle of a pub surrounded by people who were incoherently drunk while I remained stone cold sober.

The more aggressive schizophrenics made me particularly anxious. I slept on a large ward with other female patients, and although nurses patrolled I was terrified that I might be attacked while I slept. It took me a long time to get to sleep each night and I employed a technique I'd practised as a child when I couldn't sleep – lying on my stomach and placing my arms in a square on the pillow which I rested my head on, rhythmically rocking my head against my arms. I got into the habit of getting up at 4 a.m. in a bid to protect myself from any night-time marauders and spent my days exhausted.

The only person who showed any kindness to me at Grove House was a man called Billy. He was sixty-three and had spent most of his adult life in the psychiatric system. He was vague about the way they reeled him in but Borstal and stealing sweets seemed to feature. I had heard other patients say he was schizophrenic but I never saw much evidence of it. He told me about some of the other older patients who had been locked up for getting pregnant outside wedlock or because they argued with their parents in the era when that was still the case.

Billy was tall and skinny with smiley lines. His grey hair had gone thin and as soft as a baby's and his trousers were always much too big for him. He frequently forgot to hitch them up and instead walked with a compensatory waddle to prevent them dropping to his ankles.

I sat in a chair most of the time, trying to construct an invisible screen around me to keep the other patients away. I couldn't see any meeting point between their conditions and mine and I thought if I got too friendly with them I'd become contaminated by their madness. As children we knew about places like this. We used to sing songs about the nutcases in the nuthouse and made jokes about lunatics. I thought all the people I labelled lunatics carried knives and randomly rampaged through the centre of Liverpool though.

Billy was different. He was not mad and he was funny. He knew instantly that I was feeling miserable and tried everything to make me laugh. He had an encyclopaedia of jokes in his head and even though I started off turning my head away when he approached, I ended up smiling.

'There was a man who used to go into a pub every day and ask for a meat and potato pie, right?'

I nodded slightly.

'As soon as he paid for it he would rub it into his forehead, right?'

I nodded again.

'This went on for ages and then one day when he came into the pub asking for his usual meat and potato pie the man behind the bar told him they didn't have any that day, right?'

I was getting vaguely interested.

'So the man asked for a packet of crisps instead and rubbed these into his forehead just the same way he had rubbed all the pies in. One of the customers was watching him and asked: "Why are you rubbing those crisps into your forehead?" "Because they haven't got any meat and potato pies" he says.'

He searched my face for a smile and I did manage a weak one. The jokes came thick and fast after that; some were funny and some weren't. But because Billy was obviously sincere I found just hearing the words tumble out was a welcome antidote to the authoritarian doctors and nurses and the troubled patients.

We became friends and before long our bond of solidarity turned to subversive activities. One of the petty rules in Grove House was that cups of tea were only permitted at mealtimes. Billy and I couldn't understand why we couldn't have a cup of tea whenever we wanted one.

Food was served through a hatch and after meals shutters were clanged down to seal us out of the kitchen. But sometimes the kitchen staff didn't pull the shutters all the way down.

''Ere,' said Billy one day. 'Fancy a cuppa?'

'Don't be daft,' I said. 'You know we're not allowed.'

'It's called beating the system,' he said, barely able to contain his excitement. 'Look, they've left the shutters open a bit. I'll keep watch at the door and you climb under the hatch and bring out two nice steaming cups of tea for us.'

'What if we get caught?' I giggled. The idea appealed just as much to me as it did to him and the days of sneaking into the kitchen to gorge at breakneck speed on the nuns' leftover roast potatoes and gravy flooded back.

I slid under the hatch and had a quick look around. The stainless steel surfaces were shining and a smell of burnt toast hung in the air. I found some tea bags in a cupboard and squeezed the tap on the hot water urn to fill the cups. I began to panic about getting caught and decided it would take up too much time to look for milk. I passed the cups of treacly tea under the hatch and then slid out after them. Billy and I huddled in a corner where we couldn't be spotted if someone popped their head round the door and began to drink.

Billy smacked his lips together. 'You don't half make a magnificent cuppa, Clare.'

The tea tasted like nectar and both of us savoured every drop.

One night around midnight, Billy sneaked into my ward and tried to climb into bed with me. The nurse on duty was nowhere to be seen and must have been on her break. Billy was wearing a white vest and very long white Y-fronts. I felt physically sick at the thought of him getting so close to me. His breath was stale and he was breathing very fast. I didn't know why the thought of getting close to a man made me panic so much, particularly when I craved human affection. But I could taste the fear rising through my throat and knew I had to get rid of Billy at all costs.

'Budge up, Clare, I want to get into bed with you,' he whispered.

I considered screaming but thought that if I woke everyone else up I would be branded a troublemaker, so I decided to try another strategy and went into nanny mode.

'Don't be so daft. You'll get caught and then we'll both be in big trouble. Get back to your room this minute.'

My authoritarian tone seemed to work and he backed off sheepishly. I felt weak with relief when he backed off but I spent the next hour trembling and didn't sleep at all that night.

Some of the patients were given ECT. I didn't know what it was until one of them gave me a graphic explanation, but I knew that it made them frightened and disorientated.

'They take you away and force you to lie on a table. Then they tie your hands and legs down and put a horrible tasting cloth in your mouth.' Peter, the man who was enlightening me, was in his forties. He had sharp looking stubble on his face and leaned too close to me, so that I could smell the old tobacco and the fish he'd eaten for lunch on his breath. He was enjoying watching the scared look on my face and paused to build suspense.

'They wire you up to some electricity machine and then they pass God knows how many volts through your brain. They fry it like your breakfast eggs so it gets all dead and crispy and quiet.' I started biting my nails and he walked off pleased as Punch.

That afternoon, a frail young woman came back from her session weeping. 'I can't remember anything, I just can't remember,' she whispered over and over again, gripped by a terror that her mind had been amputated and was now in endless freefall from her body. Many patients tried to escape and some succeeded in hanging themselves.

I decided that if that was what they did to people here I had to escape.

The hospital was set in huge grounds. I was admitted in January and a few weeks later snow began to fall. It kept falling, deadening sound and bleaching the world outside Grove House to a pure, blinding nothingness. Every time I looked out of the window I had a sensation of being buried alive and decided that if I was going to survive I would have to run away sooner rather than later. Most of the doors were locked but I had discovered a small door at the back of the hospital that opened silently when I tried the handle. I had never noticed it before and decided that the fact that it was unlocked was a signal for me to run immediately.

I was wearing my slippers and a lightweight shirt and trousers, but I thought that bolting right away might be my only chance. I didn't even go back to my ward to get my coat out of my locker in case it aroused the nurses' suspicions. I slipped out and started to run. Opening the door felt like walking into the magical world of *The Lion, The Witch and The Wardrobe*, a book I had read and been entranced by while I was teaching at the school in St Annes on Sea. The snow was like wet putty under my feet. At first I didn't care because it felt so wonderful to be free and to feel the sharp, cold air on my face. But after about a minute it became harder and harder to put one foot in front of the other. My feet felt unbearably cold in my sodden slippers, and the snow I disturbed as I ran splashed the rest of my clothes wet. I had just reached a hedge and was working out whether I should try to vault over it or crawl under it when I heard footsteps crunching behind me.

A panting nurse came up to me and placed a rough hand on my shoulder. 'Back you come,' she said unsympathetically.

'How did you know I was here?' I asked, amazed that my plan had been ruined so soon.

She smiled knowingly. 'All I had to do was follow the footprints you left in the snow,' she said. 'You wouldn't make a very good burglar.'

She marched me back inside. The white expanse seemed even further on the way back. Hot tears slid down my face, making little dimples in the snow as they fell.

I assumed that my act of rebellion, of trying to escape, would be punished with an even longer sentence at Grove House, although, in fact, no sanctions were applied against me. However, I did become angrier than ever at my incarceration. Breakfast, lunch and dinner were always served at exactly the same moment in the day. Beyond the medication, I received little treatment and the days dragged. The only diversions on offer were a pile of dog-eared jigsaw puzzles, which looked as old as the hospital. My counsellor, Sandra, came to visit me a couple of times and she brought my friend Sue Barlow along with her.

Sue was gentle and didn't judge me. 'Breakdowns are commoner than you'd think.' She smiled. 'It happened to one of my uncles.' But she did say she couldn't quite believe that I was sitting in a gloomy place like Grove House.

'I'm flabbergasted, Clare. You're the last person I would have expected to end up here. You were the life and soul at college. We all thought you didn't have a care in the world!'

She put her arm around me and gave me a supportive cuddle. I was happy to see her and relieved that she still wanted to know me, but at the same time I felt terribly ashamed that now she knew all about the side of myself that I had tried so desperately hard to hide.

I loathed the doctor who was in charge of my care. He always seemed to be cross about something. What have you got to be cross about? I thought. You're free and you've got power. I didn't voice these thoughts though, and was sulkily silent whenever I saw him.

The snow seemed invincible. It stayed for weeks and a few days after my abortive escape I went into the grounds and, slicing my finger through the thick layer of snow which had just fallen on the doctor's car, graffitied a space in the snow which read: 'Mr Grumpy'.

Perhaps he never discovered it was me, or perhaps a new snowfall rubbed it out, but he didn't respond to this act of defiance. I wasn't expecting a reaction, the act alone had been therapeutic.

To my amazement, a couple of weeks later he told me that I could return to my flat. I had been at Grove House for two months and was thrilled at the prospect of liberation, although apprehensive about re-entering the world.

'Just keep on taking the tablets and you'll soon be absolutely fine,' he said.

No attempt was made in all the time I was at Grove House to unravel the clues leading to my breakdown and consequent suicide attempt, and no counselling was ever offered. For a profession that is supposedly based on science and logic it seemed strange to focus on the end result without looking at the journey which led to it, like never bothering to unwrap a present because there was too much Sellotape on the paper.

It seemed to me that all the doctors saw was the iceberg tip which is visible to the naked eye. Judging that tip too harshly or too definitively does an enormous disservice to so many human beings whose beginnings and middles explain how they arrived at their ends. I didn't understand myself what had led to my emotional crumbling as an adult but to have had someone attempt to join up the dots for me would have helped enormously. No one did, and I was discharged with a bottle of pills, a referral letter to my GP and an uninterested goodbye.

CHAPTER TWENTY-THREE

I was told by the Joseph Archer College that I would have to take the rest of the academic year off and begin the second year of my course again in September. The fog continued during my 'recovery'. I spent the time doing nothing at all. I lay back and let nothingness wash over me, again and again. I couldn't read, I couldn't watch TV and I shunned all social contact. Some basic survival mechanism kept me going and, as agreed, I turned up on time for college at the beginning of September. It didn't feel like a new start because I was still broken. I was simply obeying orders. I talked to no one about the breakdown because no one asked me. They didn't want to go there. It was as if that day in the classroom liquid leprosy had spewed out of my mouth. Rather than be infected, everyone kept away.

The friends that I had started the course with had by now completed it while I was still only halfway through. I felt like the class dunce. My friends were kind but distant. Like most people they felt uncomfortable around long-term, low grade emotional pain when their own lives seemed steady and bright. 'Good to see you, Clare, you take care of yourself now', or 'Let's go for a coffee some time', while wriggling out of ever setting a date, was the level they could cope with.

The proudest moment in my life had been when I was voted head girl the first time I went to college. I knew that the other girls had chosen me not out of pity but because I was lively and bubbly and cracked jokes all the time. I obviously wasn't being sensible but I fervently hoped that when I returned to college I would still be head girl. That role was rightfully mine, I believed.

It was a blow when I got back and said to one of the teachers, 'Oh, I was here last year and I'm head girl.'

She twisted her mouth around slightly, trying to make it come out with the best words. There were no good words to explain that, thanks to my stupidity in having a breakdown and my subsequent agreement to stay away for a year, my precious status had been snatched away.

'Clare, I'm afraid we had to give the job to Debbie because you've been away for so long.'

'But that's not fair,' I said. My voice had dropped about two octaves. 'The other girls picked me!'

'I'm sorry, Clare, truly, that's the way it is.'

The shame of being deselected compounded the shame about my breakdown and I tried my best, and succeeded, to sleepwalk through the year.

The girls who had been in my class the previous year had moved forwards while I had moved backwards. To include me they would have had to lean over and yank me up to their level. The physical manifestation of the breakdown had scared and troubled them and they didn't want me in their midst that much. So I crept through the year trying not to touch anything around me in case it hurt me, and they sped past me waving warily. They were moving away from a station on a high-speed train as I stood on the platform becoming blurrier and blurrier. It was a horribly lonely year.

Somehow I got through the course and received my certificate, something that gave me no pleasure. I couldn't see the point in applying for nannying jobs. Most of the other girls on the course had never had a nannying job before and were using the qualification they gained as a passport to their first job. I had proved to myself that I could get this kind of job; it seemed like a step backwards to repeat what I had done before. And I felt I didn't have the energy and patience and peaceful emptiness in my head that I had had before, which had made me so good at devoting every part of myself to the children in my care.

Ever since my mother first broke the news to me at Park Hall that my father was not Sam Malone but a 'proper gentleman' called Jorges Sherriema I had thought of him often. Beyond curiosity about who he was and what kind of personality he had, I had built him up into some kind of saviour figure. The worse my life became the more I pinned my hopes on him parachuting in all the way from Chile, scooping me up in his arms and taking away all my pain. I fervently believed that if I was just able to gaze into his face and see my own reflected back to me it would give me comfort. I decided to adopt his surname, even though I wasn't sure how to spell it, in the hope that some more substantial bond might take root and grow above the earth. It was very dislocating not to know half of the two people who made me.

As an inky bleakness wrapped itself more and more tightly around me, I became increasingly preoccupied with my unknown father. I had no idea how I could track him down, and in some ways it was easier to keep hold of him as some sort of abstract mascot than to risk the disappointment of meeting him in the flesh.

CLARE SHERRIEMA 1990–2000

I adopted the surname of my Chilean biological father, Jorges Sherriema. Later I discovered the correct spelling was more likely to be Chenefa

CHAPTER TWENTY-FOUR

I changed my surname to my father's. It soothed me for a while but without a living, breathing person to inhabit the name, the balm of calling myself Clare Sherriema soon evaporated.

I returned to my one bedroom housing association flat in Stanley Street, Liverpool, where I had lived while I was doing the NNEB course, but it was only a matter of time before I tried to kill myself again. My secret perverting-food-and-slicing-body routine was gathering momentum. The momentary relief when the blood was released from my veins was followed by days of pain while the skin scars healed. My throat hurt from the constant effort of retching and the fumes of stale vomit hung perpetually around my mouth.

The build up to ending things felt different this time. Last time suicide had presented itself to me as a pure solution. Now my self-loathing had reached a different level. I decided that I had been very foolish to go and see my counsellor Sandra immediately after taking my first overdose. I vowed that I wouldn't mess up my second attempt but would drift off quietly into the peaceful sleep of death.

I had started to smoke cannabis, which seemed to calm me down. I rolled a spliff and inhaled deeply, alternating the drug with gulps of cheap white wine and the anti-depressants I had squirreled away in my bedside drawer. I felt almost casual about taking my life. The bundle of blood and bones and organs I was wearily dragging around meant little to me and ridding myself of it would be a tremendous relief. I was certain that my footprint on the earth was so slight that no one would notice the indent I'd made after I took my last breath.

Blood was drying from where I had cut myself and was making my nightdress stick painfully to my skin. Before I embarked on what I was sure would be my final overdose attempt I had written another 'Sorry for causing everyone so much trouble' note, which I put into my drawer.

As wooziness began to take over the phone rang. I had planned to take it off the hook but had forgotten. I should have just let it ring but force of habit made me pick it up. It was my community psychiatric nurse.

'Hello, just a quick call to see how you're doing,' she said airily.

My speech was becoming slurred. 'Oh, you're a bit late, I've done it now –'

She understood. 'Open the door of your flat, I'll be round in two minutes,' she ordered.

I felt like an old hand as charcoal, stomach pumping and admission to another psychiatric hospital, St Luke's, followed. I hadn't even lost consciousness this time and certainly saw no white light beckoning. Instead I felt every unpleasant thrust of the tube down my throat into my stomach and groaned with the pain of the tube and the pain of still being alive.

St Luke's looked very different from Grove House. It was a brand new building with only four wards. There was less than a hundred patients altogether in St Luke's while Grove House had housed several hundred. However, the treatment seemed no better and this time I was determined to fight. I took an instant dislike to the psychiatrist who came to see me on the day I was admitted there. He didn't look me in the eye, which I felt was an extremely bad omen. He seemed to bask in the power he had over his patients. Every time he leaned to one side a roll of neck flesh lolled against his collar.

He nodded to the nurse at his side.

'Put her down as a Section 2,' he said, without asking me a single question about how I was feeling.

'What's that?' I said indignantly.

'It means we can detain you for twenty-eight days.' He smiled a tight smile. He looked at me as if I repulsed him.

'Twenty-eight days! No way am I staying here that long.' I tried to make eye contact with him, but he was scribbling away.

'Right, put her down as a Section 3 instead,' he said.

'That's six months,' said the nurse when I looked baffled.

They gathered together a room full of people to agree on a label for me. I had no idea what their jobs were but when I asked one of the nurses later she said that most of them were doctors at different stages of their training.

I was asked to join the circle of doctors and nurses so that I could be assessed. Being stared at by so many pairs of unsympathetic eyes made me feel sick. One of the psychiatrists, Dr Chris Barlow, understood how intimidated the whole thing made me feel

'Would you like to chat with me in private, Clare, instead of having to perform in front of all those doctors?' she asked at the end of one of the sessions.

I nodded gratefully at her rescue plan and after that I saw very little of the other doctors. She and I sat quietly in her office and talked.

She had a tray with an old-fashioned blue-and-white china teapot on it with a matching milk jug and two cups. Our meetings always followed the same course.

'Would you like some tea, Clare? Sugar? Ah, no, of course not, the nuns –' I'd told her about being force fed sugarless tea by Sister Maria.

'Are you feeling better today?'

The way she phrased the question made it much harder for me to answer honestly than if she'd asked, 'Are you feeling terrible today?' Maybe she was trying to make me feel more positive about myself. Perhaps she was willing me to say the right things to speed my discharge.

As at Grove House, the days passed slowly. There were a few staple activities for people with mental health problems like basket making and painting, which didn't interest me. The boredom of the days made me short tempered. Charlie, one of the patients, infuriated me by putting milk inside the teapot with the water and tea. It reminded me of mealtimes with the nuns.

'Don't do that, Charlie, people like to drink their tea all different ways, not just the way you think they should drink it.'

He started shouting. 'Don't you dare speak to me in that tone. Who do you think you are?' He narrowed his eyes at me.

I shouted back and he shouted more and the words got uglier. The staff turned away and allowed us to get on with it.

The next day I stood guard over the tea pot while the tea was being brewed and held my hand over the open top, even though the steam burned me, to prevent Charlie glugging half a bottle of milk in there. He slammed the bottle down, sloshing puddles of it on to the table, and grumbled out of the kitchen. I had won.

Not all the patients were like Charlie though. I met Sam only once. He didn't look more than seventeen and he was sat on the floor watching TV. He had a bag of sherbet lemons in his hand. He smiled a sweet, gentle smile and offered one to me.

Later that day I heard a piercing scream. It sounded very different from the aimless screams I sometimes heard from other patients. This was an extremely purposeful scream. Nurses came running from all directions and we were all cordoned off into the TV room. We found out a few hours later what had happened when Pauline, a particularly chatty tea lady, wheeled the trolley in and whispered a response to our clamour of questions: 'It's that lovely lad Sam. He hanged himself above his bed with his shoelaces. His mother came to visit, pulled back the curtains which he'd drawn around his bed, and found him. It's a disgrace the way this place is run if you ask me.'

None of the staff had noticed he was missing, and if his mother hadn't come in he might have stayed there for another hour or two.

Suicides did happen from time to time and some patients tried to copy the tactics of those who had succeeded in taking their own lives. They rarely managed it though because the staff were always extra vigilant for a period after these incidents.

The rest of us were sad at the death of this sensitive boy but in a peculiar way it made me feel glad to be alive. I felt slightly envious that Sam had succeeded where I'd twice failed, but also rather relieved that I was still around to discuss these events with Pauline. I looked down at my hands and appreciated the blood running through my veins, keeping everything warm and soft and living.

I didn't have the same opportunities to binge and vomit at St Luke's as I had at home and so I'd barely eaten since I'd arrived. But for the first time in weeks I helped myself to a biscuit when Pauline wheeled the creaking tea trolley into the day room.

St Luke's, on the whole, was similar to Grove House. Suicides, both failed and successful, were familiar parts of the cratered landscape. A sense of caring or compassion among the staff was often absent. We were all numbers who needed to be quietened and contained.

'You'll always be a revolving door, Clare,' said one of the stoniest nurses, who knew my history.

I didn't understand what the term meant.

'It means that you'll never get well. You'll be discharged from here soon but you'll be back, like the rest of them.'

My mouth dropped open like a fish that's been flung on to dry land but is still trying to take a few breaths.

'That's not going to happen to me,' I said defiantly. 'You watch, you won't be seeing me in here again. As soon as I get out of this place I'm going to leave the psychiatric system behind and get on with my life.'

Her harsh words made me determined to throw off the system in the same way as a professional strong man I had once seen on TV, who had a car placed over his prostrate body and had then used the strength of his body to push the vehicle off him. But the psychiatric system was heavier than any car and I wasn't a professional strong man.

While I was in St Luke's I witnessed horrible violence against those who rebelled against the regime. Would-be runaways, often skinny after spending too long in an institution, were dragged back into the inner bowels of the hospital by hefty nurses. Those who continued to kick against the system were pinned down by two or three staff, who always seemed to appear from nowhere when the buzzer sounded, and injected into passive compliance. A rumour spread that one person died as a result of some mismatch between his blood pressure level and the dose of chemical stun gun administered but we never managed to substantiate it.

The only comfort the patients found behind the heavy walls of the hospital was in each other. When one was feeling low a couple of others would try everything to elicit a smile, from bad jokes to pulled faces and clown dances.

Apart from the meetings with Chris Barlow my days were filled with nothingness and time stretched like an endlessly spreading blob of oil on a lake. But the time did end. I was given new medication, and although it wasn't explained to me what it was, it made me feel better. The black weight that had been pressing down on my skull dispersed. Instead of a crushing sensation the oxygen around my soul now felt white and light and carefree. Once again I was dispatched back into the world.

CHAPTER TWENTY-FIVE

Of course I retreated into myself. I was assigned a community psychiatric nurse called Julie, who came to visit me in my flat every once in a while. The other rooms in the house were occupied by people with mental health problems and I watched some of them with consternation. Peter and Pat were a couple who had been discharged from a psychiatric institution after spending many years there. Pat had been placed there because she had been diagnosed a 'rebel child'. Peter's route into various institutions was unclear but at some point after admission he was diagnosed with schizophrenia.

I watched Pat trying to dry wet sheets in the garden. She didn't understand that lying them down on ground which was often wet and dirty wouldn't get them dry. There was a washing line in the garden but she appeared to have no clue about what it was for.

Sometimes I would find her and Peter sitting blankly on the stairs smoking intensely in the middle of the night. They weren't distressed, but they seemed very distant from the world.

'Are you all right there you two?' I asked them in my chirpy, speaking-to-children tone.

They both nodded and carried on smoking. They were much more disconnected from life than I was and it frightened me that if I stayed in this environment I would before long slump to a point where I would be sitting on the stairs with them, staring at nothing.

Julie, the community psychiatric nurse who visited me, also visited them. She seemed to have an extremely heavy caseload and was always dashing off to deal with some crisis or other.

Peter and Pat received regular his'n'hers shots of anti-psychotic drugs when she visited. Then she patted them distractedly on the forearm, without meeting their questioning gaze, and dashed off to see her next patient. When she visited me she was always hurrying too. 'All right then, Clare, you're looking better this week, sleeping better I expect. Well I can't stay long, I've got two more patients to see then everybody's notes to write up.' I wondered if she was running from anything.

'Look, Julie, I know you're in a hurry but I'm concerned about Peter and Pat. I just don't think they're coping well with their independence,' I once ventured.

She looked distracted, but she got out her notebook and scribbled something down.

'OK, I'll mention it to my boss and see if they need moving to somewhere with more support.'

Within a week they'd gone – I don't know where to – and I felt quite lonely looking out of my window and not seeing Pat vacantly spreading sheets on the dewy ground.

Although Peter and Pat inhabited a separate world which never penetrated mine, I missed them. The rituals of bulimia and self-harming were hard-wired into my brain and when I felt low and alone it was left to them to console me. I had neither self-harmed nor binged and vomited while I was in St Luke's because I knew that it would prolong my time there, but the urge lay dormant like a virus waiting to be triggered. Solitude was my trigger.

Practice makes perfect and puking is no exception. My ritual was more or less the same as before I'd been admitted to St Luke's. I ate apples and the occasional slice of bread during the week. It was too greedy to eat the apples all in one go, so I cut them into quarters and rationed them throughout the day. I cycled for miles and miles in an effort to lose more weight, each rotation of the pedals was a message of hate to my body. Only when I got so weak and dizzy that I thought I was going to fall off the bike did I eat some stale bread. It had to be stale so that it tasted untemptingly horrible.

I starved myself for a week and then, when my sense of anticipation reached a crescendo, I jumped on a bus to the supermarket and filled my basket with calories. Unlike the bread and apple rations, everything had to be as delicious as possible. Then I rushed home, locked the door behind me, turned on the TV and lifted the phone off the hook. Everything was ready. My saliva went into wild overdrive and dribbled out of my mouth. I ripped off wrappers and began. I swallowed rather than chewed chocolate and cakes and biscuits and bread with so much jam on it that it buckled under the weight when I lifted it to my mouth.

As I gorged I remembered all the biblical stories of famine followed by feast the nuns had ram-raided into our brains. My childhood loathing of ice cream, salad cream and anything else of that colour and consistency remained so I avoided most yoghurts. But dark-coloured yoghurts, like blackcurrant, were acceptable and part of my ritual was to finish each feast with one. Once the last spoonful of yoghurt had slid down my throat I ran to the bathroom and guided my fingers down my throat. The food came back up in such big lumps it hurt my throat as much on its return journey as it had on the way down. Afterwards came serenity: I felt weak and exhausted and sore. I climbed into bed and slept dreamlessly.

My eating habits began to evolve. I was waiting longer and longer to binge between bouts of starvation and I enjoyed the power starving myself gave me. Stuffing myself and then making myself sick came to feel increasingly like weakness. Starving myself felt much purer. Without realising it I stopped binging altogether and the apple and stale bread rations were all that slipped down my throat. I had heard about anorexia, which people described as 'the slimmers' disease' and assumed that was what I had developed. I felt proud of my protruding bones and pinched skin. Perhaps it was my imagination but my skin looked a little bit lighter, an added bonus.

I wasn't left in peace with my eating habits though. The community psychiatric nurse who visited me was worried.

'You look thinner every time I see you, Clare. You must try and eat enough to keep your body working properly. You can't run a car on no petrol you know.'

I was delighted that she'd noticed I'd lost weight. I wore black most of the time, convinced that it hid the bulges of fat which in reality no longer existed. When I smiled modestly at her compliment she scribbled in her notes.

'I think I know of an excellent place which can help you regulate your eating better. I'm going to speak to the doctor and see if we can refer you.'

CHAPTER TWENTY-SIX

I was sent to a specialist eating disorders unit at a hospital in southwest London. It was 1993 and I was thirty-nine years old. I did a quick audit of my life so far and decided that starving myself skinny was my only achievement to date. I had no choice but to go along with the referral, but vowed to find strategies to outwit their best efforts to make me fat.

I'd never been to London before and I was curious. I promised myself that, with my height of four foot eleven and a half, at the very least I'd maintain my current weight of six stone three and, if possible, lose the last two stone I felt was standing between me and the lightness of being I craved.

The hospital was yet another depressed, dark Victorian building. I was supposed to stay for two years on an intensive rehabilitation programme which would break the cycle of my destructive eating habits for ever and spit out a brand-new fatted me. I had no intention of staying that long. My plan was to stay for a few weeks then call my community psychiatric nurse, tell her it wasn't working out, and return to Liverpool where I could be left to starve myself with fewer interruptions.

The programme kicked off with an initial assessment. I was placed in a huge circle of chairs and twenty pairs of eyes gazed unashamedly at me, gauging how far my bones protruded against my skin under my baggy clothes, how I kept the weight off, what kind of mental illness I had. I felt like prey in a jungle. The lion of the jungle was a professor with a long name I couldn't pronounce.

'Now, Clare, tell us what your ideal target weight is,' he purred. 'If I was a magic fairy and could wave my wand and make you any weight you wanted to be, what would it be?'

The idea of this paunchy, wrinkled man with a shiny bald patch on his head and a three-piece suit dressed up as a fairy godmother made me giggle.

'Four stone,' I said bluntly. I was anxious and irritated at being an object of pity and detached curiosity and couldn't be bothered to play the game. I just wanted the inquisition to be over as quickly as possible. I was wearing slippers with little bunny rabbits attached to the toes and kept my eyes fixed on them. I was sitting on the very edge of the chair with one foot in front of the other ready to sprint out of the room. I would have preferred to talk to a woman as I always did but he was asking most of the questions.

'No, no, no, no, no,' he tutted, pretending to sound saddened by my foolishness. I felt that actually he seemed rather pleased. I was another candidate for serious control. He turned to the woman sitting next to him who was writing notes and whispered loudly: 'Cubicle'.

She jumped a little, not wanting to appear impolite at being deafened but unable to remain totally impassive.

'My dear we're going to start you off in a cubicle,' he said smiling but still trying to look sad. The two expressions clashed. 'We find the severely anorexic do best there. No going to the bathroom by yourself, you'll have to use a commode in your cubicle; no baths, you'll have to wash with a bowl in your cubicle; no moving out of the cubicle unless a nurse wheels you in a chair; no getting rid of food, it will all be consumed in your cubicle and we'll be keeping a very close eye on that.'

It sounded horrifying but I said nothing. It was a challenge. The stakes had just got higher and I would have to become more devious if I was going to win and stay in control of my own weight and life.

There was a large blackboard on one wall with my name chalked on to it. The chalker had spelt my surname wrong.

'Hey, you've spelt my name wrong,' I shouted, transferring all my anger about the cubicle to that. 'It's not Sh'rima, it's Sherriema. It's a Chilean name.'

The jumpy woman sitting next to the professor twitched apologetically. She got up and corrected the spelling. When she stood up I noticed how thin she was. I always judged people, women especially, on the basis of body fat levels. I wondered if the professor was trying to bring her under control too.

After a few days of life in the cubicle – a bed to the side of the ward partitioned off with curtains drawn all the way round it – I felt like a turkey being fattened up for Christmas. An endless procession of food arrived at my bedside. If the nurses were in a real hurry they didn't even come right into the cubicle but instead put a disembodied hand through the curtain and plonked the latest instalment of calories on my table – three meals and three snacks a day. Fried fish, roast meat, roast potatoes, mountains of greasy pasta, a few side shows of vegetables and then puddings groaning with sugar and cream. Mostly eating was emotional agony but sometimes, when the food was something I had particularly loved in my pre-anorexia days, I found myself enjoying it.

Whenever I could, though, I stashed food in my bedside locker where they didn't seem to do spot checks. I tried to choose food that didn't smell too strong and didn't decompose too fast. I got to learn about different moulds and different smells. Bananas smelt pretty bad. First they turned black then they imploded so that the skin looked empty. White bread formed a nice plain canvas for bright greeny-yellowy moulds to bloom and the slabs of Victoria sponge cake they gave us never seemed to go off at all. I wondered what chemicals they added to maintain them in a state of perfect plasticity. Every three days I was allowed to go to the bathroom. A nurse watched me from behind a screen while I used the toilet and had a bath. It was then that I contrived to hide the rotting food in the folds of my towel and flush it down the toilet. I stayed in control in these small ways.

CHAPTER TWENTY-SEVEN

Most of us cubicle girls tried to exercise off the heavy load of calories we were fed. We weren't supposed to have any contact with each other in case we infected each other with subversive plots against 'getting better', but I sometimes peeped out of my cubicle and saw silhouettes of girls behind curtains doing exactly what I did – jumping up and down until they were drenched in sweat. Later when I was allowed on to the ward I discovered a table tennis room and I used to sneak in there with co-conspirators and play hyper-energetic games of table tennis before weigh-ins in a desperate bid to burn off a few stubborn calories. I did high jumps into the air while I was waiting for a shot and we would keep running round the table and switching the sides we served from to head off the emotional damage of a high reading on the scales.

Despite the solitary confinement rule we found ways to communicate. The partitions between the cubicles were made of very flimsy wood. If you pressed your finger against it you could feel the sponginess in the centre. I began a whispering friendship through this partition with the girl next door to me. Her name was Sarah and we became close friends. We whispered complaints about the food and the staff to each other whenever we got an opportunity.

'Hi, Sarah, what did you do with your dinner, stashed some? Yeah, me too, I'm due a trip to the bathroom tomorrow morning and those roast potatoes are going you know where.'

Sarah laughed. Solidarity against the regime was an unexpected and very therapeutic side effect of it. There were clear demarcation lines between the women who were focused on getting better and the rest of us. Those who wanted to get better tried to keep away from bad influences like Sarah and me who devoted our time to insubordination of one kind or another. We were kindred spirits. Many of the women on our unit seemed to come from much more affluent and better-educated backgrounds than I did but the desire to control our food intake forged a powerful bond between us. Sarah and I formed a supportive sisterhood to help each other outwit the doctors and nurses.

A nurse flapped in from behind my curtain and stood with folded arms as I whispered through the partition to Sarah.

'Are you talking to yourself now, Clare?' she asked, pleased with herself to have made an alarming supplementary diagnosis.

I shrugged and said nothing. I didn't want to be labelled delusional but equally I didn't want to cut off my scant opportunity for human contact.

She bustled off to tell one of the doctors and they watched me more closely after that. They prided themselves on the way they policed us yet were oblivious to at least half the tricks we got up to. Sarah and I amused ourselves with their obtuseness.

If we wanted to chat face to face we arranged to go and use the phones at the same time. Making phone calls to friends and family was one of the few permitted activities aside from enforced eating. We weren't allowed to walk down the corridor to the phones ourselves but had to be wheeled down in chairs. There were two phones next to each other and Sarah and I arrived at more or less the same time, picked the receivers up but didn't bother dialling a number, then started catching up on ward gossip.

'I woke up about 5 a.m. and did two hundred sit-ups while the nurse on the unit was on her break,' I said proudly.

Sarah looked a bit envious. 'Oh, God, I've done nothing for days. They always seem to be hovering round my bed because I lost two pounds the last time we were weighed.'

Whenever a nurse walked past we both turned our mouths into the telephone receivers and faked conversations: we competed for the silliest comments to the non-existent people on the other end of the phone.

'Oh, I'm sorry to hear the cat puked all over your new slippers, Mum,' said Sarah.

'Oh, you lucky thing, Joanne, discovered by a talent scout in the middle of Liverpool city centre and off to Hollywood next week!' I countered.

When the coast was clear we laughed so hard we both snorted, which made us both laugh more.

Eventually both Sarah and I gained enough weight to be moved on to the open ward. There we had to go and help ourselves to breakfast, although we didn't have much choice about what we helped ourselves to: a bowl of cereal, two pieces of toast, two little packets of butter and two little packets of jam were compulsory.

Sarah and I both loved the blackberry jam, but so did a lot of the other girls and usually by the time we got to the breakfast table it had all gone. We were left with the marmalade, which we both loathed.

'Why don't we go and pinch a supply from the kitchen,' said Sarah one morning after we'd lost out again. 'If they're forcing us to eat this stuff we might as well eat the flavour we like.'

I was keen to go along with the idea. My track record – Morgans Road, when I pinched the apple out of Mrs Bennett's pies, the nuns' roast potatoes and then cups of tea in Grove House – made me an expert. We giggled and laughed as we crept towards the kitchen, pressing ourselves against the wall of the corridor like we'd seen people do in films. We got into the kitchen without being detected.

'I'll keep watch at the door while you hunt for the jam,' said Sarah.

Inside the third drawer I opened I found a huge supply and started shoving little packets up my jumper.

'This is fantastic, Sarah,' I said brightly. 'We should have enough to last us here for a good few weeks.'

She was tapping me on the back as I chatted; I thought she was silently saying 'Well done for finding the jam', but in fact she was discreetly trying to warn me that we'd been found out. I turned round and saw one of the nurses standing in the doorway with her arms folded across her chest. Sarah was laughing so hard she was bent double with her bony chest knocking against her angular knees.

Ironically, the nurse didn't seem happy that we wanted more food. 'Clare, what on earth are you doing, put those back at once,' she said. 'Now get back to bed both of you, you're two very silly girls.'

* * *

I had had very little contact with my sisters and brothers since I entered the psychiatric system because I felt ashamed about what had happened to me. I simply slid out of sight and they had no idea how to contact me. I was happy to be cut off from my former life. Coming to a hospital where no one knew me, more than 200 miles from home in Liverpool, was a fresh start of sorts. Each time my life entered a new phase I felt, at least momentarily, that I had shed my old skin and become a new person. Still skinny and with my good friendship with Sarah to ease myself through the days, I was content for a while.

CHAPTER TWENTY-EIGHT

They used various group therapies to try and cure us of our deviant eating patterns. Yet again there seemed to be no effort to probe events on the long road leading to anorexia.

We used to have group sessions where we all had to sit in a circle and tell everyone what our names were. Everybody knew everybody else's names and I felt we were all being patronised by this 'getting to know you' exercise.

'My name is Fred,' I said every time I was asked something. The doctor in charge of the session gave me a withering look, which satisfied me enormously. I had outwitted him: he knew he couldn't force anything out of me that I wasn't prepared to part with.

Art therapy was another tool in the unit's arsenal. The art therapist talked to us all like small children: 'Now, girls, I'd like you to draw anything that comes into your heads.

'Don't worry about it looking like a Van Gogh, just do what comes naturally.'

Sarah and I hated the sessions and agreed to produce identical pictures of bland, inscrutable yellow smiley faces. The art teacher wasn't happy with our contributions.

'Now, Sarah, would you like to discuss your picture with the others?' she said.

'I've drawn lots of yellow smiley faces because I feel yellow and smiley,' said Sarah, rolling her eyes up to the ceiling.

None of the staff seemed to know how to respond to these small insurrections. I think that while they pitied us for our self-destructiveness they also felt unnerved by our power. Eating to remove hunger and to survive is the most natural human instinct; to subvert that we needed an eerie strength, which the staff neither had nor understood.

Some of the talking therapy was conducted in a room with a two-way mirror. As we looked into the mirror we weren't supposed to know that a group of therapists were sitting behind it observing us. But of course we did – information travels in places like that. One morning Sarah and I peeped into the room behind the mirror and saw a microphone hanging down from the ceiling. At our next session we arrived early and switched it off. Sarah climbed on to a chair and did the deed and then, giggling, we went into the therapy room and waited for the others to arrive.

Two minutes into the session a young therapist marched in and demanded, 'What's going on? We can't hear a thing.'

'That wasn't very discreet,' whispered Sarah to me behind her hand. After the session we laughed and laughed.

Despite my friendship with Sarah and the pranks we got up to which made life more bearable, I only lasted three months in the unit before I discharged myself. The staff tried various ways to keep me there. Janice, one of the therapists, seemed to take a human as well as a clinical interest in me. Every time I talked about walking out she had an interchangeable list of responses lined up.

'I'm worried about what will happen to you if you leave, Clare,' she said. 'Why don't you just stay tonight, it's getting very late and very dark now and you can think about it again in the morning.'

And when she'd got me to agree to stay until morning she sat by my bed when I woke up and said: 'Why don't you just stay two or three more days and then think about it again?'

She bought me a beautiful grey and black patterned silk scarf from Selfridges for Christmas, which I still wear, but she and I both knew that her persuasive tactics would only hold me back temporarily.

I walked out feeling free and ripped up the list of foods I was supposed to eat before I stepped on the train back to Liverpool.

Back in Liverpool I once again quickly slipped into my cycle of starving and bingeing. I felt as if I'd never been away.

I'd agreed to go back to the hospital in London for outpatient appointments and devised an elaborate plan so they wouldn't find out how much weight I'd lost. Each outpatient appointment started with a weigh-in. So, to avoid being found out for losing weight, I meticulously sewed fifty-pence pieces into the back of the waistband of my trousers and twenty-pence pieces into the sides. I sewed each one into its own tiny pouch of material so that it wouldn't make any give-away jangly sounds when I moved. I put pouches of sand inside my bra and bought Velcro weights that I wrapped around my ankles and thighs. I weighed each one out on my kitchen scales and did the sums so that I knew exactly what weight would register on the hospital scales when they weighed me.

As soon as I'd been weighed I had to go and sit and have a talk with the psychiatrist. Sitting on the thigh weights was very uncomfortable and I was so busy trying to conceal their existence that I could barely listen to what the doctor was saying. The hospital had a lot of stairs and walking up them with all the extra weights attached was quite difficult. One time I bumped into therapist Janice on the stairs. I was wearing a brightly coloured, busily patterned dress with a full skirt that I thought did a perfect job of concealing everything that was stashed into various parts of it. Janice touched my dress admiringly.

'Oh, what a beautiful dress you're wearing, Clare, it's nice to see you in bright colours instead of your usual black.'

I was convinced that if she didn't let go of the material, the sand and weights and money would all make a sudden dash for freedom and end up in an incriminating puddle around my feet. My heart was knocking against my ribs. Then, luckily, Janice innocently let go of the dress.

'Well I've got to dash to a meeting now, Clare, lovely to see you again, you really are looking better.'

At first my outpatient appointments were monthly, then, because the doctors were so pleased with my progress as a result of my artificially inflated weight, they were reduced to once every three months.

In the end, though, I couldn't bear the deceit of it all any longer. It seemed absurd that my weight remained somewhere under seven stones and the doctors kept telling me I was doing well and had gained a couple of pounds. I unpicked the special waistband, which concealed coins and some of the other materials I'd used to trick the hospital staff, and put them all in a big envelope with a covering letter saying:

'I'm so very sorry to have cheated at the outpatient appointments. I'm enclosing the things I used to make myself weigh more because I didn't want to trick you any longer. I apologise for letting you down.'

CHAPTER TWENTY-NINE

I received no response from the hospital. They'd failed and I'd failed and both of us knew it was pointless to continue trying to put flesh on my pointed bones. I did start to put weight on, however, without any therapy or external pressure.

I had a plan which I was sure would put an end to all my troubles. I was going to have a baby – the one thing I had always desired. The thought of having sex with a man to get myself pregnant repulsed me and, in any case, I didn't know any men I could approach. But I had read an article in a magazine about all the different ways to get pregnant without a man. The article explained that an increasing number of private clinics were offering these services and that quite a few of their clients were older, single women.

I knew that if I was too skinny I wouldn't be able to conceive and so I decided to reacquaint myself with my bulimic ways. I remained underweight but put on almost a stone and a half, so that by the time I walked through the door of the first clinic I was a respectable eight stones. It was 1999 and I was forty-five years old. My understanding of a woman's biological clock was rather hazy. For the previous fifteen years I had shaved a decade off my real age. Doctors, hospitals and therapists all had my date of birth recorded as 1964 and I thought that this would give me a better chance of being accepted for treatment.

I had found accommodation in a two-bedroom housing association flat. It was in a Grade II listed building and I decorated it in beautiful, bright colours, as far away as it was possible to get from the decor at Grove House. I still had several thousand pounds in the bank saved up from my nannying days and I decided that, if necessary, I'd spend every penny of it on getting myself pregnant.

I hadn't been in touch with my sisters and brothers very often since I'd started travelling around the world nannying and they knew nothing of my breakdown at college, or of my subsequent admission to a psychiatric hospital. I didn't want them to know about any of the bad things that had happened to me but felt that a joyful announcement of an impending birth would be the perfect moment to restore contact with them.

I had always adored children and knew that I'd be able to look after a baby. From the time that I was little more than a baby myself I had been thrust into a caring role. The babies and children in my care as a nanny were uncomplicated beings and, unlike the adults I knew, responded to my love with their love.

All my attempts to get pregnant were in the private sector and I found that as long as I handed the money over up front nobody asked too many questions about my mental state.

I started off with artificial insemination. This was very straightforward and not too expensive, but five attempts of syringing anonymous sperm up my vagina failed to make me pregnant. I was bitterly disappointed but determined to try other treatments. Next came intra-uterine insemination – a more invasive procedure which involved implanting sperm into my womb. Four attempts failed. The more I failed, broke my heart and lost my money, the more determined I became to succeed. IVF was my last chance. I knew that this had worked for lots of people who hadn't succeeded in getting pregnant any other way and I was newly optimistic. I was so sure this treatment would work for me that I started touring baby shops looking not only at clothes but also at prams and cots.

In one shop I got involved in a very detailed discussion about the merits of different prams.

'This one lifts off the frame and can be used as a carrycot or Moses basket,' said a very enthusiastic shop assistant. 'It's our best selling model. When are you due?'

'Oh, I'm just in the very early stages.' I smiled the kind of contented smile I thought a pregnant woman would produce.

'Congratulations to you, that's wonderful news.'

I almost bought the pram and a cot and a four-pack of snowy white babygrows there and then but managed to hold off.

I had to give a blood sample before I started the treatment, and the nurse who drew the blood noticed all the scars on my arms.

'Now, now, what's all this?' she asked. 'You can't go having babies when you're doing this sort of thing to yourself. I'll have to let the doctor know about this.'

The doctor was informed and came in to the treatment room with a sombre expression on his face.

'What have you been doing to yourself, Clare?' he asked shaking his head slowly.

I decided to choose a carefree style of bluff. 'Oh all that stuff is behind me now. I wouldn't be trying for a baby if I was still doing silly things. Look, the scars are all old, see how faded and silvery they are.' I didn't show him the fresh ones across my chest.

The doctor looked doubtful for a minute and rubbed the frown dimple in the middle of his tanned forehead. He'd already taken my money and done a consultation and questionnaire with me. If he backed out now he'd have to give me a full refund, which would be inconvenient, and not cost effective. He made a decision.

'OK, Clare, if you're sure this cutting business is all in the past we'll proceed.'

The first attempt failed so I tried again. When my period arrived on time I felt as if I was sitting among earthquake debris. There was nowhere else to go. I had no more savings and a womb and crowd of eggs that were obviously defective. My only comfort was my razor and my first and second fingers, which darted up and down my throat at increasingly regular intervals. But those things couldn't make the yearning go away. I was getting hardly any release from self-harm and bulimia now.

A couple of months later I was lying exhausted on my bed. I had just carved the word HATE across the skin of my abdomen. The word was directed at my failed eggs and womb. It was the first time I'd experimented with letters with my razor and I was quite impressed with how clearly the word stood out below my navel, another Scarlet Letter.

I felt too tired to go and mop up the mess and lay very still in the hope that the blood wouldn't trickle very far. Then I felt blood between my legs. I presumed that despite my efforts the blood was running downwards from my stomach. But the dripping seemed to have a life of its own. I felt violent, period-pain type cramps and assumed my period had started a week early. The pains were getting much more agonising and intense. I'd never experienced period pains like this before. I tried to curl up against the pain but it only made it worse. Then something slithered out of my vagina. It was the size of my hand and looked like a piece of liver. I dialled 999 and told them I'd had a miscarriage.

I peered with detached curiosity at the tiny foetus, which I'd placed in a shallow, white bowl. What had happened hadn't really hit me. I was trying to find a baby in there but could see nothing apart from a red, gooey mass, which I suppose was the placenta. Mercifully my cramps had stopped.

When two serious ambulance men arrived to take me to hospital they asked me to hand over the beginnings of my baby.

'No, no, it's my baby. I want to keep it with me for ever,' I begged.

'Well, Clare, we'll have to let the doctors have a look at it and then we'll see.'

I recognised the 'let's humour her' tone and carried on pleading with them. I thought that if I could preserve my baby in a jar and have it with me always it would bring me consolation in the dark hours. However, once we arrived at the hospital a nurse whisked the white bowl away and I never saw it again.

A doctor with a kind grey face and bits of frayed grey hair escaping from a bun at the back of her neck, examined me and saw the carnage across my abdomen. The word 'hate' was clearly visible to her.

'My goodness, Clare, what on earth have you been doing to your poor stomach?'

I poured everything out to this kind, concerned woman: 'I didn't know I was pregnant because I've kept on having periods. I've tried so many times to have a baby by all sorts of different means and I was so very, very upset that nothing worked that I wanted to show my useless womb how angry I was with it. All I've ever wanted is a little baby to love and look after. I used to be a nanny, I'm really gifted at looking after children and in my heart I do believe that with a baby to focus on all my problems would vanish.'

Although I'm too old to have a baby I believe that still.

I sobbed and sobbed. The doctor seemed tearful.

'I can see from your notes that you're under the care of the psychiatric service. I'll send a doctor down to assess you and maybe he can change your medication and give you something to make you feel a little bit better.'

I was given an ultrasound scan. I had started to believe that what I had expelled was a bit of placenta and that the baby was still thriving inside me. I looked intently at the image on the screen.

'What's that, lying there, isn't that my baby?' I asked the scanner over and over. 'My baby's still inside me isn't it?'

'No, Clare, I'm afraid your baby's gone now. It came away cleanly and your womb is as it was before you became pregnant. You don't even need to have the lining of your womb scraped because there are no bits of placenta or anything else left behind.'

Two days later I was discharged, my womb as empty as the day I was born.

JADE CHILDS 2000–2002

Jade: a green gemstone (Spanish)
Childs: a lover of children (my definition)

I needed to change both my first and last names. I chose Jade because green is my favourite colour, and Childs because I adore children

CHAPTER THIRTY

The flat I lived in for the previous nine years was one of several conversions in an old house. One of the joys of living alone was the infinite opportunity to cut, starve, binge and puke in peace, something I wanted to do increasingly as I grieved for my lost baby.

I was more isolated than ever and barely spoke to anyone from one day to the next. From time to time people in the streets, mostly teenagers, made racist remarks to me. 'Go back to your own country you Paki,' they usually jibed. Those comments forced me to break my silence.

'Get your geography right. I'm Chilean,' I snapped. They never knew what to say after that and usually gawped open-mouthed. I don't suppose any of them had ever heard of Chile. After one such incident I went home, lay on my bed and screwed my eyes tight shut.

'If you're there, God, it's not too late to swap my skin from black to white. Life has been very hard for me and I know it would really help me if I could just be white.'

There was no response.

Losing the baby and realising that I had no more chances to try for another one made me yearn more than ever for a mother in my life. I was reading the local newspaper one day when I saw an advert for the Meet A Mum organisation. The advert gave little explanation but said: 'If you would like to meet a mum write to the following address.' The advert seemed like the answer to my prayers. I assumed it was some kind of fostering service for parentless adults.

I wrote an enthusiastic letter, including my name and address but not my age, real or otherwise. 'Please could someone contact me about the advert because I would very much like to have a mum', I wrote. I received a handful of leaflets back explaining the work of the organisation. It was a kind of network for mothers of young children to meet each other. I felt ashamed that I had misunderstood the advert so fundamentally but also bereft. I had really believed that at last I was going to find the mother of my dreams.

When I first moved into the flat I spotted a tiny box room folded under the roof of one of the stairwells. It was only five feet high and six feet long by two feet wide. It wasn't suitable as accommodation but as, at my height of four foot eleven and a half, I was the only resident who could walk through the miniature door without stooping, I asked a manager at the housing association if I could use it as an extra little sitting room.

The manager agreed and the room became my Alice in Wonderland room. I had shelves installed and on them displayed lots of the little things I had collected over the years, like the toys out of Kinder eggs and lots of miniature soft drinks cans. I got an electrician to feed wires from my flat down into my tiny room to power a miniature TV and a light. I bought a lightweight, child's writing desk and lined my miniature room with the same Axminster carpet that was in my flat.

The tranquillity of my living arrangements was shattered when a new man moved into the empty flat across the landing from me in 1997. The man's name was Bill. I estimated that he was in his forties. He was more than six feet tall, so given our height difference, when I stood next to him I felt more like a little girl than usual. He had quite a handsome face with combed back hair greying at the temples and too many tattoos snaking up and down his arms. Although I slashed my own skin I could never understand why people liked to 'colour in' parts of the surface of themselves. It seemed like a profound violation to me. Bill had a four-year-old son called John, who lived with his mother, Bill's ex-partner, during the week, while Bill looked after John at weekends.

As I grew up I never lost the language of children. It served me well as a nanny and I found that children were drawn to me because I never asked them the sort of adult questions children consider stupid. Almost immediately I became friends with John. He was entranced by my Alice in Wonderland room. He loved looking at the miniature Kinder-egg toys, at the little cans and at the pictures I drew. Most of all he loved the child-sized snugness of the room. I used to sit in my Alice in Wonderland room drawing pictures of my childhood. I had begun to think about writing a book about my life but didn't feel I had the literary skills to put it together. So I decided to try to convey events in pictures. With Bill's permission John came and sat with me and did drawings of his own, which I put up on the wall of the landing between Bill's flat and mine.

Through John, Bill and I became friends. We shared cups of tea and chats about nothing in particular.

'You're great with John, you know,' Bill said to me one day.

'Well, it's just because I'm used to children and I've spent a lot of time working with them,' I said.

Bill didn't seem to have heard and carried on as if I hadn't interrupted his flow of words. 'In fact you're great all round, Clare. How do you fancy going out together, you know, dating. You're a good-looking girl, I don't know why you haven't got a boyfriend already.'

'Thanks, Bill, but I'm really happy as I am.'

'Is it me? Is there something wrong with me? Don't you fancy me?' he snapped.

My perceived rebuff seemed to be making him irate. The seductive, wheedling tone had suddenly vanished and was replaced by something deeper and nastier. He didn't sound as if he was prepared to take no for an answer from me.

'I can see it's going to be a real challenge getting you into bed, Clare. But when we do get to make love make sure you keep your glasses on because they really suit you.' He didn't smile when he said this.

I tried to back off. I was happy to be friends with Bill, and particularly with John, but the pressure to have sex with him felt unbearable. I was trapped.

He started telling me he'd dreamed about me. He'd watched me coming home from his window and opened the door of his flat before I climbed the stairs so it looked as if it had been casually open for a while. I knew he'd only just opened it because I could see the chain from his door swinging against the frame. However, I only started to pick up on these unnerving signs once Bill started pursuing me in earnest.

When he left his flat he assumed I'd be watching him. I was, but not for the reasons he hoped. Although he could never see me behind my curtains he always turned round halfway down the street and waved in the direction of my window.

I no longer left my door open and I dreaded his step on the stairs. When I did see him he fixed me with a hard stare and said things like, 'Do you know, I dreamed about you last night, Clare?' I didn't dare ask him to elaborate. I continued to play with John when he visited at weekends and tried to direct all my remarks to John rather than to Bill.

Bill claimed disability benefit for a bad back, although it never appeared to trouble him and he spent much of his spare time helping his brother move heavy furniture around in his brother's shop. But the benefits office became suspicious and one day, as he helped his brother carry a fridge freezer down four flights of stairs, two investigators from the benefits office were secretly photographing him. Armed with the evidence to confront him they appeared at the communal front door of the house. I didn't have a phone at that time and was on my way out to make a call from a nearby phone box.

'We're here to see Bill,' they said neutrally. I had no idea who they were and assumed they were friends of his.

'He's just up at the top,' I said as I ran out into the street.

When I returned home a few minutes later Bill was waiting for me. His face looked twisted.

'You fucking bitch, you've ruined everything for me. You were in cahoots with those two men from the benefits office weren't you? You got on the phone to them when I was shifting that fridge freezer and told them to come down right away. I saw you let them in, I'll get you for this you whore.'

'Bill, none of this has got anything to do with me. Of course I didn't phone those men, even if I had they couldn't get down here in thirty seconds. They must have been investigating you for a while. It's all got nothing to do with me.'

After that things became much more frightening. He used to ring my bell after nights of heavy drinking at the pub and call through the door, 'Clare, Clare, I want to put my spunk inside you.'

I stood silent and frozen on the other side of the door and prayed for him to go away. Thankfully he never broke my door down or forced his way in.

He started doing little things to irk me, like leaving his boots on my doorstep, winding rags around the banisters and damaging the spy-hole in my door. I couldn't understand why he had festooned rags around the banisters and I didn't want to get into an unnecessary conversation with him about them. It seemed very weird to me.

One day I bumped into him on the stairs and he physically threw me into my Alice in Wonderland room. The door to the room opened outwards so it was impossible for me to shut him out.

'I'm going to keep you in your precious little room and nail the door up so that no one ever finds you. You can cry all you want and starve to death in there for all I care. Have you ever seen the film *Cape Fear*, Clare?' I hadn't.

'Well what the man in that film does to the woman in that film is what I'm going to do to you.'

I managed to run past him out of the room. I had never run so fast. I got into my flat and bolted the door. My heart was beating so hard I thought it was going to explode like a firework into my chest wall.

'I've got nine brothers and sisters, Clare, and I'm going to send them all round to smash your face in,' he shouted to me as I ran off up the stairs.

I thought it was probably not a good idea to watch *Cape Fear* but I rented it out from my local video shop and watched it a few days later. It was about a man who hunted down a woman he was obsessed with and did underhand things to gradually drive her mad, so that when she complained people said it was all in her mind.

I complained to the housing association managers and they agreed to have a word with him. But I found out from another tenant in the building whom Bill had spoken to that he had made a counter-allegation about me, saying that I spied on him and was always hassling him for sex.

In the end the managers did nothing. The fragile tranquillity I'd constructed around myself with my beautiful flat in a beautiful building had fallen around my feet like rose petals in a sudden snowfall in August. I was trapped and frightened and felt like a captured lion tightly bound in ropes by hunters. I barely left the flat and couldn't see any way of escaping from Bill.

I used to wear my long dark hair in two fat, glossy plaits. It attracted many compliments because of its length and gleam, and because it was that rich shade of bluey-black which you never see on the heads of white people. I had spent six years consciously growing my hair. But my hatred for myself was becoming more solid and contained, like a pile of autumn leaves that have been floating independently across a path but which are then swept into a tight pile and rained on to seal them into one gluey mass.

I loathed my face, my body, my inability – in my opinion – to do anything worthwhile, and my lack of cheerfulness. I attributed my loneliness to all of these defects.

I decided that a fitting punishment for my repugnant self was to slice my plaits off near my scalp. As soon as the idea came into my head I had to carry it out. I saw no point in dithering and thought that, like the cutting of my flesh, this short, sharp shock would provide me with a moment of delicious oblivion.

It was harder to saw through them with the blunt scissors than I imagined. I ended up getting my prized razor blade out and speeding the job up that way. As they plopped to the floor I felt as if I had lost two limbs. Afterwards I sat holding my dead plaits. They continued to shine as bright sunshine bounced through the window, making a triangular shape on the carpet. My plaits and I sat peacefully in the triangle. They were still things of great beauty so I was enormously relieved that they were no longer attached to me, as I didn't feel worthy of them. I leaned over to my bedside table and picked up a hand mirror. I peered at the peculiar tufted face, and six-year-old Clare, newly shorn of hair and nits by my impatient mother, stared back.

Once my hair was gone I got to work on chopping at my body. My breasts and my stomach were favoured spots; then I moved on to the pills. This time a neighbour who knocked on my door and heard me groaning dialled 999 and saved my life.

I left my flat in an ambulance and never returned.

After a short spell in hospital I was placed in a group house in Wimpole Avenue with staff on the premises round the clock. I changed my name to Jade Childs because I was anxious that Bill would pursue me wherever I went, with his nine brothers and sisters forming an angry line behind him with fists poised to squash my face. I had my own room but all other facilities were communal. I wasn't happy there but felt too listless to go back to living by myself. I missed my flat but felt much safer away from Bill in another part of Liverpool with a different name. I was given the address of a day centre for people with mental health problems and went along.

There was a range of what I call pretend life activities on offer like crafts and card making, which some people took part in and some didn't. A lot of moping went on so I tried to talk to the people I could have an adult conversation with and not get drawn into more than niceties with the others. Ritual was very important. Some people got passionate about their seat and if someone else disturbed the natural order of things by sitting in it they erupted.

A man called Joe nodded his head vigorously when I said hello to him. The only way I could get his brain to turn off the nodding switch was when I started to nod too. 'Why are you nodding like a flippin' donkey, Joe?' I said every time I saw him. That was his cue to laugh and walk off, leaving me in peace.

For a while I accepted days at the day centre surrounded by people I couldn't hold a conversation with and evenings in front of bad TV. My weight crept up as I began eating forbidden foods again and gradually, imperceptibly the bad seeds took root in my head. The weight gain triggered another bout of anorexia. The anti-depressants I'd been taking didn't seem to be working so I stopped swallowing them. Living had become an overwhelming effort and going to the day centre seemed pointless.

I became skinny again but still felt a great heaviness: not the delusional obesity of anorexia but a different kind of heaviness, as if cement had seeped inside to entomb my organs. I wore three coats to hide my bones and the concrete protruding through my ribs, which I was convinced everyone could see. I locked myself in my bedroom, only leaving in my pyjamas with the coats thrown over the top once a day to buy bottles of vodka and lemonade from the off licence.

Various members of staff in the group house tried to entice me to eat sandwiches and other filling foods. I refused everything except apples, oranges and bananas. I'd made a new set of rules to live by and the key points were: to keep as still as possible – sudden movements made everything feel worse, to only drink booze, to only eat fruit, and to stop communicating with anyone.

I swore at staff who knocked on my door with offers of help. I was horrible to them and by any logical law of equality they should have been horrible back. I felt their invincible pleasantness was an affront to the natural order of things. Their niceness rankled.

I heard creaks in the wallpaper and was convinced it was trying to whisper messages to me. I strained my ears but couldn't pick out any words. Then I saw the devil with big horns and bulging eyes but no proper face in my curtains, so I set them on fire. Nobody seemed to mind. One of the staff sweetly, patiently installed a smoke alarm. I immediately unscrewed it, threw it across the room and told her to fuck off.

'Why don't you just get on a slow boat to Siberia?' I shouted. The cement was building and building inside me. In the end I had to run.

I wanted to make a dramatic exit like in a film but instead I wandered out of the front door when the staff were occupied doing other things, walked around aimlessly for a while and spent the night at a friend's house.

I slept better than I had for a long time and impulsively decided that what I needed was to get away from the group home. I asked my friend to drop me off at Lime Street Station, bought a one-way ticket to London and leapt joyfully on to the Intercity train just before the whistle blew.

ROSIE LODGER 2002–2003

Rosie: like a rose (American)
Lodger: a person living away from home (my definition)

I ran away from the supported accommodation in Liverpool, moved to the streets of London and needed a name that couldn't be traced back to my life in Liverpool. I chose Rosie because I felt like a second-hand rose with no belongings, and Lodger also because of my sense of unbelonging

CHAPTER THIRTY-ONE

I didn't know that it was one of the coldest days of the year. I stepped off the train still feeling happy, and with my three coats and the pleasure of utter anonymity the cold couldn't touch me. I wandered around the streets for a while and asked a couple of men sitting in a doorway drinking extra-strong lager where the nearest shelter was.

'There's one round the corner luv, nice hot soup and lots of food but it's not a night shelter. You're a bit late for that. All the spaces go early in the morning.'

I could see them eyeing me up, looking at my unweathered face, my untatty clothes and my undirty holdall and wondering how long I'd last in the cold jungle.

I walked off, not feeling particularly worried about how I would survive on the streets. I had left Liverpool on impulse and, as usual, hadn't thought through the consequences of what I'd done. Yet again I was running away from myself and at first that always made me feel free and cleansed of my previous self. It was like the early intoxication of a new love affair with someone unsuitable – the unsuitable person was the new version of me. Each time I ran away I forgot that the old me always came back.

It was dusk and all the Christmas lights had been switched on around Oxford Street and Regent Street. I was happy to be surrounded by so many sparkly baubles. As I walked up and down the streets packed with hurrying people I felt perfectly content. I had slept on the street in a cardboard box once before and I believed it seemed like a very useful dress rehearsal.

The circumstances had been very different though. I had camped outside a furniture shop in Liverpool for four nights before the sale started. It was when I was working at Plesseys and living in my own flat. I set my heart on the brand new sofa on offer for a fraction of its usual price. My brother Tom came down a few times to keep my place at the front of the queue while I went to the toilet at the hotel across the road. The second man in the queue also wanted to buy a sofa; companionably he agreed to take one and I the other. When I walked through the doors of the shop and handed my money over for the sofa I felt an enormous sense of achievement, as if I'd passed an exam with top marks because I'd done the hard graft of revision. It was a jolly and focused kind of sleeping rough, though, and bore no resemblance to sleeping rough in London at all.

It was getting late and all the hurrying people had disappeared off the streets. I began to feel less sure about the decision I had made to run away. I found a clean, dry cardboard box and settled into a doorway but I felt too scared to sleep.

One man urinated on me to try and get me to move out of the doorway he wanted for himself, but I refused. 'Get lost, you old misery and keep your disgusting habits to yourself,' I shouted.

As the euphoria of being invisible in London wore off the cold penetrated my three coats. I missed the warmth of my room in Liverpool. I even missed the staff who nagged me kindly. I felt as if I didn't shut my eyes at all but I probably did succumb to a few minutes sleep here and there.

As soon as it got properly light I climbed out of my box bed, propped it up neatly against the nearest rubbish bin and started walking aimlessly up and down the lavishly decorated streets of the West End. It was three days before Christmas and everyone looked happy and to me terribly rich as they shopped in twos and threes for gifts, already laden with department store carrier bags.

I walked into a little park. The sun was elbowing the icy clouds to the edges of the sky and I found a bench almost directly under the sun. I craned my neck to get my face a couple of inches nearer to the warmth of it. A young woman with shiny dark hair folded into a bun in the nape of her neck came and sat down next to me. She was wearing a fashionable shade of dark red lipstick. Her mouth stretched wide when she smiled, revealing tiny, perfect teeth. She too was lifting her face up to the sun.

'There's something special about the sun in winter,' she said in heavily accented English. 'Sun in summer is just hot but sun in winter feels like a luxury item. It's like a very good hot coffee with chilled cream swirled in.'

I'd never thought of sun in winter like that but I knew exactly what she meant. We started chatting and she told me she was a student and was spending a year in London.

She asked about me and I started telling her about running away from Liverpool and sleeping in a cardboard box. Her shining brown eyes widened.

'Oh, that's really tough,' she said. 'If I had my own flat I'd bring you back to stay with me but I'm just renting a room in a friend's flat so I can't.'

She tipped the contents of her purse on to her lap and handed me three shiny pound coins. 'Here take this and buy some hot food,' she said.

She jumped up. 'I need to go to a lecture. Take good care of yourself.' She hugged me. She smelled of earth and cinnamon. She walked off and turned back to wave. I was bathed in her kindness and suddenly felt more optimistic about the day.

I wandered into one of the soup kitchens and sat down at a table in the corner with a mug of tea. Two young women approached me smiling.

'Hello, I'm Jan,' said one. 'And I'm Yvette,' said the other.

'Hello, I'm Rosie, pleased to meet you.'

The name Rosie suddenly popped into my head. I didn't want to use any name that would help the staff at the supported house in Liverpool to track me down. They knew me by both the names Jade and Clare so I had to come up with something different. I racked my brains for a surname and, after a moment's hesitation, came up with Lodger – after all I was a lodger on the streets of London.

Jan and Yvette accepted my new name without suspicion. Both looked clean, well groomed and mentally stable: not remotely homeless.

'What are you going to do over Christmas?' asked Yvette.

I shrugged. 'Back to the cardboard box I suppose. I'm just living day to day, I hadn't really thought about it.'

'Why don't you come down to Crisis with us?' said Jan. 'They've got a shelter just for women and the food's great.'

The information about the food sounded very off-putting. The last thing I needed was to be surrounded by the intoxicating smell of calorie-jammed food. But, short of options, I agreed.

I was grateful that neither Jan nor Yvette started asking me about my background or how I'd come to be on the streets. I was learning about the unspoken rules of homelessness: don't ask, don't assume and don't judge. When I first saw some of the street drinkers lolling in doorways doing their best to get some oblivion I thought that I was different from them and that I shouldn't be on the streets. Then I remembered the way I sat and drank myself into an anaesthetised state in my room and suddenly knew that I was escaping the same pain as them. Pain can be caused by a million different things but the urge to numb it is always the same.

CHAPTER THIRTY-TWO

The three of us walked to the address Jan and Yvette had scribbled on a piece of paper. It was a cavernous, disused car showroom with a hard, sticky floor. Free-standing heaters looked forlorn in the middle of this huge space as they tried but failed to counter the chill.

But, despite the less than perfect conditions, several young women enveloped us in a warm welcome and invited us in. They were wearing an assortment of badges and I was told they were volunteers running the shelter over the Christmas period.

'Hello, I'm Rosie,' I said. The name sounded entirely natural to my ear, as if I had always lived with it.

I was offered a seat by a heater and a cup of tea. Everyone was warm and friendly and everyone was focused on giving us a nice Christmas. I couldn't believe that they cared so much about doing that for us.

Sarah, one of the Crisis staff, tucked me up in bed each night. I floated with happiness and felt loved; it was like having a real mother. I said almost nothing all week but as I endlessly sipped steaming tea I luxuriated in being safe. Nobody wanted to investigate the contents of my life, to peer at my brain chemistry, to diagnose one form of disorder or another. People just wanted me to be safe and content.

Although I was happy and did feel protected at Crisis, I was very ill. I ate only one crisp and half a biscuit in all the time I was there. Though I hadn't felt it had worked, without my medication unwholesome thoughts of death and inflicting the maximum possible damage on myself streamed through my mind. I didn't confide any of these thoughts to the Crisis volunteers but they could see that I wasn't eating and that I looked pale and ill.

'Maybe you should see a doctor, Rosie,' Sarah suggested. I agreed; a doctor visited and urged me to go into hospital.

I agreed and one of the volunteers took me to a small hospital in north London and sat with me while I talked to the psychiatrist on duty. I never discovered if the hospital was only for psychiatric patients or if it was a general hospital that included psychiatric services as part of its case mix.

I showed him the scars on my arms and chest where I'd been cutting myself. He looked calmly at the scars but I could see that the Crisis volunteer was shocked at the way I'd been butchering myself. 'Why don't you let me admit you and just have a little rest here for a few days,' said the doctor. 'You look absolutely exhausted.'

The thought of ending up in another institution after yet another failed dash for freedom made my heart sink. But Crisis was about to close and I had nowhere else to go so I shrugged and whispered 'OK.'

The doctor smiled and the Crisis volunteer looked relieved that I was going to get some medical care. But the place was short-staffed because it was the Christmas period and nobody had any time to talk. Once again I had encountered pressure from doctors to get me inside the psychiatric system, but as soon as I was behind the walls of one institution or another interest waned and very little seemed to happen to alter the state that I and others were admitted in. The drugs I was prescribed usually didn't work and the doctors always seemed to ask the same superficial questions, rather than embarking on the slow, painstaking business of excavating the truth.

Again I decided to leave the hospital. My latest reinvention of myself, which had seemed so promising in those first few hours in London when I strolled up and down Oxford Street enchanted by the Christmas lights, had failed. But I had no regrets about running away and living on the streets. I had encountered more kindness than cruelty. I packed my bag and walked out of the front door of the hospital. Nobody tried to stop me and I was free once again. But with no idea of what to do, where to go or how to survive the freedom had become meaningless.

The hospital was near Mill Hill East tube station. I jumped on the tube and decided to see where it would take me. I watched all the unfamiliar stations blur past me – East Finchley, Archway, Camden and then Euston flashed up. At last there was a name I recognised. I had arrived here from Liverpool. I got off the train and wandered around the station concourse. I had brought more than £100 with me to London when I fled Liverpool but I had spent almost nothing. I wasn't eating and the night shelters I went to were free. Cups of tea were my biggest item of expenditure. I bought one now and as I cradled it in my cold hands I started to think about Maureen, my favourite care worker at the supported home in Liverpool. She was always kind and smiley and was never too busy for a chat. Suddenly an almost physical wave of longing to talk to Maureen washed over me. I finished my tea and decided I'd call the house and see if she was there.

I was trembling as I dialled the number. As if by prior arrangement with some divine force, Maureen picked up the phone. Until now I hadn't given much thought to what the people in the house thought about my disappearance.

'Oh my God, Jade, is that really you? We all thought you were dead. Where are you? How are you?' I could hear Maureen's voice tremble as if she was about to cry.

The concern and warmth in her voice were too much for me. I no longer needed to stay in survival mode. I could let go. I cried and cried and so did Maureen. All the train travellers who walked past me as I howled down the phone must have thought that my entire family had just died.

'We've all missed you terribly,' said Maureen when she'd composed herself. 'Have you got money? Will you come home to us?'

'Yes, I'll come back now. I don't know why I ever left. This freedom business isn't all it's cracked up to be.'

The next train to Liverpool was in eight minutes. I jumped on it and slept soundly until it pulled into Lime Street Station just before 11 p.m.

JADE CHILDS 2003

Back to my Liverpool care-in-the-community name

CHAPTER THIRTY-THREE

Maureen opened the door to me and hugged me hard.

'Thank God you're safe, Jade. We've been worried sick about you. Let me get you something to eat, you look more emaciated than ever. And the doctor will have to take a look at you tomorrow.'

Suddenly I felt terribly weary. I didn't want to be fed by Maureen or prodded by a doctor. I just wanted to sleep. I woke up the next morning feeling refreshed. I was glad to be back in my old room in the attic and I felt settled, as if the urge to keep on running had left me for ever. I suppose I had reached some sort of uneasy peace with my life.

I had tentative reunions with my sisters Mary and Lucy and with my brother John. We had only been in touch erratically over the years but I promised them that I wouldn't vanish from their lives any more.

Several months after I'd got back from London I wrote to Mary at her old address including my address and phone number and mentioning that I wanted to visit to give her older son, Mark, £100 for his imminent eighteenth birthday. She called me the day she received the letter.

'Why don't you come down now, our Clare. It must be five years since you've been in touch.'

I jumped on a bus and half an hour later I was sipping tea in Mary's living room. We had hugged, but my siblings took their lead from our mother and never went for overt displays of affection. We chatted as if we had last seen each other a few days before. Mary told me her husband had died suddenly a few years before. She asked few questions about what I'd been doing and with relief I chatted vaguely about what people from Morgans Road or Park Hall were doing now. Mary gave me phone numbers for Lucy and John and later on I met up with them too. It felt good to be back in touch with the only flesh and blood I knew. I was tired of hiding away and dodging people and situations all the time. I felt I wanted to start being honest about my life and to stay in one place.

I didn't exactly like myself but I hated myself less. I had given in to myself. My skin colour didn't repulse me quite as much as it had. 'You're black, get over it,' a pragmatic little voice in my head kept saying.

As I fought against myself less, the anorexia and bulimia faded. I began to eat too much fatty, heavy food, but swallowing it all down made me feel passive and peaceful. I was letting go and it felt liberating rather than weak. The fat rolled on to my bones more quickly than it had ever done before. Getting it all off again seemed like just too much of an effort.

Going to the day centre for people with mental health problems was directionless and unstimulating but I no longer minded. There was nothing else I particularly wanted to do. After years of rebelling against myself and the system I had at last been broken into life in the psychiatric world. I received weekly injections of anti-depressant drugs, which deadened things, but that too I didn't mind. I preferred nothingness to pain.

The supported housing I was living in, which at first had felt like a prison, gradually began to feel less oppressive. I became accustomed to the rules, as if my eyes had slowly adjusted to a very dimly lit room after a period of bright, outdoor midwinter sun.

I didn't mind the other residents even though none were my friends. I got used to Julia who had the room across the corridor from me. She was locked into a variety of routines that punctuated her waking and sleeping hours. She always rose around 6 a.m., purposefully, and then slumped immediately into the armchair in the dining room, where she snored obtrusively until almost noon. She smoked exactly one packet of cigarettes every day and had each one timetabled precisely. The washing machine was one of the mechanisms by which she timed her nicotine fixes. She smoked one cigarette when a wash cycle started, pulled a chair up in front of the washing machine and swivelled her eyes round the glass window in time with the rotations of the clothes. When the washing stopped moving and the red light flashed on she reached for a cigarette.

And I kept away from Sam, another resident, who had a large collection of spiders, including a couple of tarantulas. Sam was fearless in the company of his spiders and the terror among the rest of us when he dangled one or more spiders at close range made him feel enormously powerful.

As my years in the psychiatric system wrapped themselves more tightly around me, the assumptions about Clare/Jade/Rosie's incapacity increased. Nobody needed to grapple any longer with questions of why I was where I was, why I had broken down, why anything. It was all too long ago and it didn't matter. I was rubbed out with their giant eraser. I had become the pale imprint of me they assigned to me. There was revisionism at work too. According to one of the psychiatrists I saw, this stupor was no longer a state I had sunk into. Instead it changed into something that I left the womb with. It was incurable and so, with no prospect of recovery, I was expected to buckle down and make the most of my lot. The system and I had become soldered together like an old married couple who tolerate rather than love each other, and who don't know how to function apart.

CHAPTER THIRTY-FOUR

And then one day Miranda walked in. She had just started working as a community psychiatric nurse in the area I was living in and I was one of a number of cases she was assigned.

From the moment I met her I sensed something was going to happen. She wasn't lazy, she wasn't interested in ticking boxes or in backing out of the room as soon as she'd jabbed a needle into my bottom. She was alive and passionate and enquiring and always came in agitated and animated about something. She was tall and too slim and her trousers flapped around her legs.

'I don't want to frighten people by wearing a skirt and letting them see my chicken legs,' she laughed, appearing entirely unconcerned about her legs or the effect they might have on other people. I envied that. Her eyes shone with thoughts and her large mouth was perpetually mobile, expressing joy, rage, empathy and many things in between.

'I'm feeling mad as hell today, Jade. I've just been listening to a man on the radio who has come out of jail after serving eight years for a robbery he didn't commit. Turns out the police framed him because they had messed up at the scene of the robbery and failed to gather crucial forensic evidence that would have put the right blokes behind bars. He sounded so broken. What kind of a system do we have that allows people in positions of responsibility to act in this horrible way?'

I listened and nodded. Sometimes I felt like her counsellor, letting her get things off her chest. But what I didn't realise was that she was building my trust, letting me know that she was a person who cared, who railed against injustice and things that just weren't right. I warmed to her very quickly.

The third time she saw me she came into my room with her usual sense of urgency. But this time she wasn't talking about something alarming she'd heard on the news.

She gave me a very deep look, trying to burrow behind my eyes.

'I sat down for four hours last night, Jade, reading all your files, from your first admission to Grove House right up to the latest stuff added this week.'

'Oh, right,' I said, giggling nervously at the thought of someone spending so much time focusing on me. I had got used to people flitting past me on their way to somewhere more interesting. 'Was it a boring, depressing read?'

She didn't answer, keen to get on to what she had discovered.

'You know what I think?' she said, pausing before delivering something I sensed would be dramatic. I looked blank.

'I think your files read like a whodunnit without a murderer.'

I didn't know what she was talking about.

'You suffer from reactive depression, Jade. You're not schizophrenic. So why has no one ever bothered to find out what you're reacting to?'

'I don't know,' I said, still not really understanding what she was driving at but feeling a prickle across my scalp.

'The files they've kept on you tell me your blood pressure measurements in 1981 and a precise breakdown of medication prescribed for ever but the spaces for your soul are absolutely empty. It seems to me that no one ever bothered to ask you the blindingly obvious. What were you thinking about at critical moments in your life – before your breakdown, before you cut yourself up, before you tried to kill yourself? They're so bloody busy filing everyone into boxes and making sure they're hushed that they never ask "I wonder why this person is making such a racket?" '

I tried to remember what I was thinking about or maybe what I was trying not to think about at these times but nothing came; just a strong pain inside my head that I hadn't felt for a long time.

Miranda was sitting opposite me, her bony knees brushing against my fleshy ones. She reached over and held one of my hands in both of hers.

'I think someone hurt you, hurt you very badly, probably when you were much younger,' she said softly.

She was giving me permission to look and see.

'The notes talk about a reluctance to be near men, you always request a female doctor. There's no mention of any relationships with men. Why is it that you don't like men, Jade?'

I shrugged. Nothing came to mind.

'And the name changes – always running away from yourself. I think it's time for you to make peace with the real you. But you can't do that and heal your pain unless you understand what has caused it,' said Miranda.

'But I don't feel any pain,' I said. 'I'm puzzled more than anything. I don't know why I suddenly had a breakdown in the middle of a lecture all those years ago. I don't know why I'm always so unhappy, why the anorexia came, the bulimia, the suicide attempts, the cutting . . . I just don't understand. It would be nice to understand though.'

'Did the nuns ever hurt you, or any of the priests who visited Park Hall?'

I racked my brains but couldn't remember ever having anything much to do with any of the priests who drifted in and out of Park Hall.

'The nuns were pretty cruel to us. I always wanted cuddles and affection but we never got anything like that from them. They were strict and used to knead me with their sharp knuckles sometimes. Do you think that's why all these things have happened to me?'

'Well I'm sure the way they treated all of you children didn't help. But was there anything else, Jade? What about your father or one of your brothers? Did they ever hurt you in any way?'

'I've never met my real father so he can't be to blame, but Sam, me mum's husband, wasn't very kind to me. He hated me because I wasn't his and the fact that I was black rubbed his nose in it. He was always saying to me mum, "Get rid of that black bastard." I remember him beating me when I was about three years old because I'd eaten some tomatoes I wasn't supposed to eat out of the larder. And he hit me mum all the time. Could that be it?'

'I'm sure that didn't help but it's probably not the cause of all your troubles. What about your brothers? Did they ever do anything to you you didn't like, touch you in a way that made you feel odd, or any visitors to the house, family friends? I think something awful happened, Jade, and I think you've pushed it down and down and down inside you in the hope that you'll never be able to find it again.

'But if there's poison you must seek it out. You must find what you've buried. You don't want it stuck inside you somewhere, you want to pull it out like a rotten tooth and then you'll get strong again and can start living properly and honestly. You deserve that, Jade, everyone does. I'm saying to you that you're allowed to remember, you're allowed to tell me about it. Don't carry the blame, you're the innocent one.'

I tried to think hard about Damian and John and Tom, but they hadn't been cruel to me. As a family abandoned by my mother and then trying to survive with the nuns we more or less stuck together. Tom, particularly, was the one I adored, gentle and innocent and needy. I had tried my best to be his mother.

I kept thinking. I couldn't bear to look at Miranda. Something was swirling noisily through my head. It was ice cream and salad cream and yoghurt. I kept hearing Miranda's words 'stuck inside you' and 'pull it out' over and over. And suddenly it was there, back in my head. All the information I'd been frantically trying to recall to stop Miranda's questions.

'Oh my God. Oh my God,' I whispered. 'I know why I can't bear to eat ice cream or salad cream.'

Miranda gripped my hands tightly and then held me softly while I cried. It was like having a mother at last.

I think I cried for an hour and a half. I'd never heard myself cry like that before. I sounded like an animal, not a pathetic little creature caught in a trap but a strong animal emitting big lion roar sobs, expelling toxins in lumps of stringy snot and powerful tears which bounced off my cheeks.

A few straggled words came out but not much.

'Don't think about it any more if you can't bear to,' she said. 'We can talk about it bit by bit. Would you like to have a little rest now, get some air perhaps?'

But now my mind felt like those exceptionally clear blue skies you get after a muggy, violent grey storm.

'No, no, I must tell you everything now in case it goes again and then I might never be able to find it. I do remember everything. Now I don't understand how I could ever have not known all this.'

'Whatever terrible thing it was that happened to you, Jade, I don't think there were enough compensatory things in your life to allow you to heal. I think with no father, an absent mother who appeared to be ambivalent towards you, the nuns who showed you no affection, the foster parents who didn't really want you – it was all too much. You never had the love to pull you through. You caved in and that terrible thing was buried alive in mind rubble. If you've truly remembered now, you can lay whatever happened to rest and move on.'

I wanted to talk urgently. 'The people who came to give the lecture at college the day I had the breakdown were from the NSPCC. They were teaching us how to spot the signs of sexual abuse in children. When they started speaking I couldn't bear to hear about what abusers did even though I was still blocking out the secret I was forced to keep about my childhood. They said: "Children who are abused are often threatened or bribed to keep the abuse a secret."

'I suddenly remembered that I'd been instructed to keep a big secret. Then I couldn't think any more and wanted to throw the chair to silence this man who wouldn't stop talking. Although I couldn't remember or couldn't bear to remember the details of the secret I knew that it was something painful and violent in my already blighted childhood. But now I feel I can look what happened in the eye. For the first time I feel safe enough to do that.'

It was my mother's boyfriend, Peter, the only person who ever showed me any kindness, who instilled a lifelong terror of men in me.

'He became my mother's boyfriend when I was four and he always wanted me to sit on his knee. Then he used to stroke my legs. It was affectionate and nice and I got a taste of the attention I'd never got from my mother. Then, a couple of months after he arrived, he started creeping up to my bedroom.

'Often I would be fast asleep. My mother was usually out, although she never explained where she vanished to at night-time. The neighbours told me years later that she and her friend Pat used to go up on to the ships when they docked at Liverpool and spend the nights with the sailors. The others were always asleep when Peter appeared. Mary quite often spent the night with Marie and Damian, John and Tom slept in bunk beds in another room. I was so tiny and suddenly this fat giant had climbed into bed next to me exhaling stinky alcohol fumes across my face.

'I lay there puzzled rather than afraid while he stroked me softly between my legs. He buried his huge wet tongue in my ear making my eardrum recoil.

' "You're my princess," he rasped. "This is our secret and if you keep quiet about it I'll buy you as many sweets and chocolates as you want."

'Despite the smell and weight of him next to me, my heart leapt. Never in my life had I had access to as many sweets and chocolates as I wanted. Getting enough to eat and, even better, getting sweets was my top priority and always a struggle. He held me so securely in the bribe that it never occurred to me to tell anyone what was going on. And, at first, because I was so utterly starved of affection, I didn't mind being touched. He was very gentle to me and so quiet that the others fast asleep in the bed never stirred. He didn't come all the time, maybe about once a month for a couple of years. I was happy because at last I had a guaranteed supply of sweets. If Peter wanted it all to be a secret that was all right with me.

'One night when I was six years old he crept into my room and pulled his big hard stick of a penis out of his pants. I had no idea what it was or that men had those things between their legs. At first I thought it was some kind of a toy he'd stuck on with Sellotape.

' "Suck on this little princess and I'll make ice cream come out of the end for you."

'He forced me down between his legs and jammed his penis into my mouth. I was sick all over the blankets. White stuff did come out of the end of it but it tasted nothing like ice cream. From that moment my earlier feeling of being the chosen, privileged one fell away. I wanted to keep as far away as possible from Peter. I always pretended to be asleep when he crept into our bedroom, but he touched me whether I was asleep or awake and sometimes physically pulled me down the bed so that my head lay between his hairy, sweaty thighs. I never saw him approach any of my siblings, who slept soundly. He only seemed interested in me.

'This went on for about a year. I didn't know what terror was before but now it was everywhere in me. He didn't stay at our house every night and I forced myself to stay awake until the early hours when I knew he was unlikely to turn up. I dreaded his heavy step on the creaking stairs. After he had forced me to have oral sex with him four or five times, I devised a plan to avoid him. I darted into the cupboard in our bedroom and pulled the door shut behind me if I heard him coming in time. He never found me in there. I was extremely frightened and don't know how I managed to squeeze myself into such a tiny little ball that I could fit in there but the adrenaline of the fear helped me to fold myself up more compactly than I had thought was possible. When I heard him going back down the stairs I opened the cupboard a chink and eventually, flooded with relief, I tiptoed out and went back to bed.

'One night Peter crept in as usual. I was seven by then and I hadn't managed to get into the cupboard in time. I pretended to be asleep but he shook me so vigorously that I could only have managed to keep my eyes shut if I was dead.

' "You're a big girl now, princess, and we're going to do something that big girls do," he whispered.

'I trembled at the sound of it but I assumed that as Marie was the same age as me she would be doing whatever it was that Peter had in mind too. Because Marie came from a nice family and was just one week older than me, I thought that if she was doing it, it must be all right.

'Peter picked me up off the bed and very tenderly carried me downstairs. He laid me gently, like a piece of precious china, on the sofa I'd been born on. But there was nothing gentle about what he did next.

'My mother, as usual, was out and Peter must have been fairly certain that she wasn't due back at all that night, because the new thing he wanted to do was to rape me. I had no idea what rape consisted of, nor had I ever heard of the word. I was always very tough as a child and very rarely cried but what he did hurt so much that I screamed and begged him to stop.

'He didn't stop though. He just carried on until he had finished, his enormous belly squashing me, suffocating me. He was very drunk and seemed totally unaware of my cries. As he thrust his way inside me I felt a simultaneous splintering inside my head and inside my vagina. He was ripping apart my insides and ripping apart my childhood.

'Afterwards he looked pleased with himself. He leaned close to me and whispered, panting slightly, "If you ever, ever tell anyone about our little secret, princess, you'll end up in jail and you wouldn't want that would you?"

'I'd thought it wasn't possible to feel any worse than I did, but hearing those words was like an electric shock. Stunned, I curled up in a tiny ball on the sofa and sobbed silently. I was too scared to move. Peter walked out of the room.

'The next day he was very kind to me. He gave me money as well as sweets. Maybe he felt remorse or maybe he was trying to soften me up for the next time he planned to rape me. But the bribes didn't comfort me.

'Instinctively I knew that Peter had gone against nature that night and had crossed some terrible line that should never be crossed. Soon afterwards he vanished from my mother's life as suddenly as Sam had. Perhaps he did feel guilty or perhaps he found a new little girl to rape.'

Words were spilling out very calmly and coherently, as if they'd formed an orderly queue inside my head for years and had finally been given the signal to cross an invisible barrier into my mouth.

'I suppose that's why I'm still afraid of falling asleep, whether I'm here or out on the streets in London,' I said to Miranda. I hadn't been looking at her much while I was talking. Instead I'd fixed my eyes on a particular flower on the curtain opposite me. I kept thinking, If I just keep looking at that flower I won't lose my nerve and I'll get all this out. But now I looked at her and I could see she was trying to hide tears.

Even when I felt the coast was clear of Peter, sleep was not something I could drift into naturally. I devised a technique of lying on my stomach with my hands folded underneath my forehead. I would rhythmically bang my forehead against my folded arms and hum a tune or manically sing 'La la la' to try and rock myself to sleep.

Sitting with Miranda everything had come back at once – the cupboard where I felt terror and found safety, the hard, tearing pain of Peter forcing himself inside me, the sweets, the soft coaxing and, always, that merciless hardness against his soft belly.

Peter had stolen my childhood; then the vulture nuns had picked the carcass clean. The theft of my life as a child had made it impossible to have a real life as an adult. At last I understood everything and now I could start to mourn what I had lost.

EPILOGUE

I am now fifty-two years old. People tell me I have retained a childlike quality although I am well into middle age. They make the remark casually, some kindly, some patronisingly; none knowing why I am still attached to Winnie the Pooh T-shirts and cinema films aimed at the very young.

The truth is that my childhood was too damaged to allow me to shed its skin naturally when I emerged from my teens. Some people who have been physically, sexually or emotionally abused in their childhoods go on to become abusers, career paedophiles. Perhaps Peter was one of them, determined to have his payback time. Neither he nor my mother ever said anything about his childhood so I'll never know if it held any clues which would explain why he went on to become an abuser.

However, I believe that many more, like me, become broken human beings who have no desire to harm others but who are irreversibly harmed themselves. I have become a map of my abuse. The brutalised initiation into the adult world of sex at the age of six, the lack of parents as a steadying compass to guide me through the most basic aspects of growing up, the institutionalised years and, above all, the absence of love – the one constant in my formative years – have all conspired to stunt any fluid, elastic movement through life.

Basic, natural, human responses were trampled out of me by Peter, and I was damaged just like a seed trampled before it has had a chance to put down roots and feel the sun and rain.

Childhood should be a secure staircase into the adult world. The first step firmly laid down in babyhood so that the second may rest sturdily on top of it when a child starts to walk and talk and so on. You need to have a childhood before you can shake it off. Never having the real thing has strangled me into replaying the trappings of it across the decades. In short the theft of my real childhood has left me floundering in a perpetual ersatz one. My physical growth into an adult tricked people into thinking that I was an adult. I struggled to act the part but didn't have the infrastructure, like a body without bones. Taking my childhood by force not only denied it to me, it has also denied me full entry into the world of adults.

Mostly the years with my foster parents and with the nuns felt like neither childhood nor adulthood – they were simply a series of starvations. Although I can't start my childhood again I have developed mechanisms to protect the cavities where my childhood should have been from the harshness of the light. I have learned how to insulate myself, and now that I'm stronger I can start to move beyond the events of my childhood.

I still feel queasy every time I glance at my dark skin. The synonymous nature of black and bad was drummed in too deeply for too many years for me to feel at ease with it or to enjoy what I know objectively are its advantages, not least the fact that it makes me visibly, visually, a part of my father. These days I know rationally that people pay a lot of money on sunbeds and take expensive holidays to hot countries to turn their skin the same shade as mine, but I can't quite make peace with my skin. I try to avert my eyes from it as much as possible and have retained those early longings to be white. If I woke up tomorrow with white skin I still can't help feeling that my life would improve.

My brothers and sisters were all affected by our childhoods in different ways. My younger brother, Tom, whom I adored, moved to America in the mid-1980s. In 1991 I got a phone call out of the blue from his friend saying he had shot himself dead. I was devastated. He was four years younger than me and I had been a good approximation of a mother to him. He cried every night when he was put to bed as a toddler: my big brother Damian told me I used to get into bed and stay with him until he fell asleep. As soon as I climbed in beside him and cuddled him he shut his eyes and fell asleep. In August 2003, there was another phone call; my oldest brother, Damian, had been found hanged.

I don't know exactly why my brothers killed themselves. Tom had written to me shortly before he died sounding very depressed. 'Life is shit', he wrote. As for Damian, after his death one of his children told us that he'd been abused as a child but they didn't know by whom.

Childhoods like ours have consequences, and all of us are destined to live out our lives managing those consequences in our different ways.

I don't believe I'm bitter about the way things have turned out, but I am wistful, and I long for two things: above all to be cocooned in a loving family, protected from the world in the strong, gentle arms of two perfect parents. My mother didn't live up to that expectation although I believe I loved her in the same unsatisfactory, convoluted way she loved me. Because I have never met my father, my view of him is untarnished by reality. If Jorges, my father, is still alive, and happens to be the kind of safe, dependable, morally pure man I have fantasised about, an antidote to Peter, I would joyfully leap into his arms if he appeared on the horizon to claim me.

My other longing has always been to become a mother. I hoped that by having a baby I could break the cycle; that by giving all the love I wanted to have lavished on me as a child I could neutralise the past and warm the future. Although the years of making my womb useful have moved past me, the longing remains, in the same way as someone still feels pain in their calf after their leg has been amputated.

I've never wanted to have a relationship with a man and I always keep as far away from men as I can, but who knows if things could have turned out differently if I'd had my first sexual experience in my late teens or early twenties – a gentle progression from teenage sweaty kisses in the cinema and harmless flirting. I might have been happily married today.

Before my breakdown and journey along the corridor without end that is the psychiatric system, I had overcome many aspects of my childhood. I had forged good friendships and had satisfying jobs as a nanny. For a little while my life was a success because of my personality and my ability. In the psychiatric system those qualities were leached out of me. Even though some shout, some are mute, some rock back and forth, some weep, some are locked, some unlocked, there is a grey standardisation to our humanity. Everyone is monochrome. Writing this book has made me want the colours back.

The drugs we are all fed in the system, sometimes force-fed, manufacture a perfect stupor in us, a pallor in the soul, a passive acceptance of our fate as a recipient of services for ever. Even now I am scared of making decisions and ask others to take responsibility instead. My experience of the psychiatric system has been one of no expectations, no encouragement to break out and wave goodbye, and no help in reclaiming our identity.

I only ever knew one person who got out. She suffered from depression and graduated from attending the day centre to becoming a very sensitive, capable mental health social worker. I know I became more ill as a result of being in that loveless environment for so long. I used to have the confidence to control twenty children, now I don't think I could manage one.

While some people who find themselves in the psychiatric system show outward signs of their inner turmoil, I rarely displayed anything like that. Fellow psychiatric patients and outsiders have often remarked, 'What are you doing in this place? You don't seem mad.' The comments are lacking in compassion for those whose troubled minds manifest themselves in their speech and movements but, even so, perhaps I should have taken them as a cue to move on.

My wounds will never heal into the perfect skin of a newborn baby, but turning, for the first time, to look over my shoulder at the life I have lived so far has been a balm for the open sores. I can say that truly I have survived. I have survived the abuse, the beatings, the overdoses, even the bright white light calling me over to the other side, so it is reasonable for me to think that I am strong and perhaps that I am destined to be a survivor of whatever is thrown in my path.

Looking back at my life has given me the impetus to change it. I know I will continue to need support but I want a real room of my own now. I want to work again and to have back the control that one person after another has taken from me. No more escapes and no more disguises, I am returning to myself.

People from different periods of my life know me by my various different names and I like that. Clare for family and childhood friends, Jade for my Liverpool psychiatric system life and Rosie for friends I have made in London. I like having different names for different parts of myself. In a strange way these names have helped me find out who I really am.

There are many traits I inherited from my parents and many events which shaped me that I have spent all my life wishing were different, but at last I understand that what I have is all I have. It has taken me more than fifty years to make this peace with myself but at last I have done it and now I can start to learn how to be happy.

CRISIS

Fighting for hope for homeless people

Crisis, where Rosie and Diane met, is the national charity for single homeless people and works year-round across the UK helping people fulfil their potential and transform their lives. Crisis helps rebuild the lives of homeless people by helping those trapped in the cycle of homelessness and raising awareness of their plight. The charity estimates that there are around 380,000 hidden homeless people in Britain, living in hostels, temporary bed and breakfast accommodation and squats, or sleeping on the floors of friends and family. Rosie is donating money made from this book to a special project with Crisis – Crisis Skylight – a centre where homeless people take part in free practical and creative workshops giving them the opportunity to build skills, confidence and self esteem.